- ✉ Postal address
- ☎ Telephone number
- ✎ email address
- 🚗 ✈ Directions b

## SCORECARD

Shows metres from back tee, indicating gold, green, yellow or red rating of holes. (To convert distances from metres to yards, add 10%, or take approx 1 more club.) Gold holes are generally featured in photos and captions; the reason for a hole being red is given in a caption.

| | m | p | | m | p |
|---|---|---|---|---|---|
| 1 | 356 | 4 | 10 | 356 | 4 |
| 2 | 385 | 4 | 11 | 500 | 5 |
| 3 | 171 | 3 | 12 | 194 | 3 |
| 4 | 516 | 5 | 13 | 368 | 4 |
| 5 | 348 | 4 | 14 | 338 | 4 |
| 6 | 149 | 3 | 15 | 206 | 3 |
| 7 | 487 | 5 | 16 | 386 | 4 |
| 8 | 321 | 4 | 17 | 490 | 5 |
| 9 | 403 | 4 | 18 | 415 | 4 |
| | 3136 | 36 | | 3253 | 36 |
| | | | | 6389 | 72 |

## SUMMARY DESCRIPTIONS

A short description of each course is shown in a box highlighted in a pale sand colour.

Summary description box

**Particularly enjoyable courses** If the box colour is rich sand colour, the course is one the editorial team regard as particularly enjoyable (not just for design, so much as for the whole experience from reservation and arrival to 19th hole).

Particularly enjoyable course

Rated courses have 2 pages, main text, 3 photos and captions; unrated courses have 1 photo and caption only. All have summary descriptions.

A course name in *italics* denotes a course included in this guide (except on the Contents and map pages, where it denotes a *particularly enjoyable course*).

## ABBREVIATIONS

| | | | | | |
|---|---|---|---|---|---|
| **Adva.** | = | Avenida (avenue) | **m** | = | metres |
| **C** | = | Calle (street) | **p** | = | par |
| **Ctra.** | = | Carretera (road/highway) | **r** | = | right |
| **IH** | = | Course designed by club, in-house | **rbt** | = | roundabout(s) |
| | | | **urb.** | = | urbanización |
| **l** | = | left | | | (a residential community) |

THE POCKET GUIDE TO
GOLF COURSES

# SPAIN
# & PORTUGAL

# THE POCKET GUIDE TO
## GOLF COURSES

# SPAIN
# & PORTUGAL

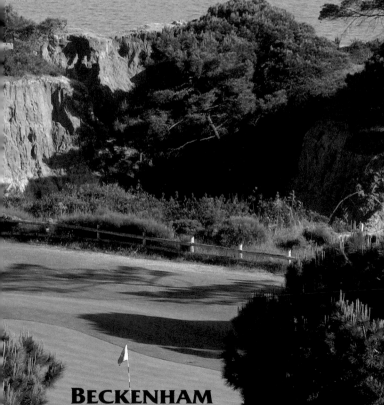

## BECKENHAM

First published 2004 by Beckenham Publishing
Limited, Calamint House, PO Box 3339, Manchester
M8 4XX, UK

A catalogue record for this book is available from the
British Library.

ISBN 0 9548040 0 7

10 9 8 7 6 5 4 3 2 1
2008 2007 2006 2005 2004

Design: Robert Updegraff
Print production consultant: Geoff Barlow
Printed in Italy

Photographs © Beckenham Publishing Limited 2004
Uccello *A Hunt in the Forest* reproduced by kind
permission of Ashmolean Museum, Oxford.

look@pocket-golf.com  www.pocket-golf.com

# Acknowledgments

Although the views given in this book are
the personal consensus of the editors, we
could not possibly have compiled it without
the generous support of so many, including
the numerous golfers whom we have met
during our research. Our thanks go to all
who have helped us, and especially for the
engaging support of members of the Lowe
family. We are indebted to the rest of
Beckenham's editorial team and our panel
of amateur and professional players, who
have between them (and us) played on
every course listed. Special mention also to
those involved in the non-golfing aspects,
namely: Juan de Zavala and Mariola
Blazquez, and (more recently) Arnie &
Hilary Cohen, in Madrid and Manchester,
respectively, for their invaluable assistance;
Anna Harvey, our copy editor, for her
punctilious dedication, common sense and
guidance (less mistakes became fewer, now
none – except any that are our own);

**Half title photograph:** *RSHE Club de Campo (Sur) p3:17, from the right.*
**Title page photograph:** *Pine Cliffs p3:6 from behind green – the demanding back
tee is just left of the 'P' in Portugal; the edge of the normal tees is just visible at the
extreme left of the photo, very slightly lower.*

All information provided in this book was, to the best of our knowledge, accurate as of 31 July 2004, and is based on data
supplied to us. Readers or clubs who wish to update information in this book should email us at look@pocket-golf.com
Significant changes will be posted on our website: www.pocket-golf.com

Robert Updegraff and Geoff Barlow for making the design and production process so creative, efficient and pleasurable – and thanks particularly to Bill McCreadie, without whose tolerant and freely given advice, this book would never have made its way through the publishing maze. Most of all, we have appreciated more than we could ever fully acknowledge the support and, all too often, long-suffering patience of our closer friends and families.

We cannot name everyone who has helped us, but would particularly like to mention the following:

Rafael Alonso'Lasheras, Malcolm Black, The Cat, James Collier, 'Bepo', Chris Davies, Lee Davis, Andreas Doring, Freddie fforde, John fforde, Nic fforde, Peter Fowler, Baden & Eva Foster, Isabel Gancedo, Román García-Guaita, Antonin García-Ureba, Colin Gregan, Ellie Gulliver, Jeff Hall, David Head, John & Gilly Hendry, Edmund Hendry, Roger Holmes, Clare Horton, John Huggan, Robin Hurlstone, Michael & Marcela Johnston, John & Jane Kettlewell, Siân King, Charles & Frances Lochrane, Caroline and Peter Long, Jordan Lott, Michael Lovett, Allen Lowe, Rhod McEwan, Paul Maleedy, Helena Mak, Jose Melo, Barney Miller, Sam Millhouse, Stella Millhouse, Michael MacLoughlin, Mel Morris, Andrew Moss, Rory O'Callaghan, Pablo Oliart, Peter O'Malley, Stuart Parfitt, Asunción Pascual, Idris Pearce & Anne Meyer, Sara Pearce, Sarah Sanderson, Enrique Satrústegui, Helen Shaw, Antonio Henriques da Silva, Armando Silva, Nick Slate, Jaime Uriate, Derek & Diane Woodward, Uri Zakay, Reyes Zavala

Finally, thank you to all the golf clubs for allowing us to play and photograph their courses, without which this book could not have been possible.

**Below:** *a side-on panorama, showing the presence of gold-rated Furnas' p3:2 (tee above right of pink shrub bottom right; green left), the treachery of the undulations around long p4:17's green (centre) and the unfolding avenue of p5:18's fairway (into distance, centre right) – all created by the ranks of Japanese cedars, natural undulations of the site and water (in front of 18th tee, left of pink shrub). The view the other way from our camera position at the Mirador (signposted) is spectacular: 100s of metres down into the extinct volcanic caldera, the village of Furnas and its beautiful lake.*

# CONTENTS
*(Particularly enjoyable courses are set in italics.)*

# PORTUGAL

## LISTINGS – USEFUL INFORMATION

# THE BECKENHAM RATING SYSTEM

## Overall course ratings

We set out to point to excellence rather than weakness. For this reason we have not adopted a '1-10' or 'marks out of 100%' system, where low ratings would inevitably have to be given in some cases, nor (for the same reasons) a star system in which every course is rated.

We therefore award between 1 and 3 stars to courses whose design quality is particularly commendable:

★★★ for courses which approach perfection – with the potential to require anything and everything from the golfer, whilst being fair; they must also stand up as a work of art, have presence and no weak holes. There may be fewer than 50 such courses in the world – none in Iberia, to date, though the original 9 holes at *Furnas* would have qualified, had they not been extended to 18. *Courses worth crossing the world to play.*

★★ for excellence: as for ★★★, but with perhaps the occasional blemish or weak hole causing the distinction – the art and presence factors are still prerequisites. *Courses worth crossing a continent to play.*

★ for courses representing very good design quality – as for ★★, but with perhaps some more blemishes, e.g. some weak holes and/or scoring less in the art/presence department. *Courses worth crossing a country to play.*

↗ rating is given to courses we recommend for a fuller experience of the best in golf course design. *Courses generally (but not always) with the potential for elevation to a star rating.*

We recommend the other (unrated) courses in the book to the travelling golfer as generally being in the higher ranks of golf course design, or worth playing some other reason. We only include courses at this level, if they are sufficient in quantity and proximity to an airport to render their locality suitable as a golf 'destination'. The exceptions are the Costa del Sol (west of Málaga) and Algarve & Lisbon areas, where we have included all courses in what is collectively Europe's most popular golf destination. For readers touring by car we have also selected a few courses, a little more strung out by themselves, on the main routes south.

## Individual hole ratings

Here we have used a very simple system, based on 'traffic light principles': *green – yellow – red*, from strong to weak with yellow representing an 'average' hole. (This average relates to the whole population of golf courses around the world, not just in Iberia.)

Additionally, above green we have devised a special '*gold* rating' for those few holes that are so well designed and integrated into their surroundings it is difficult to imagine how they could be improved. *A hole worth playing the whole course for – just so you can play that hole.*

## Criteria used in The Beckenham Course Rating System

We rate the golf courses (from the viewpoint of a right-handed, male scratch amateur, playing the back tee course for the first time – subject to a knowledgable caddy's advice where appropriate) on two different levels:

**i)** the golf course as a whole, which we assess for:

**Variety** – the extent to which the course provides a diversified mixture of golfing tests and design features to provide a breadth of challenge;
**Stylistic integrity and consistency** – the extent to which the course has a commonality of features and therefore stands together as a whole, rather than consisting of a compilation of disparate parts;
**Fairness** – the extent to which the course and its challenges are openly presented, so that playing errors are due to the player himself making such errors, rather than due to a feature of the course of which the player is not given reasonable notice;
**Routing** – the extent to which the physical relationship between the layout of the course and the land on which it is set enhances and/or diversifies the golfing challenge (e.g. through changes in the direction of play) and its aesthetic and physical experience; and, to a lesser degree,
**History** – the extent to which the course has been used for important events, or has otherwise enhanced the game of golf;

**ii)** each individual hole, for:

**Playing challenge** – the extent to which the player's physical golfing skills are tested whilst playing the hole; these skills include delicacy of touch as much as sheer physical strength;
**Mental challenge** – the extent to which the player is required to think his way around playing the hole (e.g. a strategic hole will score more than one where no choices are given to the player);
**Use of land** – the extent to which the design makes good use of the natural features of the land, or, if artificial, the golfing quality of the land created;
**Aesthetics** – the quality of the visual, sensual (and occasionally aural) impression provided whilst playing and walking the hole;
**Green and greensite** – the design quality of the putting surface, and the topography and golfing defences incorporated in the design of the complex immediately surrounding it;
**Negatives** – give the assessor the ability to downgrade a hole because of particular features which detract from its qualities (e.g. noise pollution, blind shots, reverse cambers, blind bunkers, too steeply uphill, etc.).

***Important note:** because the hole ratings only make up approximately half of the overall score in rating a course, comparison of courses by their respective numbers of different coloured holes is not a particularly meaningful exercise (e.g. Quinta do Lago (North), unrated, has 9 green holes whereas La Manga (North), rated ↗, has 8).*

# How to use this book

## General guide

To quickly choose a course you haven't played before, use the star and hole rating system plus the summary description (i.e. the words in the sandy coloured box). For our opinion on the holes of a course you already know, refer also to the hole-by-hole colour ratings (on scorecard). For more detail on featured holes, read the photo captions (gold holes are always included). For an explanation of why a hole is red, refer to the smaller print. For more about rated courses, read the main text.

## Key
**Name of course Star rating** (if applicable) – see page 8

# MÁLAGA ★
**Colt/Simpson** | **1926/64** | **€€**      **H:** M 28, L 36, J 28/36

Name(s) of designer (if two names '&' means co-designers, and '/' means different designers at different years of design shown).

Price band – for most expensive green fee (i.e. high season weekend, 2004 prices):

| | |
|---|---|
| € | below €60 |
| €€ | €60 – €100 |
| €€€ | €100 – €200 |
| €€€€ | more than €200 |

Maximum **H**andicap requirements (if none, none) for **M**en, **L**adies and **J**uniors (boy/girl – if different); if no junior information given, assume same as for adults. **Best always to take your handicap certificate.**

*Important note:* there is a huge variety of green fee discounts and packages, which change regularly and would therefore be misleading to include in this book. Our price band system should be used as a general guide as to which courses are more or less expensive relative to the rest.

**Trolleys:** pull trolleys are generally available to hire at courses in Iberia
**Buggy\*:** available/compulsory/advisable/caddies available, but no buggies

- 🛒 **Reservation essential**
- ❸ **Number of different tees normally offered at each hole**
- 📇 **Handicap certificates required**
- >27 🌡 7/8 **Months with average daytime temp. above 27°C (80°F)**
- <13 🌡 1/2/12 **Months with average daytime temp. below 13°C (55°F)**
- 🎣 **Driving range on site**
- ◯ **Balls to rent at driving range**
- ✔ **Clubs for rent on site**
- 🎓 **Teaching available on site**
- ⁝⁝⁝ **Easy to lose balls – take plenty**

*\*Important note:*
*'Buggy advisable' denotes a particularly hilly course. If a course is hilly, but reasonably walkable for those fit to do so, we do not show the buggy advisable symbol.*

- ✉ **Postal address**
- ☎ **Telephone number for reservations** – best always to reserve (some courses do not accept visitors every day of the week and several have annual closures; we do not publish these, as they often change).

**✉ email address for reservations; web site url**

**🚗 ✈ Directions by road from appropriate airport** N.B. 'follow road' means follow straight on, straight over all roundabouts, junctions etc. until further instructions; 'sign' means sign for club. We suggest you use our instructions in conjunction with a local map whenever possible. Spanish roads are generally well marked with km signs, which we often use to guide you. All distances are approximate.

**Scorecard** – shows metres from back tee, indicating gold, green, yellow or red rating of holes. (To convert distances from metres to yards, add 10%, or take approx 1 more club.) Gold holes are generally featured in photos and captions; the reason for a hole being red is given in a caption.

|  | m | p |  | m | p |
|---|---|---|---|---|---|
| 1 | 356 | 4 | 10 | 356 | 4 |
| 2 | 385 | 4 | 11 | 500 | 5 |
| 3 | 171 | 3 | 12 | 194 | 3 |
| 4 | 516 | 5 | 13 | 368 | 4 |
| 5 | 348 | 4 | 14 | 338 | 4 |
| 6 | 149 | 3 | 15 | 206 | 3 |
| 7 | 487 | 5 | 16 | 386 | 4 |
| 8 | 321 | 4 | 17 | 490 | 5 |
| 9 | 403 | 4 | 18 | 415 | 4 |
|  | 3136 | 36 |  | 3253 | 36 |
|  |  |  |  | 6389 | 72 |

**Summary description** of course in box highlighted in a pale sand colour.

**Summary description box**

**Particularly enjoyable courses** If the box colour is rich sand colour the course is one the editorial team regard as particularly enjoyable (not just for design, so much as for the whole experience from reservation and arrival to 19th hole).

**Particularly enjoyable course**

Rated courses have 2 pages, main text, 3 photos and captions; unrated courses have 1 photo and caption only. All have summary descriptions.

A course name in *italics* denotes a course included in this guide (except on the Contents and map pages, where it denotes a *particularly enjoyable course*).

### Abbreviations

| | | | |
|---|---|---|---|
| **Adva.** | = Avenida (avenue) | **m** | = metres |
| **C** | = Calle (street) | **p** | = par |
| **Ctra.** | = Carretera (road/highway) | **r** | = right |
| **IH** | = Course designed by club, in-house | **rbt** | = roundabout(s) |
| | | **urb.** | = urbanización |
| **l** | = left | | (a residential community) |

*Important note: Spanish principal road numbers are in the process of being changed as we go to press: we have included new numbers wherever possible and (where relevant) also referred to old numbers. The most relevant change is that the N340 coast road is now the A7 (but not apparent in Catalunya as of July 2004). However the A7 still uses the N340 km signs, even though the A7 starts at Algeciras whereas the N340 was measured from Cádiz.*

*For photographers who are prepared to be on location at sunrise, golf courses may seem easy prey, as this reverse view of PGA Catalunya p4:4 suggests – taken with a Nikon D100 + AF-S Nikkor 24-120mm 1:3.5-5.6G VRIF-ED lens (24mm, 1/350s, f10, ISO 400) at 6.55am on 1st May 2004. However, too many golf course photographs are taken by non-golfers, whose clients are in the main non-golfer*

# PREFACE

Our purpose is to set new levels for golf course guides. As we go to press, there is no single volume which deals exclusively, selectively, authoritatively and in pocket book format with the most popular golf destination in Europe. Most existing publications on the subject are funded directly or indirectly by parties with vested interests. We have no such connections.

In addition, we have established a new system of rating not just golf courses but individual holes (including awarding 'gold hole' status to fewer than 50 outstanding holes over Iberia, and 'red hole' status to even fewer of the weakest) – all of which should fuel debate. Clubs given red holes should not take umbrage: readers are positively encouraged (and indeed might well be interested) to play courses with red holes just as much as those with gold holes – and two have both!

We have included as many photographs as space will allow. One of the problems with golf course photography is that the focal point is nearly always the flag, which, with a shot taken from the player's viewpoint, is always likely to be in the distance. This results in many excellent reverse-view golf course photographs, bringing the flag to the foreground – normally not particularly helpful to the player. Whilst seeking to include the best images, because this is a guidebook, as a golfing photographer I have not been prepared to sacrifice conveying a sense of what is required of the player, for the sake of including better images – even when time and the elements were against us. The photos in this book, and many others from our substantial library, may be purchased from www.pocket-golf.com.

*property/tourist-orientated marketing executives. As this shot conveys, the resultant images, though generally excellent and occasionally inspirational, are often meaningless to a golfer who wants to know about the challenges of the course. There are, of course, a few well-known and highly talented specialist golf photographers – but they are very much the exception.*

We have structured the book to be used at different levels and for different types of readers – from the travelling golfer, local or holiday house resident, to the armchair tourist, and from players to golf design enthusiasts. To get the best out of it, please carefully read 'How to Use this Book' (pages 10-11). We have made a point of avoiding interminable hole by hole descriptions. We have also included a certain amount of verbal entertainment, e.g. crossword addicts might like to muse over the last sentence in the main text on *Pedreña* (Seve's home club); chocaholics should not eschew *Golf del Sur*; we have spiced up *Vilamoura (Victoria)* for football and pop fans – and there are more... Answers on www.pocket-golf.com.

We are very aware that there is ultimately no right answer to what is or is not good golf course design... We accept that those who disagree with us may have just as valid reasons for disagreeing with, as we have for holding, our opinion – no doubt cases could even be made for some red holes being gold and vice versa (or some being both!). We welcome your comments to look@pocket-golf.com.

We have invested more than two years in this project, the most comprehensive survey of its kind: we have rated, photographed, videoed and played on all 18 (and most 9) hole courses in the book, with a panel of professional and amateur players from scratch to high handicap, male and female, providing instant feedback. So here is the consensus opinion of some well-travelled golfers – players of all standards, designers and critics.

William fforde, Editor
Marbella, Spain, July 2004

# INTRODUCTION

For some twenty years I have roamed the world competing with and against many of the finest players of our time. From golfing artistes such as Ballesteros and Olazábal, technicians like Faldo and O'Meara, through to the power and finesse of Woods, Els and Singh, I have been fortunate to encounter the full range of golfing skills at first hand. But it is my fascination with the courses I have played and visited that has been the most enduring facet of my involvement with the game. Whilst many sports can lay claim to all those things interesting about competition and technical skill, few are able to watch these evolve in such a diverse range of arenas as our noble game.

When I was on tour full-time I picked up a bit of a reputation as the man most likely to praise or find fault with the design. I am sure I was right to point out weaknesses – from a desire to see improvements, and to rekindle the spirit and artistry of Donald Ross, Colt and MacKenzie who, back in the halcyon days of golf construction (before the Great Depression), set the golfing world alight with courses that, even today, are ranked among the best on the planet. If they could create such beauty and functionality with the minimum of fuss and equipment then, why should we not do even better now?

## Assessment principles

Our basis of assessment has followed generally accepted principles, dating back to those published by MacKenzie (opposite), which lie behind most other course rating surveys. What makes ours different is that we give ratings for every hole, as well as for the course as a whole.

The key criteria assessed include the playing and mental challenges of each hole, its use of land, the quality of its greensite (i.e. the green and the area immediately around it, including greenside hazards, etc), its hazards and its aesthetics. In rating courses, we have also taken into account the variety and consistency of their design, their routing and fairness, and (to a lesser extent) their history. All this, plus the extent of our team's knowledge about the development of golf course design over the past 150 years, has given our research greater depth than many other studies have been able to achieve.

## Debate

However, whichever principles one adopts, ultimately we are dealing very much with a subjective matter: there is no right answer as to which course is better than another – it is a matter of personal taste and judgment. That is what makes it all the more interesting. What we have done is to stick our necks out, to say what our particular team of well-travelled golf design experts feel. More than anything we hope to encourage debate, and that it will lead to the consumer requiring higher standards. We look forward to c feedback from readers and hope that this will encourage us to publish further volumes covering other parts of the golfing world.

This book should therefore open up discussion of what is – and what is not – acceptable design. I would love to walk into a clubhouse, and find all the golfers having an informed exchange of ideas on the holes they would like to play and how to improve standards back at their home club. No one person will completely agree with another (and indeed I would be surprised if everyone agreed with all our ratings). This of course will only add fuel to the discussion. If such debate grows and standards continue to improve, I shall be happy.

Golf is a great game, and provides endless fun for all. This joy can be heightened significantly when you pit your skill against a really well-designed course. We have to aim high to make courses fun for all players – without the need to be dumbed down, or tricked up. They must remain inspirational and challenging, just as they are.

## MacKenzie's Principles

I will conclude with those 13 principles essential to good design set down in 1920 by the late Dr MacKenzie in his book 'Golf Architecture'. MacKenzie was possibly the greatest golf designer that ever lived, and I am sure it is no accident that his wartime expertise was camouflage. The best golf design leaves you with a feeling that any alterations to the land are so natural that they have been completely disguised.

Here is a summary of Dr MacKenzie's principles:
1) two 9 hole loops;
2) a large proportion of 2 shot holes and at least four 1 shot holes;
3) minimal walking between greens and tees;
4) undulating ground but no hill climbing;
5) every hole different in character;
6) a minimum of blind shots;
7) beautiful surroundings and minimal artificiality;
8) heroic carries and alternative routes;
9) an infinite variety of strokes required;
10) a complete absence of having to look for balls;
11) interesting even to a scratch player always seeking ways to improve;
12) enjoyable for high handicappers;
13) equally good in winter and summer.

Of course, changes in technology have changed the game significantly since 1920 – as with many other sports. But have the characteristics of good design changed? Very little, I would say.

What makes good art has not changed just because of changes in how one creates and uses a work of art – and, for all the huge technological input into the infrastructure of a modern layout, ultimately course design is not a science, but an art.

Greg Turner, Tour Editor
Queenstown,
New Zealand, July 2004

# SPAIN

Golf in Spain instantly evokes the Costa del Sol, which is where the consumer has the most choice, with some 40 courses over a coastline of some 100km. Unfortunately, primarily because of the soaring value of land, golf courses have been left with inadequate sites, too often resulting in poor quality. Happily, the three newest courses have reversed this trend (and, of course, there are some older exceptions). Madrid has some outstanding courses, but the

golf tourist area with the highest standards is the North East (i.e. Barcelona & Costa Brava). Golf in the islands is growing fast. Finally, do not underestimate the North: some wonderful courses, fewer tourists and Basque food is the best... Avoid inland courses in winter and summer months, and be prepared for occasional lengthy periods of heavy rain everywhere during the peak golf season (even on the Costa del Sol, which sometimes seems inappropriately named – particularly during mid-autumn and mid-January to mid-April).

*Smoke from an autumnal bonfire adds depth to a morning view of San Sebastián's p4:5 and the Basque mountains beyond.*

# EMPORDÀ (FOREST) ★★

von Hagge   1990   €€        **H:** M 28, L 36, J 28/36

✉ Empordà Golf Club, Ctra. de Palafrugell a Torroella, 17257 Gualta, Girona

☎ +34 972 760 450

✎ reserves@empordagolfclub.com   www.empordagolfclub.com

🚗 ✈ Girona: AP7 north towards France; exit 6 onto C66; 8km past La Bisbal d'Empordà l onto GI652 past Torrent; onto C31, skirting Pals, for Torroella; club by km346 on l.

| Blue | | | Yellow | | |
|---|---|---|---|---|---|
| | m | p | | m | p |
| 1 | 364 | 4 | 10 | 479 | 5 |
| 2 | 165 | 3 | 11 | 309 | 4 |
| 3 | 379 | 4 | 12 | 171 | 3 |
| 4 | 498 | 5 | 13 | 485 | 5 |
| 5 | 152 | 3 | 14 | 158 | 3 |
| 6 | 292 | 4 | 15 | 335 | 4 |
| 7 | 566 | 5 | 16 | 377 | 4 |
| 8 | 171 | 3 | 17 | 363 | 4 |
| 9 | 491 | 5 | 18 | 410 | 4 |
| | 3078 | 36 | | 3087 | 36 |
| | | | | 6165 | 72 |

Two grand-scale, challenging loops of 9 start and finish on open ground, but otherwise weave through a magnificent, beautiful and dramatic umbrella pine forest. Lavish bunkering and some water defend fairly large, often sloping/raised greens.

*After 5 holes surrounded by trees, on the tee of p3:8 your eyes will be drawn, almost magnetically, by the open vista over the long bunker left of the green. Try not to let that description apply to your ball, tempting though it may be to steer away from the trees. The long green is joined to almost mirror image p3:12.*

*The sharp banks separating raised green from fairway at right to left dogleg shortish p4:11, and the ranks of pines behind, typify Forest's many combinations of good looks and quality design.*

We can think of many courses where the design is no match for the aesthetics, or vice versa, but (with the exception of the apartment backdrop to watery 18) the Forest course is a feast for both eyes and play. The challenge of the opening two links-style holes (right to left dogleg p4:1 with fairway undulations and a bunker almost all round the green, and effectively bunkered raised and mounded p3:2) proves this before the pines begin to cloak the fairways at 3, a long p4 to a raised, well-bunkered green. Indeed, the transitions from open land to forest and

back provide some of the best holes, with the two tiers of the 17th green as the sting in this particular tail. The course has several tree-defying doglegs, including strategic p5:4 – if you draw it round the corner with your drive, the green becomes temptingly reachable over another (bunkered) corner with your second. With courses of the calibre of *PGA de Catalunya* and *Platja de Pals* nearby, consider basing a golfing holiday around a flight to Girona (don't miss its cathedral and old Jewish quarter) and the Costa Brava.

*A reverse view (from 18) of the photo left, showing p3:12 (and p3:8 beyond) through the forest, below the Pregnant Woman's nipple (see Links page 33).*

# PGA DE CATALUNYA ★★

Coles & Gallardo   1999   €€

✉ PGA Golf de Catalunya, Ctra. NII km701, 17455 Caldes de Malavella, Girona

☎ +34 972 472 577

✎ info@pgacatalunya.com
www.pgacatalunya.com

🚗 ✈ Girona: N156 (airport exit road); r onto B10 towards Barcelona; course approx 3.5km on r (km701.5).

| | m | p | | | m | p |
|---|---|---|---|---|---|---|
| 1 | 396 | 4 | | 10 | 397 | 4 |
| 2 | 354 | 4 | | 11 | 173 | 3 |
| 3 | 489 | 5 | | 12 | 491 | 5 |
| 4 | 380 | 4 | | 13 | 365 | 4 |
| 5 | 191 | 3 | | 14 | 408 | 4 |
| 6 | 375 | 4 | | 15 | 461 | 5 |
| 7 | 487 | 5 | | 16 | 186 | 3 |
| 8 | 170 | 3 | | 17 | 423 | 4 |
| 9 | 427 | 4 | | 18 | 415 | 4 |
| | 3269 | 36 | | | 3319 | 36 |
| | | | | | 6588 | 72 |

Excellent tree-lined course on near ideal site for inland golf – undulations, mature woodland, Pyrenean vistas, water, beauty... Many downhill tee shots lead to flowing fairways, strategic bunkers and provocatively sloped, reasonably large greens – all with few uphill shots. Appears seductive, plays tough.

*Downhill medium-long p5:3 is reachable in 2 by long hitters: but is it worth the risk? Go left, and you're in water, right and you're in sand, playing towards water. Think strategy...*

Aesthetics are so important in judging a golf course. Indeed, if you were only allowed to play one course for the rest of your life, would you choose the course where you had your best round, or the course whose beauty has enticed you into playing it time and again – however badly? PGA de Catalunya, set in a pine forest with stunning views of often

*This view from the tee of medium p5:7 illustrates the challenge: if you can drive over the two trees on the left (a carry of 200m from the back) you shorten the hole, making it reachable in 2. Otherwise best to lay up short of the approach bunkers.*

snow-clad distant Pyrenees, simply begs you for one more caress. Most of us will be seduced into hacking our way round, but talented golfers will themselves seduce this beauty and score. But one is looking for brains as well: Neil Coles & Ángel Gallardo were up to that – PGA de Catalunya is a seriously good layout, confirmed by the fact that it held 2 Tour events in its first year (though we should note that it is owned by European Tour Courses). There's plenty of water, but only twice severely penal – at 12 and 13. The course is conveniently close to Girona airport, but you are more likely to be disturbed by croaking frogs, quacking ducks and the occasional cuckoo, than by jet engines. Aesthetics aside, PGA de Catalunya's principal design qualities are that it is strategic and honest, requiring accurate golf on undulating, sometimes windswept, fairways and greens to score well, not least if you occasionally visit its lush rough. Construction of a 2nd course began in 2004.

*This may surprise you, but we rate 11 highly – a rare example of a truly strategic p3. Normally p3s cannot be that strategic, because there is only one shot to the green. Here, the green is wide, but the safe shot is always to go for the middle, regardless of pin position, often leaving testing putts – the putting surface runs downhill away from the tee: with the pin at the back, be sure to stop your ball rolling into the lake; with the pin at the front, it's pleasantly back uphill. We love the designers' deceit with the wooden banking on the left, which fools the first time back tee player into thinking that there is water in front of the green to the left: there isn't!*

# PUERTA DE HIERRO (ARRIBA) ★★

Colt/Trent Jones Jnr   1912/2001   €€€

✉ Club Real de la Puerta de Hierro, Avda. de Miraflores s/n, 28035 Madrid

☎ +34 913 161 745

Only playable as guest of a member.

🚗 ✈ Madrid: M10, then M30; l into Paseo de Castellana; r before 1st underpass into Avda. de Monforte de Lemos; immediately l into C. de Sinesio Delgado; r into club 600m after tunnel.

| | m | p | | | m | p |
|---|---|---|---|---|---|---|
| 1 | 178 | 3 | | 10 | 375 | 4 |
| 2 | 511 | 5 | | 11 | 197 | 3 |
| 3 | 375 | 4 | | 12 | 425 | 4 |
| 4 | 354 | 4 | | 13 | 369 | 4 |
| 5 | 468 | 5 | | 14 | 416 | 4 |
| 6 | 171 | 3 | | 15 | 449 | 5 |
| 7 | 349 | 4 | | 16 | 323 | 4 |
| 8 | 284 | 4 | | 17 | 166 | 3 |
| 9 | 415 | 4 | | 18 | 550 | 5 |
| | 3105 | 36 | | | 3270 | 36 |
| | | | | | 6375 | 72 |

Classic excellence: the best older course in Spain – consistently fair, spacious and attractive holes flow round undulating, majestic wooded park on edge of city centre. Well-bunkered, deceptively testing sloping greens. A very private club with an excellent 19th.

*The view from the tee of downhill p4:3 is reminiscent of a renaissance painting, but in reverse: the Arcadian landscape (abundant with pheasant, partridge and rabbit) is the foreground, not the background (the mixed architecture of urban Madrid). Testing 2nd shot.*

*Long p4:9 combines so many come-and-play-me-again features: visually enticing, downhill with flowing land, testing bunkering and a sporting green.*

One of Spain's oldest courses belongs to one of its most exclusive clubs: Puerta de Hierro lies on beautiful, rolling woodland, yet part-bordered by urban ring roads NW of Central Madrid, with wide-ranging views of the Royal Palace and other landmarks from across several centuries. Looking the other way from the elegant, traditional clubhouse at p3:1, you may sense that you are viewing a work of art, not just another golf course. Revised and restored over the years by several masters (including Simpson and Harris) and remodelled by Trent Jones Jnr, Arriba is a vintage pre-WW1 Colt canvas (built within a year of St George's Hill, the course he considered his best). It provides a flowing visual feast, achieved principally by the way the dramatic, dazzling white bunkers guide the eye along the fairways to tricky, sloping greens, nearly all backed with banks and pines. The 1st loop

*Big hitters could drive shortish p4:8, but the huge variety of pin positions on a far from flat green, set at an angle behind visually and tactically superb bunkering, yet with space to play safe short/left, make that a huge gamble.*

of 9 takes us over the higher part of the estate, constantly changing direction, before the 2nd 9 routes us in a broad loop – up to 11 and 12, dropping spectacularly at 13, and thence back. All this without being tired by long uphill holes, or green to tee treks. In 8 and 9 Arriba contains the best back-to-back short-long p4 combination in Iberia. Enjoy also the deliciously shaded putting green (behind the excellent greensite of 18), and clubhouse cocktails… Mine's a negroni!

# RSHE Club de Campo (Norte) ★★

von Hagge  1997  €€€                    **H:** M 28, L 36, J 28/36

✉  Real Sociedad Hípica Española Club de Campo, Ctra. de
   Burgos km26.4, San Sebastián de Los Reyes, 28709 Madrid
☎  +34 916 571 018

✎  deportes@rshecc.es   www.rshecc.es

🚗 ✈ Madrid: M11; r onto A1; exit to club at km26; cross
highway; straight over next 2 rbt to club.

| | m | p | | m | p |
|---|---|---|---|---|---|
| 1 | 412 | 4 | 10 | 488 | 5 |
| 2 | 149 | 3 | 11 | 395 | 4 |
| 3 | 532 | 5 | 12 | 365 | 4 |
| 4 | 352 | 4 | 13 | 369 | 4 |
| 5 | 365 | 4 | 14 | 142 | 3 |
| 6 | 326 | 4 | 15 | 389 | 4 |
| 7 | 180 | 3 | 16 | 514 | 5 |
| 8 | 372 | 4 | 17 | 181 | 3 |
| 9 | 582 | 5 | 18 | 351 | 4 |
| | 3270 | 36 | | 3194 | 36 |
| | | | | 6464 | 72 |

Grand-scale mounded layout over undulating land naturally suited for a golf course. Artificial landscaping and rolling fairways blend in well with tree-lined surrounds. Often incisively bunkered, with some wickedly sloping greens. The best modern course in Madrid, if not Iberia.

To simplify a long story, the take-over of Madrid's Club de Campo by the city council resulted in the re-establishment of a separate club using the equestrian name of a society which had fused with the rest of the Club de Campo in 1941. Driven on by the desire to own their own land, RHSE aggrandised themselves with a truly glorious site for golf 25km north of

*Early morning light and irrigation spray at longish p4:11 serve to heighten the dramatic effect of some of RHSF's key features: greenside (and fairway) mounding, penetrating bunkers, sloping greens and water (bottom right).*

*Medium short p5:10 is a tremendous strategic hole, influenced by pin position, water and the tree in front of the green. From a high tee, you may drive to the top of a bunkered ridge (whence this view, and a higher but longer second right of the tree), or (as a longer hitter) bounce the ball down to a lower level (whence a shorter second with the tree more in play). Or a testing lay-up towards the left-hand bunkers: too short, you risk water and the tree is in the way; too long, sand!*

central Madrid, next to the Jarama motor circuit. It was most fitting that they selected Robert von Hagge (the 'von' being a personal self-aggrandisement, in complete harmony with his style) as the designer of their two courses.

Norte and *Sur* are a lavish pair, which appear to have been a wise (and no doubt significant) investment by the 6,000 or so members of the club.

Norte is the tougher test of golf, but both will challenge your brain as well as your playing technique. With uphill and downhill holes, valley carries, doglegs left and right, water and some

*The slightly featureless uphill drive at medium long p4:8 is more than compensated for by the view which greets you over the brow. Say no more…*

dramatic bunkering, all in two harmonious loops, Norte is very much a three-dimensional course. The treacherous greens have some fiendish potential pin placements for championship play, but one gets the feeling that the club rightly has its members at the forefront of its priorities: the luxury of being able to set up the course for top players is only one of its many facets. If you can only try one course, choose Norte, but preferably play both.

# SOTOGRANDE ★★

Trent Jones Snr   1964   €€€          **H:** M 25, L 30, J 25/30

✉ **Real Club de Golf Sotogrande, Paseo del Parque s/n, 11310 Sotogrande, Cádiz**

☎ **+34 956 785 014**

✎ recepcion@golfsotogrande.com   www.golfsotogrande.com

🚗 ✈ Gibraltar: A383 from La Línea; after 9km r onto A7; km130 exit for Sotogrande/Valderrama; 1st r at rbt; after 500m at rbt l for Sotogrande Costa; follow road for 2.8km to club entrance on l.

|   | m | p |   | m | p |
|---|-----|---|----|-----|---|
| 1 | 356 | 4 | 10 | 405 | 4 |
| 2 | 473 | 5 | 11 | 330 | 4 |
| 3 | 304 | 4 | 12 | 522 | 5 |
| 4 | 208 | 3 | 13 | 189 | 3 |
| 5 | 321 | 4 | 14 | 453 | 5 |
| 6 | 466 | 5 | 15 | 392 | 4 |
| 7 | 382 | 4 | 16 | 355 | 4 |
| 8 | 185 | 3 | 17 | 157 | 3 |
| 9 | 330 | 4 | 18 | 396 | 4 |
|   | 3025 | 36 |   | 3199 | 36 |
|   |      |    |   | 6224 | 72 |

The first Trent Jones in Europe, this excellent, grand-scale, tree-lined out and back course over mainly mildly undulating ground is fair, and pretty roomy. Large, well-bunkered, sloping greens, sometimes defended by water, reward accurate shot-making. The best Costa del Sol design.

**N.B. There is also a 9 hole course (1299m).**

*Gold-rated p4:7 is a downhill right to left dogleg, with a pretty green surrounded by bunkers and defended on the right by a lake; trees form the backdrop. The less you get round the corner with your drive, the more you play towards the water with your approach shot – but it will never completely escape your mind!*

*Understated p5:2 is a gently undulating dogleg, sweeping right to left around two carefully placed bunkers to a raised green protected by sand and framed by cork trees. Plenty of room to enable you to play it well – or not so well. The hole wins gold for its strategic qualities – several options to plot your way around all that sand.*

Sotogrande has always been an up-market place, but one has to admire the foresight of the original promoters. Not only was it the only significant development (which continues to this day) in the hitherto unexploited west of the Costa del Sol, but they brought in a famous American course designer for his first work in continental Europe. An American-style course on a grand scale, albeit with Mediterranean clothing, is what they got: Sotogrande is now the grandee of the Gibraltar area, just as *Las Brisas* (also by Trent Jones Snr) is for Marbella. The feeling of space at both is refreshing in comparison with many of the courses along the coast, especially those closer to Marbella. Sotogrande is actually a hybrid: there are quite distinct differences between the Mediterranean and American elements – 2-11 and 15-16 are 'Hispano-American', i.e. Trent Jones' style is imposed on undulating ground bedecked with cork and olive trees, whereas 1, 12-14 and 17-18 would not be out of place in Florida (i.e. generally flat, framed by clumps of palms, some very tall – especially left of 17,

*The undulating tree-lined fairway and bunkered raised sloping green of p4:9 typify the Mediterranean elements of Sotogrande's design.*

where they make a towering statement to balance the water on the right). Both elements respect careful driving, as the generally large, amply-bunkered greens reward accurate iron shots with birdies. Yet for the rest of us, there is still at least a sporting chance of a par – gross, or net(?!). In attaining ★★, the world class quality of the Hispano-American holes just outweighed the negating inconsistency of the Florida sweep on the way home. Although there are others with potential to outrank it (either through maturity or enhancement – e.g. *La Reserva* or *Málaga*), Sotogrande is currently the best design on the Costa del Sol.

# LAS BRISAS ★

Trent Jones Snr   1968   €€€          **H:** M 248, L 32, J 36

✉  Real Club de Golf Las Brisas, Apdo. de Correos 147, 29660
    Nueva Andalucía, Marbella, Málaga

☎  +34 952 810 875

✎  secretaria@lasbrisasgolf.com     www.lasbrisasgolf.com

🚗 ✈ Málaga: r out of airport exit road onto A7 for Cádiz; r at
km229 for AP7 Benalmádena/Algeciras; end of Marbella bypass
(km178) take r split onto A7; exit junction 176 (Istán) after tunnel; l
at rbt; over bridge, straight over (i.e. do not veer left); 2nd r, up hill,
at next rbt; straight over next rbt; over hill past Aloha Golf; straight
over mini-rbt; r fork over hill; exit r out of Aloha Golf along Avda. del
Prado for 500m; l at rbt into cul-de-sac; follow road up to club.

|    | m    | p  |    | m    | p  |
|----|------|----|----|------|----|
| 1  | 365  | 4  | 10 | 361  | 4  |
| 2  | 389  | 4  | 11 | 188  | 3  |
| 3  | 436  | 5  | 12 | 467  | 5  |
| 4  | 189  | 3  | 13 | 338  | 4  |
| 5  | 532  | 5  | 14 | 361  | 4  |
| 6  | 345  | 4  | 15 | 382  | 4  |
| 7  | 158  | 3  | 16 | 203  | 3  |
| 8  | 447  | 5  | 17 | 291  | 4  |
| 9  | 316  | 4  | 18 | 362  | 4  |
|    | 3177 | 37 |    | 2953 | 35 |
|    |      |    |    | 6130 | 72 |

The definitive Marbella Trent Jones: grand-scale, yet slightly understated, spacious design over gently undulating ground adorned with specimen trees. Effective bunkering, water carries and sometimes small, sloping greens combine to require accurate shot placement to score well.

*Medium p4:6, seen here from the tee, is much more difficult than it looks: the bunker which appears to be in front of the green conceals a small pond which runs down into a watery gulley which eats back across into the fairway.*

*Short p5:12 is a tremendous strategic hole: a broad right to left sweep, water all down the left and bunkers at driving distance on the right (foreground). It is not just a question of deciding whether to go for the green in two, but being able to hold it as well, as it is raised above its surrounds (and bunkered left). There's room to lay up (possibly the smarter option) longer or shorter of pin high, according to pin position.*

Long praised as the best course close to Marbella, and one of its oldest, Las Brisas stands out as the aristocrat amongst the otherwise generally rather semi-detached alternatives nearby. Granted, it was built before the time land became too expensive to justify an alternative to residential use, so Trent Jones Snr was given a good piece of ground to work with, and the freedom not to have to route his design between building plots, which gives the layout the feeling of an oasis within some of the most dense accumulations of pretending-to-be-up-market housing in the world. Las Brisas is not without its weaknesses, e.g. after a classy start, holes 3-5 are very slightly bland. However, this is more than compensated for by its many strengths: short by modern standards it may be, but this reflects its inclusion of a wide range of hole lengths within each par category, most

*The main question at heroic short p5:8 is simple: do you go for it in 2 and risk the water in front of the green? The hazard is further from the putting surface, wider and wetter than it looks: even carried, you still have to contend with well-placed bunkers and slopes.*

notably two short p5 gems in 8 and 12, both inspiring dangerously sporting strategic to-go-for-it-or-not decisions over water. Don't throw caution to the winds here: respect Las Brisas – it's no breeze.

# CLUB DE CAMPO (NEGRO) ★

Arana   1957   €€€ (weekdays much cheaper)   **H:** M 28, L 28, J 28

✉  Club de Campo, Villa Madrid, Ctra. de Castilla km2, 28040 Madrid

☎  +34 915 502 010

✎  deportes@clubvillademadrid.com
www.clubvillademadrid.com

🚗 ✈ Madrid: M10, then M30; exit 20 for M500 (Ctra. de Castilla); r at rbt onto M500; after 0.5 km r into club; l after entrance; after 800m l by red British phone box, up hill.

|   | m | p |   | m | p |
|---|---|---|---|---|---|
| 1 | 427 | 4 | 10 | 376 | 4 |
| 2 | 404 | 4 | 11 | 192 | 3 |
| 3 | 189 | 3 | 12 | 407 | 4 |
| 4 | 474 | 5 | 13 | 427 | 4 |
| 5 | 372 | 4 | 14 | 481 | 5 |
| 6 | 404 | 4 | 15 | 343 | 4 |
| 7 | 494 | 5 | 16 | 386 | 4 |
| 8 | 352 | 4 | 17 | 153 | 3 |
| 9 | 162 | 3 | 18 | 331 | 4 |
|   | 3278 | 36 |   | 3096 | 35 |
|   |   |   |   | 6374 | 71 |

Two occasionally dramatic undulating loops, with views of nearby central Madrid, emanate from hilltop clubhouse through historic woods. Generally well-bunkered with every green multi-tiered. Long and challenging, even with slightly weaker design of closing stretch.

**N.B.** There is a second course (Amarillo, 6011m) and 9 holes p3.

*This view from the tee of excellent left to right medium long p4:10 shows how it turns round the fairway bunker. You feel there is plenty of room for your drive down the right of the fairway, but, with the pin anywhere towards the back or right of the tiered green, you will have to carry trees and sand with your second shot unless you drive well left of the bunker. Sight of greensites through tree trunks on doglegs is one of the several arborial attractions at Club de Campo.*

*Take one club more than you think at long p4:6. After a downhill drive towards the stream (foreground), the hole turns a little left and sharply uphill to a well-bunkered sloping green.*

On the hills NW of Madrid's Royal Palace lies an ancient forest: once a royal hunting ground, it is now partly occupied by the Club de Campo, Madrid's largest sporting club. Enhanced over the years, Negro, the main course, is a classic Arana design, which has stood well the test of time – and many European Tour events. Despite the quirky tree in front of the tee at tightly bunkered 17, Negro has an excellent collection of short holes, especially seductive 9, which is played over a valley to a typically tricky sloping green nestling amongst trees near the clubhouse. Tree-lined 3 and 11 are both long and well bunkered, again with greens full of testing undulations. 1-9 (Ballesteros) on Amarillo, Club de Campo's other course, disappoint, but 10-18 (Arana, enhanced by Piñero, 2002), are a better match for Negro. The whole complex (with many other sporting facilities, including a driving range and a 9 hole p3 course) is owned by Madrid's city council. Despite the entrance fee at the gate, the overall package is good value.

**Below** *The tiers on the green of medium p3:9 are clearly visible over the trees which you will need to carry with your tee shot – the other problems of missing the target are evident.*

# EMPORDÀ (LINKS) ★

von Hagge   1990/2004   €€           **H:** M 28, L 36, J 28/36

✉ Empordà Golf Club, Ctra. de Palafrugell a Torroella, 17257 Gualta, Girona

☎ +34 972 760 450

✎ reserves@empordagolfclub.com   www.empordagolfclub.com

🚗 ✈ Girona: AP7 north towards France; exit 6 onto C66; 8km past La Bisbal d'Empordà I onto GI652 past Torrent; onto C31, skirting Pals, for Torreolla; club by km346 on l.

| | Green | | | Red | |
|---|---|---|---|---|---|
| | m | p | | m | p |
| 1 | 380 | 4 | 10 | 330 | 4 |
| 2 | 372 | 4 | 11 | 164 | 3 |
| 3 | 158 | 3 | 12 | 535 | 5 |
| 4 | 328 | 4 | 13 | 364 | 4 |
| 5 | 359 | 4 | 14 | 391 | 4 |
| 6 | 168 | 3 | 15 | 148 | 3 |
| 7 | 391 | 4 | 16 | 300 | 4 |
| 8 | 546 | 5 | 17 | 398 | 4 |
| 9 | 380 | 4 | 18 | 505 | 5 |
| | 3082 | 35 | | 3135 | 36 |
| | | | | 6217 | 71 |

Challenging layout on former rice field subjected to generally remarkably effective neo-Scottish makeover, with disarming eccentricities sometimes reminiscent of old-fashioned links. Large, sloping, often raised greens. Some water. Bunkering often lavish.

The Links course comprises Empordà's original Green 9 and its remarkable 4th loop (Red), completed in 2004, which recalls some of the surprisingly irregular, yet completely natural, undulations of more northerly links, and does so rather more daringly than on the Green. We like the split fairway of the first hole (10): the risk of the long carry over mounds to the left fairway is rewarded with a much easier second to the three rolling tiers of the green; going right is easier from the tee, but then you face bunkers. Meanwhile, at a different level, the overall width of the double fairway target gives confidence to weaker players playing what may well be the first shot of the day.

We leave it to you to savour the rest, including the sandy glories of long p5:12 and the elusive greensite of dogleg p4:13, its sloping putting surface set up in the air as if on an acropolis. A higher rating may well be possible if the front 9 were stylistically enhanced to match the new holes…

**Above** *The snow-clad Pyrenees form a backdrop to long p5:12, a hole where you have to thread your ball between a series of bunkers all the way to the green.*

**Right** *Empordà (Links)'s p4 16th, is at the edge of the pine forest used by Empordà (Forest). The main obstacle here is the pine in front of the green, whose other defences and undulations are self-evident.*

*The distant hills seen from Links' p4 9th fairway are known locally as the 'Pregnant Woman', whose one visible nipple is a mediaeval hilltop fortress. It cannot be a coincidence that the routing allows about 1/3rd of all of Empordà's holes to aim at this spectacle. The eccentric green over the sleeper-tied banks of the water acts as hors d'oeuvres for the back 9.*

# GOLF DEL SUR ★

Gancedo   1987   €€                    **H:** M 28, L 36, J 28/36

✉   Golf del Sur, Urb. El Guincho, 38639 San Miguel de Abona, Tenerife

☎   +34 922 738 170

✎   golfdelsur@golfdelsur.net     www.golfdelsur.net

🚗 ✈ Tenerife Sur: TF1 towards Playa de las Américas; l at exit 24 down hill towards sea; follow signs to club.

| South | | | North | | | Links | | |
|---|---|---|---|---|---|---|---|---|
| | m | p | | m | p | | m | p |
| 1 | 352 | 4 | 1 | 459 | 5 | 1 | 338 | 4 |
| 2 | 193 | 3 | 2 | 131 | 3 | 2 | 170 | 3 |
| 3 | 381 | 4 | 3 | 415 | 4 | 3 | 449 | 5 |
| 4 | 268 | 4 | 4 | 289 | 4 | 4 | 302 | 4 |
| 5 | 482 | 5 | 5 | 473 | 5 | 5 | 143 | 3 |
| 6 | 135 | 3 | 6 | 302 | 4 | 6 | 337 | 4 |
| 7 | 284 | 4 | 7 | 330 | 4 | 7 | 355 | 4 |
| 8 | 319 | 4 | 8 | 191 | 3 | 8 | 238 | 4 |
| 9 | 543 | 5 | 9 | 359 | 4 | 9 | 137 | 3 |
| | 2957 | 36 | | 2949 | 36 | | 2469 | 34 |
| NS | 5906 | 72 | NL | 5418 | 70 | SL | 5426 | 70 |

Unforgettable black bunkers combined with natural golf holes make for a memorable, challenging, undulating layout with some testing greensites, tricky putting surfaces, palm tree hazards and a little water. Take care, especially in the wind: this delicious course can often eat you.

**Left** *L8 is one of the very best natural and simple short p4s in Iberia – its raised green is reminiscent of Royal Dornoch (regular background aircraft noise included!).*

*S8 is a mild left to right dogleg medium short p4, lined on the right with a long and original bunker containing mounds topped with hazelnut clusters of rocks (eerie: are they tombstones from a primaeval cad burial ground?!).*

An intriguing collection of 27 dark, alluring golf holes greets visitors to this unique course just a lemon whisper away from Tenerife's southern airport. Its lava bunkers are black magic, surely making Golf del Sur unique (at least at the time of its construction) in Europe – acknowledged indeed by an assortment of Tour events here over the years. The 27 holes are laid out over rolling (but not too arduous) ground, with sea views, generous fairways, palms (often clumped into side bunkers) and some testing greens. Each of the 3 layers (South, North and Links) in Golf del Sur's box holds its weight, full of different flavours (N.B. Links included – wonderfully natural). In a street of such quality, inevitably 1 or 2 corners may seem relatively own brand (e.g. doubly blind, round tree downhill left to right dogleg p5:N1, despite its testing green; and p3:S6 is a little bland after 4 good holes). But savour Golf del Sur for yourself: nothing's fudged here!

*For black magic read all gold at p3:S2 (a signature hole if ever there was one): a long narrow tricky sloping island green surrounded by grains of dark chocolate lava.*

# MÁLAGA ★

Colt/Simpson  1926/64  €€          H: M 28, L 36, J 28/36

✉ Real Club de Campo de Málaga, Apdo. 324, 29620 Málaga
☎ +34 952 381 255
✎ Book by phone  www.parador.es

🚗 ✈ Málaga: exit airport slip road r for Cádiz onto A7; r at km230 for Coín/Parador de Golf; l at rbt, under highway; r for Málaga /Cádiz; straight on under road bridge for Parador del Golf (effectively straight across rbt after bridge).

|   | m | p |   |   | m | p |
|---|---|---|---|---|---|---|
| 1 | 447 | 5 |   | 10 | 380 | 4 |
| 2 | 337 | 4 |   | 11 | 196 | 3 |
| 3 | 284 | 4 |   | 12 | 497 | 5 |
| 4 | 414 | 4 |   | 13 | 165 | 3 |
| 5 | 381 | 4 |   | 14 | 442 | 5 |
| 6 | 174 | 3 |   | 15 | 383 | 4 |
| 7 | 355 | 4 |   | 16 | 447 | 5 |
| 8 | 346 | 4 |   | 17 | 334 | 4 |
| 9 | 186 | 3 |   | 18 | 405 | 4 |
|   | 2924 | 35 |   |   | 3249 | 37 |
|   |   |   |   |   | 6173 | 72 |

The oldest course in the south of Spain, on gently flowing sandy ground adjoining beach. Two loops of 9: earlier holes generally more inland and tree-lined; from 7 more in touch with the sea. Reminiscent of classic links, design mostly retains old-fashioned bunkering and oozes appeal.

N.B. A further 9 holes (2271m) were opened in 2004 (but we doubt Colt or Simpson would have wished to be have been associated with them).

*Reaching the raised green of longish p5:12 in two is even harder than it looks; the mounding short of the green conceals a deep swale.*

*The appearance of Málaga today is largely the work of Tom Simpson, whose post-Civil-War-destruction-and-neglect restoration plans, extending Colt's original 9 holes were finally completed in 1964, the year of Simpson's death. But the atmosphere of holes such as long p4:14, running towards the balmy sea, has surely remained unchanged. It is also likely that the raised undulating green and its surrounding bunkering were Colt-inspired. With water all round the sides and back of the greensite, nothing is balmy when it's your turn to play.*

You may think that we are biased towards rating older courses higher than newer ones, but you would be wrong. For example, we have probably rated *Oporto* and *Sant Cugat* higher than some might have expected (and no doubt others below aspirations!). There are plenty of good reasons for this apparent phenomenon: there is less need for advertising hype and housebuilding around such courses, as their original cost will have been well defrayed by now. (The quality of new courses is so often overstated by marketeers, leading to disappointment when playing – Málaga is run by the Parador hotel chain, and was always too good a course to fall into this trap.) It is also because better land was available, and at lower prices – this was certainly true for Málaga, on what would then have been regarded as otherwise fairly useless sandy ground by the sea (the spaciousness of *Las Brisas*

*Shortish p4:3 exemplifies the more inland feel to the initial holes: the trees provide more wind protection – a good thing, as sand surrounds the raised green.*

within now over-developed real estate is a more recent example). Finally, the pre-computer-bulldozer designer was forced much more to work with the land allocated – result: more creativity, generally more suited to the land... more success (the character of many of Málaga's greensites and approaches could really only have been conceived in situ). With some informed modifications (particularly from 6 to 10) Málaga could be Andalucía's best, as well as its oldest – and still no bias!

# PEDREÑA ★

Colt 1928 €€€                    **H:** M 28, L 36, J 28/36

✉ Real Golf de Pedreña, Ctra. General s/n, 39130 Pedreña, Cantabria

☎ +34 942 500 001

✎ Book by phone – private club

🚗 ✈ Santander: N636 from airport; r onto S10/A67 (north) for Santander; after 1km U-turn onto S10 (south) for Bilbao; after 7km becomes A8 for Bilbao; take 1st exit (no. 11) onto S430 for Pedreña, approx 6km; club is on r of town over hill, accessible via any one of several small side roads.

| m | p | | m | p | |
|---|---|---|---|---|---|
| 1 | 335 | 4 | 10 | 192 | 3 |
| 2 | 190 | 3 | 11 | 494 | 5 |
| 3 | 357 | 4 | 12 | 151 | 3 |
| 4 | 394 | 4 | 13 | 352 | 4 |
| 5 | 286 | 4 | 14 | 317 | 4 |
| 6 | 380 | 4 | 15 | 212 | 3 |
| 7 | 154 | 3 | 16 | 477 | 5 |
| 8 | 353 | 4 | 17 | 355 | 4 |
| 9 | 435 | 5 | 18 | 330 | 4 |
| | 2884 | 35 | | 2880 | 35 |
| | | | | 5764 | 70 |

Excellent strategic, fairly hilly, classic out-&-back design, mainly astride rocky outcrop with very beautiful sea and mountain views, mostly lined with mature trees. Good bunkering and sloping greens will test your short game. A couple of blindish shots, but little water.

There is also a 9 hole course (2655m).

*Uphill medium p4:13 is generally regarded as Pedreña's best hole: a superb raised greensite and a pleasantly surprising stunning sea view...*

1928 was the year in which Harry Colt, Hugh Alison and John Morrison formalised their business partnership into Colt, Alison & Morrison Limited. Incorporation was unusual in those days for a professional partnership, and the timing was not particularly

*Reachable-in-two p5:11's excellence is understated – you drive over a brow, semi-blind, which makes the vista even more stunning as it unfolds down the curves of the fairway. The subtle bunkering will trouble your thoughts, however many shots you plan to take to reach the delicately sloping green.*

fortunate (but did Colt, a lawyer, have foresight – and therefore good reason – in that particular year?). In fact, the three had been collaborating for some time and by then Colt's earlier association with MacKenzie (who had gone to the USA, and died there in 1932) had waned, at best. When we credit 'Colt' with the design of a course, some of the attribution must (to a greater or lesser extent) go to the other three (though increasingly minimally to MacKenzie after WW1). The two other great Spanish courses are *Puerto de Hierro (Arriba)* and *Málaga* (completed by Tom Simpson): Pedreña is probably (and undeservedly) the least well-known – as a golf course. But, for European golf, starting from here: beach (and links land everywhere) saw the emerging riches of Spain...

*Aesthetics are a key ingredient to the assessment of golf courses and play a significant role in Pedreña's high rating, as this view of medium p4:8 demonstrates (though it looks rather different at low tide). Colt scores gold for use of land, and design of hazards and greensite: you drive slightly uphill (N.B. anything much off-fairway right will be lost); then a spectacular medium to short iron over the valley to a raised, bunkered green. Playing and mental challenge? That right bunker will so often get you, or cause you to go into the left one...*

# PLATJA DE PALS ★

F Hawtree   1966   €€          **H:** M 36, L 36, J 36

✉ Golf Platja de Pals, Arenales de Mar s/n, 17256 Pals, Girona
☎ +34 972 667 739
✎ recep@golfplatjadepals.com   www. golfplatjadepals.com

🚗 ✈ Girona: AP7 north towards France; exit 6 for C66; 8km
past La Bisbal d'Empordà left onto GI652, past Torrent, for Pals;
over 1st rbt onto C31; r at 2nd rbt onto Ctra. de Pals; l after
approx 2km, following signs.

| | m | p | | | m | p |
|---|---|---|---|---|---|---|
| 1 | 289 | 4 | | 10 | 328 | 4 |
| 2 | 313 | 4 | | 11 | 132 | 3 |
| 3 | 315 | 4 | | 12 | 421 | 4 |
| 4 | 377 | 4 | | 13 | 363 | 4 |
| 5 | 479 | 5 | | 14 | 462 | 5 |
| 6 | 159 | 3 | | 15 | 183 | 3 |
| 7 | 370 | 4 | | 16 | 498 | 5 |
| 8 | 523 | 5 | | 17 | 369 | 4 |
| 9 | 148 | 3 | | 18 | 493 | 5 |
| | 2973 | 36 | | | 3249 | 37 |
| | | | | | 6222 | 73 |

Difficult, unusual, narrow course, lined with umbrella pines combined with small well-bunkered greens, several raised. Suits straighter hitters, but an attractive challenge for all as long as reasonably on game. A little water.

**Supercalifragilisticexpialidocious!**

*Uccello's A Hunt in the Forest (1465) – a different sport but evocatively similar.*

*Shortish p3:11 is remarkable: surely Hawtree did not intend the trees to close in front of the tee? But there they are – and over you go... It works!*

*Imagine you are playing in the Tour School. First tee. Pressure. (Practised on the range: a few drives went 5m off line; seemed OK; we'll soon warm up.) Hmm, what have we here?! Bunkerless short p4. Driveable, actually. Small narrow green, raised all round, except on the right, where trees deflect anything played from that side. Driver? No thanks. OK, 5-iron to nice wide bit of fairway. But what about the second hit? Got to be straight. Uneven rolling fairway. Mustn't take 5 on such a silly little hole??? ??? ??? Andrews Liver Salts before bed, please...*

This unique course needed a unique word to describe it. Platja de Pals is not everyone's spoonful of sugar, as it is one of the narrowest serious golf courses anywhere, especially the section south of the clubhouse (1-6, 9-12). This characteristic was presumably dictated by the amount of land available and because it comprised a dense umbrella pine forest. (There are more than enough umbrellas here to last Mary Poppins a lifetime – but sadly, when you need the space, none of them flies away.) Indeed, this is no place even to fly a kite: the space between tree trunks sometimes may even be 35m, but with the umbrella canopy it plays much less. Yet the height of the foliage above the ground allows distant vistas beneath. Narrow it may be, but short it is not, even though the first 3 holes average less than 300m. So Platja de Pals is difficult and, if its tightness forces one to cut back off the tee, this in turn makes it play even longer. Some respite, however: bunkering not excessive, greens generally smallish and on a single plane (occasionally with banks two-a-penny), and at 16-17 the course opens up with two generous fairways, so if you want a clean sweep, try to feed the

*Twisting medium p5:18 is challengingly strategic. The bunkering, for a 500m hole, is not over the top, but the sand is well placed. You also have to think your way around those trees. Concentrate.*

birdies here… A Tour School and a pay-&-play course, it has tested most standards, and generally wins. Finally, enjoy the colour contrast: red flags, sun-lit green v shaded forest – Uccello, not Van Dyke!

# EL PRAT (RED) ★

**Norman 2003 €€€**　　　　**H:** M 28, L 36, J 28/36

✉ Real Club de El Prat, Plans de Bonvillar 17, 08227 Terrassa, Barcelona

☎ +34 937 281 000

✎ rcgep@rcgep.com　www.realclubdegolfelprat.com

🚗 ✈ Barcelona: C32, B10, B23, AP7 for Girona, l onto C58 away from Barcelona; exit 16; l at lights onto service road marked Mercavallès (not onto N150); r after 500m; club entrance l after 2km.

| | m | p | | m | p |
|---|---|---|---|---|---|
| 1 | 546 | 5 | 10 | 537 | 5 |
| 2 | 350 | 4 | 11 | 170 | 3 |
| 3 | 140 | 3 | 12 | 325 | 4 |
| 4 | 324 | 4 | 13 | 205 | 3 |
| 5 | 355 | 4 | 14 | 354 | 4 |
| 6 | 214 | 3 | 15 | 294 | 4 |
| 7 | 380 | 4 | 16 | 434 | 4 |
| 8 | 412 | 4 | 17 | 400 | 4 |
| 9 | 506 | 5 | 18 | 490 | 5 |
| | 3227 | 36 | | 3209 | 36 |
| | | | | 6436 | 72 |

This lavish, grand-scale, beautiful and heavily bunkered course, meanders in and out of a majestic pine forest, and should only improve with age. The well-conceived design's attention to detail requires shots to be placed carefully to score on top class greensites.

**6 red:** whilst not a bad golf hole in itself, it is completely out of style with the rest of the course; maturity of trees planted around it may mitigate a little over time.

*The first hole you will play completely within the pine forest is medium-length p4:2. A reasonable drive should carry the bunkers on the right, but the further you can go towards the left-hand bunkers, the more the second shot is opened up, as the hole turns slightly right towards a raised green, bunkered on both sides.*

*The trend towards longer courses makes shorter p3s all the more refreshing. Set in a glade, 140m p3:3 is a good and deceptively difficult example: the green slopes away to the rear and more to the left than appears from the tee. Note the 7 tee markers, which make this longish course playable at all levels.*

You don't have to play many holes at El Prat (Red) to realise that you are on a thoroughly well-conceived and executed golf course design. The grand scale is immediately evidenced by the bunkering at long p5:1, which brings us directly from the clubhouse to the magnificent pine forest which forms the heart of this course. But the design doesn't assume that the forest alone will render a quality golf course: within the woods, just as outside them, the fairways move – sometimes with subtlety, occasionally more dramatically.

The greensites are not only generally attractively bunkered, but are also defended by run-off areas, all of which requires precise execution of approach shots, particularly if the pins are placed aggressively. Notice also how the routing makes a strength of what could have been a weakness: the pine forest is insufficient to accommodate the

*11, a longish p3 across a small valley to a raised, bunkered green, may be rated yellow, but we include it here for its backdrop view of the spectacular Montserrat mountain.*

entire course, and is situated some 500m away from the clubhouse. Instead of routing one complete run of holes within the forest, the design gives you 3 separate visits (1st green to 5th tee, 7-9th tees, 13th green to 15) with final glimpses at 17-18. Tree growth around the other holes will make the final concept more harmonious. Making the opening and closing holes of each 9 p5s keeps the best land in close contact.

# PUERTA DE HIERRO (ABAJO) ★

Trent Jones Jnr   1999   €€€

✉ Club Real de la Puerta de Hierro, Avda. de Miraflores s/n, 28035 Madrid

☎ +34 913 161 745

Only playable as guest of a member.

🚗 ✈ Madrid: M10, then M30; l into P de Castellana; r before 1st underpass into Av de Monforte de Lemos; after 100m l fork into C de Sinesio Delgado; r into club 600m after tunnel.

| | m | p | | m | p |
|---|---|---|---|---|---|
| 1 | 205 | 3 | 10 | 428 | 4 |
| 2 | 383 | 4 | 11 | 495 | 5 |
| 3 | 333 | 4 | 12 | 406 | 4 |
| 4 | 357 | 4 | 13 | 176 | 3 |
| 5 | 524 | 5 | 14 | 487 | 5 |
| 6 | 161 | 3 | 15 | 321 | 4 |
| 7 | 398 | 4 | 16 | 322 | 4 |
| 8 | 500 | 5 | 17 | 211 | 3 |
| 9 | 424 | 4 | 18 | 373 | 4 |
| | 3285 | 36 | | 3219 | 36 |
| | | | | 6504 | 72 |

Set on generally lower, slightly less undulating terrain than Arriba, a long and demanding mainly tree-lined course with generally raised, sometimes spectacularly bunkered, greensites with treacherous putting surfaces. Two superb holes to finish. (Back 9 suffers from traffic noise.)

**Above** *Medium p5:8 turns from right to left over a brow, whence this view: drive here, and the green comes into range, but anything off line will be thrown into sand or rough.*

For us (traditionalists, admittedly) there is no doubt that Puerta de Hierro has the best 36 hole design in Iberia, albeit in a very close run with nearby *RHSE Club de Campo* and *Empordà*, perhaps with maturity to be joined by the new *El Prat* courses. Whilst (maybe controversially) we believe that it must play second fiddle to *Arriba*, Abajo is a completely new course, mostly over the lower

*Right to left longish p4:2 illustrates Abajo's style well: lavish bunkering (the fairway hazards being mainly an aiming point) and hard-to-find raised sloping green.*

ground at Puerta de Hierro, using the land for the original 3rd nine, and some more behind the clubhouse. Trent Jones Jnr was required to retain many trees because the land is owned by the Crown, adding to the design challenge. Abajo's undulating, often irregularly shaped, greensites contrast with the (at least apparently) more receptive banks around *Arriba's*, as they are nearly all raised – even a slightly misdirected approach can be thrown off into greenside bunkers, tangly rough or worse. For Abajo Trent Jones was given perhaps the best and the worst ground available at Puerta de Hierro: the generally superior front 9 were partly cut into hilly land mainly within the grand sweep of *Arriba's* back 9, whilst Abajo's back 9 is very slightly squashed between *Arriba's* close and the Madrid ring road. Abajo is the more masculine course, complementing the softer touch of *Arriba*, and is probably a harder test of golf. The best composite course would perhaps be the front 9 of each.

*Longish uphill p4:18 is beautifully and treacherously bunkered: the dazzling contrast of white sand, strong primary colours and dark shade in Madrid's searing summer sun add to the richness of the challenge (especially with an excellent 19th beckoning). A rare example of how uphill golf holes can be excellent, given sensitive treatment of levels: the tee on lower ground is sufficiently raised to give a clear view of the hole, and the undulations in the fairway enable one to see just enough of the demanding 3-tiered putting surface.*

# LA RESERVA DE SOTOGRANDE ★

Robinson   2003   €€€                    **H:** M 28, L 32, J –

✉ La Reserva de Sotogrande, Avda. de la Reserva s/n, 11310
Sotogrande, San Roque, Cádiz

☎ +34 956 695 208
Book by phone

🚗 ✈ Gibraltar: A383 from La Línea; after 9km r onto A7; exit
at km130 for Guadiaro, underneath A7 and across onto road for
Castellar CA533; club entrance approx 1km on r.

|   | m | p |   | m | p |
|---|-----|---|----|-----|---|
| 1 | 355 | 4 | 10 | 395 | 4 |
| 2 | 403 | 4 | 11 | 502 | 5 |
| 3 | 358 | 4 | 12 | 406 | 4 |
| 4 | 521 | 5 | 13 | 429 | 4 |
| 5 | 418 | 4 | 14 | 164 | 3 |
| 6 | 222 | 3 | 15 | 496 | 5 |
| 7 | 512 | 5 | 16 | 145 | 3 |
| 8 | 187 | 3 | 17 | 433 | 4 |
| 9 | 400 | 4 | 18 | 375 | 4 |
|   | 3376 | 36 |   | 3345 | 36 |
|   |     |   |   | 6721 | 72 |

Undulating, occasionally dramatic and tree-lined, well-constructed strategic course on grand scale with wide views over Sotogrande estate towards sea and other courses. Spectacular bunkering, testing (generally lateral) water and greenside challenges. Large undulating greens put premium on putting.

*Uphill medium p5:11 is right out of the top drawer: a wide driving area if you are laying up, but to have a chance of reaching the carry-all-the-way-or-don't-bother green in two, you must place your tee shot down the left, whence your second is longer than it looks. But this is also a great three-shotter: having played safe down the right, the fairway bunkers come into play and require a precise lay-up. However many shots you have played to reach the green, state of your art putting will be required to avoid three more…*

*Downhill right to left longish dogleg p4:10 becomes shortish by cutting the corner over the olives on the direct line. When we played it, it was the 1st hole and made so much more effective an opener than 1, that we almost thought of gold...*

One of the latest designs of Cabell Robinson, La Reserva immediately ranks with the quality Costa del Sol courses. Indeed, it has the potential to mature into one of the best designs in Iberia – provided that, rather like at *Praia d'el Rey* (also by Robinson), the new housing development proposed for various sections of the surrounding land does not unduly affect its aesthetic appeal. Robinson ran Robert Trent Jones Snr's Spanish office from 1970 and was thus involved with most of the courses designed under that label in Spain, except the original *Sotogrande*. Since 1987 Robinson has worked on his own account and La Reserva will surely be a testament to his skill. He was given a good site, but the very natural feel to the course belies the fact that Robinson had to move a huge amount of earth here to eradicate some deep valleys within the site. It is to Sotogrande S.A.'s credit that they were prepared to make the investment in quality, so lacking in many Costa del Sol courses, whose designs have suffered as a result. Compared with many other of his layouts, Robinson has shown more incisiveness in his bunkering here, which, combined with its insertion into some wonderful, sometimes understated, undulations and its interrelationship with the slopes of the greens, is a main key to La Reserva's success. Another (Player) course is planned.

*Long p3:6 is another strategic hole, in that, although a very long one-shotter, there is room to play short and chip onto the teasing slopes of the green, and hope to single putt.*

# RSHE CLUB DE CAMPO (SUR) ★

von Hagge   2000   €€€

✉ Real Sociedad Hípica Española Club de Campo, Ctra. de
Burgos km26.4, San Sebastián de Los Reyes, 28709 Madrid

☎ +34 916 571 018

✎ deportes@rshecc.es   www.rshecc.es

🚗 ✈ Madrid: M10; r onto A1; exit to club at km26; cross
highway; straight over next 2 rbts to club.

|   | m | p |   |   | m | p |
|---|-----|---|---|----|-----|---|
| 1 | 370 | 4 |   | 10 | 397 | 4 |
| 2 | 487 | 5 |   | 11 | 158 | 3 |
| 3 | 157 | 3 |   | 12 | 268 | 4 |
| 4 | 398 | 4 |   | 13 | 472 | 5 |
| 5 | 277 | 4 |   | 14 | 369 | 4 |
| 6 | 326 | 4 |   | 15 | 348 | 4 |
| 7 | 173 | 3 |   | 16 | 512 | 5 |
| 8 | 358 | 4 |   | 17 | 176 | 3 |
| 9 | 495 | 5 |   | 18 | 380 | 4 |
|   | 3041 | 36 |  |    | 3080 | 36 |
|   |     |   |   |    | 6121 | 72 |

**More feminine than RHSE
(Norte), and set on only
marginally less interesting
land, a flowing layout mainly
over two facing wooded
hillsides with some attractive
but testing bunkering, water,
undulating fairways and one
vista of too many houses.
Tricky sloping greens.**

'Second Course' is generally a slightly dubious attribution: one thinks of
the 9 or 18 out the back to which society host clubs often sentence you
after that lingering post-lunch kummel. Not often does one find another
18 to keep the post-prandial appetite whet. Notable UK 36 hole
exceptions are Sunningdale, The Berkshire and East Sussex National (but

*Early evening shadows emphasise the contours of p5:13, just reachable in two by
longer hitters. But the slopes on the green, tilted from right down to left, with a bank
left of the pin as shown here, mean that getting up in two is only half the battle...*

*The 75m long, rather too enticing bunker, which adorns the left approach to reachable-in-two downhill p5:2, is the first of several lengthy patches of sand at RHSE (Sur). With the pin front right, as here, it doesn't look too threatening, but back left, behind the bunker, it's another proposition entirely...*

notice we do not say which course should be savoured before lunch!). In Iberia, we would include nearby *Puerta de Hierro*, *Empordà* and the new *El Prat* (and, we should say, remain silent on a few others – further from, and closer to, Madrid). However, RSHE (Sur) should be positively added to the approved list: play it any time (kummel, sangría or neither) and you should be satisfied. Whether you wish to play the slightly more demanding *Norte*, or the, in some ways, more subtle *Sur*, is more a matter of your mood – if you are lucky enough to have the choice, that is. We do say that you should play the *Norte* if you only have time for one – really because it shows off rather

*This view of downhill medium p3:17 is from well right of the direct line from the tee. The long green is angled across the line of play: it slopes and then tiers away down to the back. Anything drawn finds sand, and a hook is worse: water awaits below left...*

more blatantly von Hagge's larger-than-life style. But maybe you should ignore us and choose the *Sur*: here you might find, relatively speaking, just the smallest hint of understatement – does it perhaps let you into more of his mind...?

# EL SALER ★

Arana   1968   €€                    **H:** M 36, L 36, J 36

✉  Parador de El Saler, Avda. de los Pinares 151, 46012 El
   Saler, Valencia

☎  +34 961 611 186

✎  saler-golf@parador.es   www.parador.es

🚗 ✈ Valencia: N111 towards Valencia; r onto V30; r onto
V15-CV500; l into club 100m after km13 (i.e. beyond El Saler).

| # | m | p | | # | m | p |
|---|-----|----|---|----|-----|----|
| 1 | 391 | 4 | | 10 | 365 | 4 |
| 2 | 344 | 4 | | 11 | 519 | 5 |
| 3 | 486 | 5 | | 12 | 181 | 3 |
| 4 | 173 | 3 | | 13 | 318 | 4 |
| 5 | 471 | 5 | | 14 | 378 | 4 |
| 6 | 404 | 4 | | 15 | 516 | 5 |
| 7 | 327 | 4 | | 16 | 390 | 4 |
| 8 | 328 | 4 | | 17 | 195 | 3 |
| 9 | 143 | 3 | | 18 | 426 | 4 |
| | 3067 | 36 | | | 3288 | 36 |
| | | | | | 6355 | 72 |

One of Spain's most
distinctive courses, with two
well-routed loops of 9, each a
gently undulating mixture of
pine and duneland links-style
golf, exposed to the winds.
Several outstanding holes.
Bunkering and greensites
match the challenge.

*Málaga* and El Saler, the two golf courses owned by the Parador hotel
group, together represent the nearest to British-style links in Spain (for the
record, *'Alcaidesa* Links' is not a links). Although neither has links
turf, they are also both serious tests of golf (and with proper links
turf, El Saler would surely attain ★★). El Saler requires an ice-cool
nerve, particularly in the wind, which bends even the strongest

**Below** *Medium-short p3:13 brings you to the more wooded inland
area of the course. Take care past the fairway bunkers, the raised,
sloping green will reject anything short.*

*This view of testing p3:17 (ice plant in flower) gives you the feel of El Saler's open links holes (5-9 & 16-18). 17 plays straight towards the sea. Its sloping, raised green is bunkered all round. You are rewarded with sea views from the 18th tee (above bushes, left).*

pines double (indeed, trees can only survive on the more inland half of the course). But it is another kind of 'ice' which may seriously ruin your card: off fairway, El Saler's duneland is rampant with ice plant, vibrant with colourful large daisy-like flowers, opening with the spring sun. These rubbery soft spiked 'uñas de gato' ('cat's claws' in Spanish) embrace an errant ball and you will need to sharpen your niblick to a razor to get out of them. Once onto the greensites, to a player, golfers at El Saler raved about the consistent subtlety and quality of their design: they are nearly all distinctive, but in the same general style, and mostly above the level of the fairway; here you will make or break your score. As you approach the 19th, let's hope you're thinking of 'links on ice' in celebration rather than frustration...

*Given our strong Kiwi connection, we cannot resist saying that shortish right to left dogleg p4:8 is similar to Paraparaumu 8, which doglegs the other way on that celebrated North Island links. 8 at El Saler wins gold for its strategic qualities with a tee under the dunes (in distance, above bunker): in every season and every wind, every time you play it you can think of a different way to reach the green, whether in two shots or one (even with the wind behind, almost certain madness). Successfully past the fairway hummocks, you will find that the putting surface slopes away from you left, with greenside bunkers beyond. Our Kiwis may have already awarded platinum to Paraparaumu, but we have yet to write that script...*

# ULZAMA ★

Arana/Segalés   1966/1991   €€        **H:** M 28, L 36, J 28/36

✉ Club de Golf Ulzama, Valle Ulzama, 31799 Guerendiain, Navarra

☎ +34 948 305 162

✎ info@golfulzama.com   www.golfulzama.com

🚗 ✈ Iruña/Pamplona: N121; r onto N135 past A15; becomes NA32; after skirting Huarte, l for Ultzama at Ostiz; club approx 5km on r (after Ripa). (Bilbao: A8 to San Sebastián; A15, A16 to Pamplona airport, etc.)

|   | m | p |   | m | p |
|---|---|---|---|---|---|
| 1 | 355 | 4 | 10 | 490 | 5 |
| 2 | 125 | 3 | 11 | 367 | 4 |
| 3 | 345 | 4 | 12 | 211 | 3 |
| 4 | 298 | 4 | 13 | 352 | 4 |
| 5 | 535 | 5 | 14 | 371 | 4 |
| 6 | 176 | 3 | 15 | 180 | 3 |
| 7 | 407 | 4 | 16 | 370 | 4 |
| 8 | 341 | 4 | 17 | 360 | 4 |
| 9 | 492 | 5 | 18 | 457 | 5 |
|   | 3074 | 36 |   | 3158 | 36 |
|   |   |   |   | 6232 | 72 |

Northern Spain's hidden gem: the newer back 9 enhance the fabulous original 9 – all in an oak forest with serene hill views on rolling terrain wonderful for golf. Some tight bunkering and in places fairly narrow. Limited water carries. Fair.

*Simple beauty belies the difficulty of the subtle slopes of the slightly sloping green at medium p3:6. Play it well and you won't realise how hard it can be sometimes to get a 3 here.*

**Above** *This view of medium long p4:16 is exemplary of the way the terrain at Ulzama rolls within the oak forest. The raised green is further than it looks.*

**Right** *The glorious 12th! It may not feel like that, once played: this is a deceptively long p3, with a sloping green bunkered on either side. At least it is downhill and relatively open – fair for such a demanding hole.*

Ulzama, set in a Navarre forest south of the mountains, could well once have been a hunting ground for game birds. But some 40 years ago the principal predator became the bulldozer, carving a flat but pleasant drive through the cover (a brace of independent 9s – the second having been added more recently). From the 1st tee of this golfing gem, you must be your own gamekeeper: birdies are still here for the taking – duck and partridge for sure, and hopefully (we kid you not) the occasional eagle. But don't be fooled, Ulzama is a demanding and lengthy test of your sport, with fairly tight tree-lined fairways, which require you to be a good shot to score. On the plus side, the aquatic risk (for game, but hopefully not yours) is confined principally to the pond front right of the green at short p4:4, though there are also a few ditches. Once you have seen the other dangers of this beauty (sloping greens, the odd blind shot, doglegs, etc.), don't grouse unduly if you do succumb. A course of this calibre surely stages tournaments: dare we suggest shotgun starts?!

# VALDERRAMA ★

**Trent Jones Snr   1974   €€€€   H:** M 32, L 24, J 32/24 Min. age 16

✉ **Golf Club Valderrama, Avda. De la Cortijos s/n, 11310 Sotogrande, Cádiz**

☎ **+34 956 795 775**

✎ **greenfees@valderrama.com   www.valderrama.com**

🚗 ✈ Gibraltar: A383 from La Línea; after 9km r onto A7; km130 exit for Sotogrande/Valderrama; 1st r at rbt; after 500m at rbt, r over motorway; through security, approx 700m on r at rbt, up hill.

| | m | p | | m | p |
|---|---|---|---|---|---|
| 1 | 356 | 4 | 10 | 356 | 4 |
| 2 | 385 | 4 | 11 | 500 | 5 |
| 3 | 171 | 3 | 12 | 194 | 3 |
| 4 | 516 | 5 | 13 | 368 | 4 |
| 5 | 348 | 4 | 14 | 338 | 4 |
| 6 | 149 | 3 | 15 | 206 | 3 |
| 7 | 487 | 5 | 16 | 386 | 4 |
| 8 | 321 | 4 | 17 | 490 | 5 |
| 9 | 403 | 4 | 18 | 415 | 4 |
| | 3136 | 36 | | 3253 | 36 |
| | | | | 6389 | 72 |

Difficult, tree-lined, fabulously conditioned, thinking man's Trent Jones course with small, testing, well-bunkered, often raised, fast greens. Drama and Ryder Cup/European Tour pedigree add to what is inevitably a memorable experience. Private club.

**Medium p5:17 red:** on one level as a golf hole this is arguably a supreme strategic challenge with a penal greensite (basically – do you go for the severely raised green in 2 or 3 shots – water in front, swale behind, green sloping towards water?). However, it is red primarily because the severity of the fairway and greensite mounding, open banks around the green and lack of encroaching trees all make it rather too much out of character with the appearance, playing style and feel of the rest of the course. (This may be good for tournament drama and stadium provision, but the rest of Valderama is not a stadium course.) Its relative severity (and consequent difficulty) does not help.

*Longish p3:12 could not be omitted from this book: a 'do or die' hole with a raised, bunkered green. Under a little peer pressure, Beckenham team player Malcolm Black solved the problem by acing it with a perfect 3-wood on 20th January 2004.*

*One of the very best inland opening holes in the world, medium p4:1 makes you think from your very first shot: where is the pin, where to place your drive (or perhaps more sensibly for some, a 3-wood), and whence in theory (and then in practice) your second shot? The left sweep of the fairway around the trees, and the way (from this view) the green slopes up to the right, behind the front greenside bunker and tree, have much to do with it.*

The name Valderrama and the history of Europe's retention of the 1997 Ryder Cup (Montgomerie at 18) and many top pro championships, are well known to most golfers. This heavily wooded layout's conception was as Sotogrande's 2nd course, christened 'Los Aves'. Its reformation arose from the faith of Jaime Ortiz-Patiño, who has owned it outright since 1985. Trent Jones Snr, the original designer, was commissioned to redesign it to the standard he would have attained in ideal terms. The order of playing the 9 hole loops was reversed, creating a strong finish, and major alterations were made to 4, 7, 11, 12, 15, 16 and 17. One of Patiño's objectives was to create a course which would challenge top professionals and club members alike: 'difficult par easy bogey' with many different tees to match abilities, was Trent Jones' response. Patiño appointed himself Course Superintendent and went to school in America to study the art. He has remained in charge ever since. Benign autocracies generally

*Slight left to right dogleg, downhill medium p4:13 is a superb exhibit of the bunkerless p4 genre: the trees at the turn of the dogleg (i.e. tree front right, and top left, in this view), and those by the green are hazards enough: you simply can't play this hole without being influenced by them.*

work well at golf clubs: narrowly missing ★★, the result has been astounding – and Valderrama is widely regarded as the best-conditioned course in continental Europe. (Easy to say that this can be bought, but to achieve excellence in the extremes of Andalucía requires tireless dedication – and the occasional prayer.) As you play this course, enjoy also just being in an award-winning sanctuary for flora, wildlife and golfers alike.

# ATALAYA (OLD) ↗

von Limburger  1968  €€          **H:** M 28, L 36, J 28/36

✉ Atalaya Golf & Country Club, Ctra. Benahavís km0.7, 29688 Estepona, Málaga

☎ +34 952 882 812

✎ atalayagolf@selected-hotels.com  www.selected-hotels.com

🚗 ✈ Málaga: r out of airport exit road onto A7 for Cádiz; r at km229 for AP7 Benalmádena/Algeciras; end of Marbella bypass (km178) take r split onto A7 past San Pedro; km169.1 r onto MA547 for Benahavís (exit immediately after bridge over Río Guadalmina); club entrance approx 700m on l.

|   | m | p |   | m | p |
|---|---|---|---|---|---|
| 1 | 313 | 4 | 10 | 339 | 4 |
| 2 | 161 | 3 | 11 | 487 | 5 |
| 3 | 412 | 4 | 12 | 207 | 3 |
| 4 | 338 | 4 | 13 | 372 | 4 |
| 5 | 544 | 5 | 14 | 343 | 4 |
| 6 | 323 | 4 | 15 | 336 | 4 |
| 7 | 218 | 3 | 16 | 141 | 3 |
| 8 | 460 | 5 | 17 | 518 | 5 |
| 9 | 320 | 4 | 18 | 310 | 4 |
|   | 3089 | 36 |   | 3053 | 36 |
|   |   |   |   | 6142 | 72 |

Testingly-bunkered parkland course over gently rolling terrain with an established feel (most holes separated from each other by mature trees). Excellent, undulating, often raised greensites. Some longish p3s and p5s. A few water carries. A Costa del Sol classic.

*It's a challenge to avoid sand at excellent medium p3:2. The pin is shown on the front lower tier of the green, which rises behind the left-hand bunker.*

We like this course not just for the design of each hole but for its space: back in the late 1960s, land values were not at so high a premium as in the early 21st century. This allowed golf course developers to use flatter and more spacious sites, compared with many of the relatively extreme

*Long p4:3 is foreshortened in this view: the hole rises slightly to a brow near the fairway bunker before dropping away towards the raised green.*

locations often used more recently. The extra land available allowed trees to be planted between fairways at a width that gives the sense of dimension normally expected (hoped for?!) by most golfers. The course was upgraded under the supervision of Derek Brown and Ignacio Soto in 1996, when all the fairways were regrassed – showing off von Limburger's classic design and its memorable greensites in renewed light. Several other Costa del Sol courses would surely benefit from similar treatment (as has also been demonstrated, for example, in 2003 and 2004 at *Guadalmina (Sur)* and *La Quinta* (B), and earlier at *Mijas (Olivos)*). (*Atalaya New*, set on adjoining higher and more undulating ground, is no match for Atalaya Old, though it provides a shorter test with some good views.)

*Morning shadows across medium p4:6: from a tee in a chute of trees you drive into the relatively open fairway, whence not much more than a pitch to a raised and well-bunkered sloping green.*

# BONMONT ↗

Trent Jones Jnr   1990   €€          **H:** M 28, L 36, J 28/36

✉  Club de Golf Bonmont, Urb. Bonmont Terres Noves, 43300
   Mont-roig del Camp, Tarragona

☎  +34 977 818 140

✎  golfbonmont@medgroup.es   www.medgroup.es

🚗 ✈ Barcelona: AP7 past Tarragona towards Valencia; exit 37; r
onto T312 for Mont-Brió del Camp; follow road, until l at rbt 500m
after km6 for Mont-Roig del Camp; skirting which, straight over rbt for
Móra; club on l at km21.

|   | m | p |   | m | p |
|---|-----|---|----|-----|---|
| 1 | 479 | 5 | 10 | 338 | 4 |
| 2 | 347 | 4 | 11 | 376 | 4 |
| 3 | 398 | 4 | 12 | 409 | 4 |
| 4 | 368 | 4 | 13 | 189 | 3 |
| 5 | 166 | 3 | 14 | 458 | 5 |
| 6 | 420 | 4 | 15 | 292 | 4 |
| 7 | 501 | 5 | 16 | 168 | 3 |
| 8 | 190 | 3 | 17 | 491 | 5 |
| 9 | 396 | 4 | 18 | 385 | 4 |
|   | 3265 | 36 |   | 3106 | 36 |
|   |      |    |   | 6371 | 72 |

With equally spectacular mountain and sea views, this well-routed, undulating Mediterranean parkland course challenges all golfers, especially where water, gullies and dry river beds come into play; paucity of rough mitigates (just!). Take care on the large greens.

*Uphill short p4:15 looks quite tempting from the tee, but the bunkers foreshorten its length and the greensite takes no prisoners. Best to play strategically short. Rely on a good pitch and hopefully only 1 putt...*

*Late afternoon sun reveals considerable mounding around the bunkers and the more subtle slopes of the fairway of uphill short p5:14. Its reachability in 2 by more than just ultra-long hitters often makes you try too hard... Result: sand!*

More than a handful of fruit groves must have been uprooted to landscape this demanding course, set around several gullies between the mountains and the Costa Daurada, southwest of Tarragona. The result is a successful example of golf course routing, worthy of its designer's name: only 4 tees are not aimed directly at either the dramatic mountains or the sea, whose brilliant azure generally contrasts with the rich green of the interlying trees on all but a few days of the year. All achieved with a change of direction on almost every tee, which, given the often windy location, heightens the test. It is a pity that the Barcelona-Valencia motorway also intervenes, but the distraction lasts only a few holes (basically 5-8). Bonmont is long and its challenges include water, gullies and dry streams on 11 holes, rolling fairways and occasionally incisive bunkering also influence play. The back 9 is much hillier – buggies may be hired just for this loop.

*This view down the rolling fairway to the green of medium p4:4 illustrates the sometimes graphic impact of Bonmont's bunkering style. An excellent hole which requires very careful positioning when the pin is placed agressively.*

# EL BOSQUE ↗

**Trent Jones Snr   1973   €€**          **H:** M 28, L 36, J 36

✉ Club de Golf El Bosque, Ctra. De Godelleta km4.1, 46370 Chiva, Valencia

☎ +34 961 808 009

✉ golfoffice@elbosquegolf.com   www.elbosquegolf.com

🚗 ✈ Valencia: airport exit onto (old NII, becomes) A3 for Madrid; exit 337 onto VV3061 for Godalleta; club 300m on r after km4.

| | m | p | | m | p |
|---|---|---|---|---|---|
| 1 | 331 | 4 | 10 | 376 | 4 |
| 2 | 365 | 4 | 11 | 444 | 5 |
| 3 | 482 | 5 | 12 | 196 | 3 |
| 4 | 170 | 3 | 13 | 379 | 4 |
| 5 | 345 | 4 | 14 | 159 | 3 |
| 6 | 347 | 4 | 15 | 494 | 5 |
| 7 | 492 | 5 | 16 | 366 | 4 |
| 8 | 185 | 3 | 17 | 400 | 4 |
| 9 | 390 | 4 | 18 | 328 | 4 |
| | 3107 | 36 | | 3142 | 36 |
| | | | | 6249 | 72 |

**Unmistakably Robert Trent Jones Snr, an undulating, lush parkland course with often small and raised, irregularly-shaped sloping greens, good bunkering and plenty of water carries. From the back tees this can be a long and challenging test.**

For all the different names – fruits de la forêt, bosvruchten, fruits of the forest, frutas del bosque, etc. – in these globalised days shops worldwide will sell you a remarkably similar product, using fairly common ingredients (perhaps with more or less sugar, E additives or whatever?). The same principles apply to much of Robert Trent Jones Snr's golf course wares (and

*Attractive downhill, almost double dogleg, short p5:11 twists around the tree and bunker. You are tempted to go for the green in 2, but if the pin is behind the bunker front left of the green, be sure to stop the ball: unwise to overshoot here!*

*Only when you walk right up onto the green of down-and-up medium p4:18 do you see the full extent of the challenge: the green, below the clubhouse walls, is unbelievably thin, and set directly across the line of play. Precision in length is paramount.*

all had to meet his standards to bear his trademark): some are very tasty indeed. El Bosque is Trent Jones Snr with Mediterranean parkland additives: attractive and enjoyable. Set on rolling ground below a hill which dominates a residential estate not far east of Valencia, it features familiar Trent Jones Snr flavours including some clover leaf bunkering and unusually shaped greens, a few of which (e.g. 1, 12, 14 and especially 18) are very shallow or narrow; several are also undulating and/or tiered. The course is also well spiced with doglegs (at 1, 3, 6, 7, 9-11, 17, 18), some with 'signpost' bunkering (i.e. bunkers you are more likely to find yourself aiming at, than ending up in). The trees are generally more ornamental than in play (unless you are particularly wild off the tee) and include familiar Mediterranean species, such as umbrella pines, olives (some wonderfully gnarled with age), etc. All plus that most familiar Trent Jones Snr ingredient: water (e.g. 8-9, and 12-15, which is where the course really gets going).

*Penal design was often used by Trent Jones Snr: at p5:15 a very long second is required to carry the water in front of the green – or lay up. No other choices.*

# EL CORTIJO ↗

Stirling  1999  €                    **H:** M 28, L 36, J 28/36

✉ El Cortijo Club de Campo, El Cortijo de San Ignacio s/n,
Autopista de Sur GC-1 km6.4, 35218 Telde, Gran Canaria

☎ +34 928 711 111

✎ golf@elcortijo.es   [No website]

🚗 ✈ Gran Canaria: north on GC-1 autopista towards Las
Palmas; El Cortijo has a private exit r off the autopista approx
600m after km7; under autopista and follow signs to club.

|   | m | p |   | m | p |
|---|---|---|---|---|---|
| 1 | 356 | 4 | 10 | 539 | 5 |
| 2 | 458 | 5 | 11 | 414 | 4 |
| 3 | 388 | 4 | 12 | 301 | 4 |
| 4 | 199 | 3 | 13 | 191 | 3 |
| 5 | 413 | 4 | 14 | 273 | 4 |
| 6 | 129 | 3 | 15 | 412 | 4 |
| 7 | 428 | 4 | 16 | 444 | 5 |
| 8 | 281 | 4 | 17 | 157 | 3 |
| 9 | 491 | 5 | 18 | 434 | 4 |
|   | 3143 | 36 |   | 3165 | 36 |
|   |   |   |   | 6308 | 72 |

Disarmingly good layout in
unlikely setting between
industrial and residential
estates. Often large and/or
undulating greens. Some
good bunkering. Water and
some strategically placed
palm trees influence play.
Can be windy.

Cacophony might be the first thought that hits you on arrival at a layout
sandwiched between industrial and high density residential properties
just inland from a coastal motorway. But as a golf course El Cortijo is a
harmonious, if occasionally disarming, success. Set on a former banana
plantation with two independent 9s (1-9 seawards, 10-18 inland around

*This view of long p4:7 clearly illustrates the juxtaposition of excellent golf with
urban landscape. From a raised tee, but with an uphill second to a sloping
bunkered green, 7 is a serious test for any player. You may do well to play this one
as a bogey 5 and hope to 'birdie'.*

*Shortish p4:8, seen here from the 7th green, is a test for your golfing brain. Some longer hitters might be tempted to 'have a go' at the green, but it is tightly bunkered and much deeper than it looks. A swale runs across the putting surface towards the back, which makes back pin positions particularly challenging.*

both sides of and over a hill), the quality of design is maintained throughout – and might have been even better, without the long but fairly gentle climb from the 10th tee to the 12th green. The tune of 'Yes, we have no bananas' may therefore seem appropriate, as the main above-ground vegetation is now the soaring palm, which forms an interesting aerial hazard (notably at 2, 5 and 18), occasionally even resulting in a ball lost – 'palm caught'. Be sure also to pay particular respect to the quality bunkering and greensites. In reality, you will probably get used to the setting fairly quickly and focus on your play. Even that climb to the 12th green is rewarded by a wide-ranging sea view, followed by the challenge of long downhill p3:13. Lay out your score carefully, and your result here could be pure music.

*This view of medium short p5:2 shows the effect of the palms as 'aerial bunkers'. With the pin on the right, the best strategy may well be to lay up and trust your short game – but it's a tricky green...*

# GUADALMINA (SUR) ↗

Arana 1965 €€€                     **H:** M 28, L 36, J 28/36

✉ Guadalmina Club de Golf, Urb. Guadalmina Alta, 29678 San Pedro de Alcántara, Málaga

☎ +34 952 886 522

✎ Book by phone www.guadalminagolf.org

🚗 ✈ Málaga: r out of airport exit road onto A7 for Cádiz; r at km229 for AP7 Benalmádena/Algeciras; end of Marbella bypass (km178) take r split onto A7; through San Pedro de Alcántara; r 200m after 'Marbella' bridge; l after 700m (just before greens thru trees on r); immediately r into club car park.

| | m | p | | m | p |
|---|---|---|---|---|---|
| 1 | 376 | 4 | 10 | 385 | 4 |
| 2 | 171 | 3 | 11 | 158 | 3 |
| 3 | 351 | 4 | 12 | 283 | 4 |
| 4 | 410 | 4 | 13 | 321 | 4 |
| 5 | 372 | 4 | 14 | 168 | 3 |
| 6 | 524 | 5 | 15 | 323 | 4 |
| 7 | 444 | 5 | 16 | 480 | 5 |
| 8 | 396 | 4 | 17 | 424 | 4 |
| 9 | 182 | 3 | 18 | 345 | 4 |
| | 3226 | 36 | | 2887 | 35 |
| | | | | 6113 | 71 |

**Remodelled in 2002, including some outstanding new putting surface designs (though within weaker greensites), this predominantly tree-lined, residential layout gives us, for one rare moment of ecstasy, the closest golf to the sea on the Costa del Sol.**

**13 red:** short p4 with a lake exactly at average tee shot length – and no realistic strategic alternative to playing two midirons to reach the green. This may have been done to prevent drives going into adjoining residences, but is not how golf should be played. A routing adjustment would have been the better solution.

A borderline case: the ↗ rating is just earned – for two reasons, both of which you should enjoy: i) the experience of playing golf right on the beach – unique on the Costa del Sol (surprising, until you consider real estate values) – for one green (10) and one complete hole (11), which is at least a match for its location (although the new 9 holes at *Málaga* run right by the beach, they are some way from the waves), and ii) the enhancements of the 2002 remodelling: the putting surfaces have been superbly reshaped (sometimes disarmingly so). 36 putts here is a very good score... The rest is not quite to the same standard, resulting in few green-rated holes, even though several rank at the higher end of the yellow spectrum.

**Above** A view of p3:11 – out to sea at dawn. Not just a pretty seaside picture: the back tees are by the beach-side fence, just out of shot left. The bunker runs the length of the hole and tricks you into playing too far right (out of shot), where run-off areas, a bunker and the green slope all heighten the risk of overhitting your subsequent recovery onto the beach. (The 10th green is in the foreground.)

**Left** Water, trees and bunkers at deceptive longish p4:8 – the green is further than it seems.

**Below** Behold, the sea! The fairway of p4:10 emerges through a narrow gap between houses and a hotel to a green by the beach. The morning shadows reveal the subtleties of the putting surface.

# LA MANGA (NORTH) ↗

**Putman   1972   €€**         **H:** M 28, L 36, J 28/36

✉ La Manga Club, Los Belones, 30385 Cartagena, Murcia
☎ +34 968 175 000
✎ golf@lamangaclub.com   www.golf.lamanga.com

🚗 ✈ Alicante: N338 – A7 – AP7 (exit 77) to end of AP7; exit
800 l onto MU312; exit 13, r at rbt for Portman; club 2.5km on l.
(Murcia: MU30 – A30 – CT32 towards AP7; exit 800 B r onto
MU312, as from Alicante.)

| | m | p | | m | p |
|---|---|---|---|---|---|
| 1 | 307 | 4 | 10 | 293 | 4 |
| 2 | 105 | 3 | 11 | 333 | 4 |
| 3 | 437 | 5 | 12 | 534 | 5 |
| 4 | 177 | 3 | 13 | 158 | 3 |
| 5 | 368 | 4 | 14 | 321 | 4 |
| 6 | 485 | 5 | 15 | 480 | 5 |
| 7 | 360 | 4 | 16 | 183 | 3 |
| 8 | 160 | 3 | 17 | 359 | 4 |
| 9 | 316 | 4 | 18 | 377 | 4 |
| | 2715 | 35 | | 3038 | 36 |
| | | | | 5753 | 71 |

Hillier, but generally more approachable than La Manga (South) despite rather more barrancas, a palm-lined, bunkered resort course with reasonably large, generally multi-level greens. Some water. The first choice of many visitors to La Manga, though reaction to the upgrading of the South may change this.

*A view down medium p4:5 from right of the tee, through trees that ought not to trouble your drive. This hole demonstrates the attractions of the North Course: shorter and more three-dimensional than La Manga (South) it may be, but there is plenty of danger, even before you reach the often tiered greens.*

Whilst famous golfers (Palmer, Player, Casper, Faldo, Ballesteros, Laura Davies and Marie Laure de Lorenzi – to name but a few) won over the longer and slightly more demanding *La Manga (South)* in the 1970s and 1980s, La Manga (North) (opened simultaneously, providing what the regional newspaper then claimed to be the only facility in Spain with two championship standard courses) has remained the favourite of members and resort visitors. Feedback suggests that this is because it is a little shorter and more amenable to the amateur. It was also the

first of the two original La Manga courses to be upgraded to the standards recently completed on *La Manga (South)*. However, when you play it, consider also the effect of the hillside into which it is set: the resulting uphill and downhill holes, some threaded across barrancas, provide more instant drama, fun and therefore satisfaction (or

*At only 105m from the back, p3:2 is as testing as it is short: once over the bunkers you face a triple-tiered green. Unless you land on the correct tier, par will always be difficult..*

frustration!). But next time maybe you will want the more technical demands of *La Manga (South)*, or the more wooded challenge of *La Manga (West)*? With three courses of different flavour, La Manga is blessed indeed.

*From the course's highest point, downhill medium p3:4, with its sandy surrounds, is a challenge in any wind. No tier on this green, nor is it flat!*

# LA MANGA (SOUTH) ↗

**Putman 1972 €€**                    **H:** M 28, L 36, J 28/36

✉ La Manga Club, Los Belones, 30385 Cartagena, Murcia
☎ +34 968 175 000
✎ golf@lamangaclub.com  www.golf.lamanga.com

>27 7/8
<13

🚗 ✈ Alicante: N338 – A7 – AP7 (exit 77) to end of AP7; exit
800 l onto MU312; exit 13, r at rbt for Portman; club 2.5km on l.
(Murcia: MU30 – A30 – CT32 towards AP7; exit 800 B r onto
MU312, as from Alicante.)

| | m | p | | m | p |
|---|---|---|---|---|---|
| 1 | 394 | 4 | 10 | 342 | 4 |
| 2 | 197 | 3 | 11 | 360 | 4 |
| 3 | 358 | 4 | 12 | 141 | 3 |
| 4 | 460 | 5 | 13 | 550 | 5 |
| 5 | 201 | 3 | 14 | 340 | 4 |
| 6 | 537 | 5 | 15 | 397 | 4 |
| 7 | 372 | 4 | 16 | 358 | 4 |
| 8 | 359 | 4 | 17 | 178 | 3 |
| 9 | 503 | 5 | 18 | 452 | 5 |
| | 3381 | 37 | | 3118 | 36 |
| | | | | 6499 | 73 |

Fairly spacious but long, well-established popular hotel resort course, rejuvenated and enhanced in 2003–4. Set on gently sloping ground with palms and several water hazards, large-scale amply-bunkered sloping greens have potential to test tourist and tournament players alike.

La Manga holds an important place in the annals of Iberian tourist golf development. Its brief history and its conversion from a private enterprise to an institution owned and managed by public companies well illustrate the often misunderstood risks of golf investment. The original and essential ingredient was vision – that of Gregory Peters, an American businessman, who employed Californian Robert Putman to

*The gentle slopes, and reasonably spacious feel, of medium but testing p4:14, enhanced with an expansive bunker on the right, are common features of the South Course.*

*Heavily-bunkered longish p3:17, surrounded by just a few of the 3,000 palm trees planted in 1972, will test any player in any round. The green is slightly raised above the approach and, as remodelled, water is much more in play – not a place to miss the target, whether you are 1 up (or down) on the tee (foreground).*

design two courses. Despite a catastrophic flood just beforehand, La Manga opened in October 1972, with Gary Player as Director of Golf and a 5 year contract for the Spanish Open on the South Course from 1973 to 1977, following which the company collapsed and Peters left the resort. After a difficult period, La Manga was acquired in 1987 by P&O, who supported the construction of a 5 star hotel, opened in 1993 and now managed by Hyatt, whose name has been branded into the resort. Surrounding property, leisure and other sport development has proceeded in tandem. Over its 32 year history, to retain its place at the top of the market, the South Course has twice been upgraded (Arnold Palmer, 1992, and the 2003/4 in-house revamp – with maturity, its rating may well be upgradeable). Reflect on this and enjoy the scene of vision, labour, heartache, loss, profit, disaster, success, drama and pleasure. It was all worth it, wasn't it?!

*The left to right slope of the remodelled green at long p5:6 is self-evident in this view (from well right, over water, in front of the 3rd tee).*

# LA MANGA (WEST) ↗

Thomas 1996 €€ **H:** M 28, L 36, J 28/36

✉ La Manga Club, Los Belones, 30385 Cartagena, Murcia
☎ +34 968 175 000
✎ golf@lamangaclub.com   www.golf.lamanga.com

🚗 ✈ Alicante: N338 – A7 – AP7 (exit 77) to end of AP7; exit 800
l onto MU312; exit 13, r at rbt for Portman; club 3.5km on l. (Murcia:
MU30 – A30 – CT32 towards AP7; exit 800B r onto MU312, as from Alicante.)

>27 ⛳ 7/8
<13 🌡

|   | m | p |   | m | p |
|---|---|---|---|---|---|
| 1 | 309 | 4 | 10 | 322 | 4 |
| 2 | 203 | 3 | 11 | 357 | 4 |
| 3 | 472 | 5 | 12 | 360 | 4 |
| 4 | 246 | 4 | 13 | 177 | 3 |
| 5 | 288 | 4 | 14 | 312 | 4 |
| 6 | 452 | 5 | 15 | 456 | 5 |
| 7 | 156 | 3 | 16 | 189 | 3 |
| 8 | 378 | 4 | 17 | 479 | 5 |
| 9 | 434 | 5 | 18 | 381 | 4 |
|   | 2938 | 37 |   | 3033 | 36 |
|   |   |   |   | 5971 | 73 |

And now for something completely different: compared with other two palmy La Manga courses, the West is in a hillier pine forest (especially 2nd 9) with some excellent doglegs in a tighter setting. Attractively-bunkered, tricky greens. Rewarding or destructive, depending on your game… (N.B. Served by a different clubhouse.)

**17 red:** water hazard on left above fairway level, making hole semi-blind, is completely unnatural and just doesn't work.

The West course adds a completely different dimension to La Manga, in that it is set over much more undulating (and indeed) hilly ground than *La Manga (North)* and *La Manga (South)*, with its back 9 very much in a forest. The West is in fact a hybrid: the older front 9 was opened in 1986, and originally known as the Atamaría (after the original village

*Medium short p4:14 turns around this bunker and tree some 225m sharply downhill from the tee. There are many options here: choose your strategy and try to stick to it…*

around which La Manga has grown) and then La Princesa. The back 9 was constructed in 1991 and also had two names: Las Sabinas and then La Princesa II. In 1996 the courses were amalgamated and renamed The West. Although maturity is lessening the differences between them, one can see that the weaker front 9 was set on slightly more open and less steep ground – the forest really closes in from the 10th tee. The two nines are both perhaps a test more suited to a serious, rather than solely resort, player. The back 9, in particular, require consistent accuracy if you wish avoid hunting for balls. But play this course well and you will feel very satisfied. Perhaps you should savour it last of the three: then the panoramic view from its 18th tee becomes a retrospective of the whole resort.

**Above** *Strategic short p5:15 is a beautiful gem: played from a high tee into a valley, you must first decide whether to risk all and carry a stream at driving length to give you the best chance of getting up in two – not for the faint-hearted at 233m; then whether to play left of, right of, or over the trees which divide the fairway 50m from the green, whose two front bunkers are only hinted at from this view. It is probably wisest to play it as a 5 and hope to be sufficiently well-positioned after 2 to set up a chance of a birdie…*

**Below** *Uphill and demanding medium p3:13 plays longer than it looks, especially with the pin on the upper tier (as seen here). Set in one of the most attractive corners of the whole of La Manga, do not allow yourself to be unduly distracted by its aesthetic charms.*

# MARBELLA GOLF ↗

Trent Jones Snr   1989   €€                    **H:** M 26, L 34, J –

✉ Marbella Golf and Country Club, Ctra. de Cádiz km188, 29600 Marbella, Málaga

☎ +34 952 830 500

✎ Book by phone    marbellagolfcc.com

🚗 ✈ Málaga: r out of airport exit road onto A7 for Cádiz; r at km229 for AP7 Benalmádena/Algeciras; exit 214 for A7 for Fuengirola/Algeciras (not AP7 autopista); r at km188 (immediately after El Rosario exit); over 1st rbt keeping parallel with A7; r at 2nd rbt; 1st exit at 3rd rbt leads to club.

|    | m    | p  |    | m    | p  |
|----|------|----|----|------|----|
| 1  | 281  | 4  | 10 | 136  | 3  |
| 2  | 477  | 5  | 11 | 344  | 4  |
| 3  | 139  | 3  | 12 | 396  | 4  |
| 4  | 264  | 4  | 13 | 497  | 5  |
| 5  | 322  | 4  | 14 | 353  | 4  |
| 6  | 462  | 5  | 15 | 349  | 4  |
| 7  | 391  | 4  | 16 | 186  | 3  |
| 8  | 191  | 3  | 17 | 504  | 5  |
| 9  | 366  | 4  | 18 | 295  | 4  |
|    | 2893 | 36 |    | 3060 | 36 |
|    |      |    |    | 5953 | 72 |

Currently the best 'mountain defile' course on the Costa del Sol, with some spectacular downhill tee shots, good bunkering, excellent greensites, commanding views and testing water. Trees come into play on lower sections.

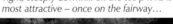

*Tight, steeply downhill off the tee p4:12 is most attractive – once on the fairway…*

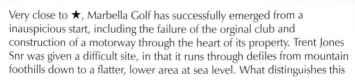

Very close to ★, Marbella Golf has successfully emerged from a inauspicious start, including the failure of the orginal club and construction of a motorway through the heart of its property. Trent Jones Snr was given a difficult site, in that it runs through defiles from mountain foothills down to a flatter, lower area at sea level. What distinguishes this

*To have a motorway built across your course is not very funny, but in some ways (guided by Robinson) this has been the making of the course: an arduous uphill p5 opener has been replaced with a close to red, cheeky short p4 and glorious strategic shortish p5:2: a long drive left over the trees (visible lower left corner) leaves you well positioned to reach the well-bunkered green in two. Played as a double-dogleg three-shotter, club and position both your drive and second very carefully.*

layout is the skill with which the routing makes best use of the land available – especially compared with other courses on similar sites nearby: rarely does one find a course with so many spectacular and/or heroic shots, both downhill and uphill (p3:10 excepted). There is nothing more inviting than a high tee shot into/across a valley – Marbella Golf offers 9 such opportunities, 3 of which are at short p4s (all the more tempting). But beware: this is one of the more difficult Costa del Sol courses, and certainly not one to choose to play for a medal competition unless you are a serious player. If you're just visiting and want some fun, why not take a good supply of ammunition, expect to lose quite a bit of it, and go for every shot, particularly if your playing partners agree to take the same attitude? When (if!) you get to the greens, your putting will be well tested on shapes and contours worthy of their designer's name. Lovely clubhouse. (N.B. Marbella Golf is a relatively private club and has no links to *Marbella Club*: play Marbella Golf, if you have to choose.)

**Right**
*Longish
p4:7, on the
lower part of
the course, is
one of its
best: after a
drive over
water to the undulating
fairway, the second is
over a dip to a green
which slopes from left
down to right.*

# MASPALOMAS ↗

**P M Ross 1968 €€**  **H:** M 30, L 30, J 30 [Minimum age 14]

✉ Campo de Golf de Maspalomas Golf, Avda. de Neckerman
s/n, 35100 Maspalomas, Gran Canaria

☎ +34 928 762 581

✉ reservas@maspalomasgolf.net  www.maspalomasgolf.net

🚗 ✈ Gran Canaria: GC1 towards Playa del Inglés/Maspalomas;
exit 47 towards Maspalomas; past 1st 2 exits to rbt; straight across
into Avda. de Neckerman; club 500m on l.

| | m | p | | m | p |
|---|---|---|---|---|---|
| 1 | 367 | 4 | 10 | 378 | 4 |
| 2 | 362 | 4 | 11 | 450 | 5 |
| 3 | 155 | 3 | 12 | 323 | 4 |
| 4 | 488 | 5 | 13 | 384 | 4 |
| 5 | 328 | 4 | 14 | 373 | 4 |
| 6 | 397 | 4 | 15 | 327 | 4 |
| 7 | 506 | 5 | 16 | 188 | 3 |
| 8 | 209 | 3 | 17 | 343 | 4 |
| 9 | 393 | 4 | 18 | 446 | 5 |
| | 3205 | 36 | | 3212 | 37 |
| | | | | 6417 | 72 |

Scottish links feel (bunkering included) on a popular flatish layout, with some testing greensites, sometimes raised – generally better than first impressions suggest, edged by beautiful flora and dunes, whence recovery often difficult.

As it adjoins 400ha of dunes, no surprise to find strong Scottish links
(designer's name included) at Maspalomas. The modesty of the
clubhouse (often made up for by the volume – in two senses! – of the

*In some lights even Gran Canaria background colours can have a rather tartan hue: this is perhaps most felt at reachable-in-two, strategic p5:11, where the potentially menacing shadows of the cross bunkers may well bring to the foreground of your mind the contradiction of more northerly golf in the most southerly climes of Europe. The green only appears benign: it has borrows, and the ground falls away behind.*

*You cannot see most of these bunkers from the tee at long p3:8 – there are good practical reasons for keeping the sand out of the wind, so we couldn't unduly fault this.*

ubiquitous canaries) and relatively monochrome p4:1 understate the challenges. When you see the slightly eccentric split-level fairway at p4:2, and the dunes at p3:3, it dawns that, despite the overall label 'flat', here is a course which can test every colour of your game (just as it has in the past tested Tour players'). The Caledonian feel continues with bunkers (grass as well as sand) in the direct line of play, distinctly tiered greens and unevenly undulating fairways. But, for all the Scottish comparisons (and even temperature apart), one is actually on a volcanic island, with occasional waste areas of sand or pumice, tropical vegetation (recovery difficult!), trees, and intense light (but not when we were there!) – and those canaries. The same designer also brought Turnberry to its championship glory (oh, and gave us an unknown little Azores course by the name of *Furnas*...).

*Place your drive carefully at shortish p4:15, or the bunkers will have you. Indeed, consider a 3-wood, so your full second can grip the raised green.*

# MIJAS (LAGOS) ↗

Trent Jones Snr   1974   €€                    **H:** M 28, L 36, J 28/36

✉ Mijas Golf International, Ctra. Vieja de Coín km3.5, 29650
Mijas Costa, Málaga

☎ +34 952 476 843

✎ teetimes@mijasgolf.org   www.mijasgolf.org

🚗 ✈ Málaga: r out of airport exit road onto A7 for Cádiz; r at
km229 for AP7 Benalmádena/Algeciras; exit 214 for A7 for
Fuengirola/Algeciras (not AP7 autopista); r at exit 700m after
km210 for Coín; r at rbt onto MA426; course on r after 2.5km.

| | m | p | | m | p |
|---|---|---|---|---|---|
| 1 | 508 | 5 | 10 | 405 | 4 |
| 2 | 160 | 3 | 11 | 176 | 3 |
| 3 | 342 | 4 | 12 | 349 | 4 |
| 4 | 392 | 4 | 13 | 525 | 5 |
| 5 | 564 | 5 | 14 | 350 | 4 |
| 6 | 399 | 4 | 15 | 194 | 3 |
| 7 | 377 | 4 | 16 | 389 | 4 |
| 8 | 209 | 3 | 17 | 342 | 4 |
| 9 | 352 | 4 | 18 | 334 | 4 |
| | 3303 | 36 | | 3064 | 35 |
| | | | | 6367 | 71 |

Challenging, popular and easy-walking, spacious parkland course on a grand scale with forgiving rough. Pedigree bunkering, water carries, and sloping greensites provide the spice. Slightly disappointing finish. Does the rather tired feel hint at investment incommensurate with use?

*There is a big difference between front and back tees at many holes at Mijas (Lagos), especially at p5:5, but also here at medium p4:3, which runs down between bunkers to a well-protected green. But from whichever tee you play, the fairway bunkers (on left as well as right) await you, narrowing the fairway the further you go. This view over the right-hand bunkers foreshortens the hole: the closest bunker is 40m from the green.*

*The fairway bunkers are perfectly positioned at uphill medium p4:12: the closest is 200m from the tee, the furthest 273m to clear. So play left or right of them if you can.*

Some readers may feel that the two Mijas courses should be rated equally, if not with *Olivos* above Lagos. We would understand this, but they are perhaps more likely to be golfers for whom condition is more important than design. It is within our remit to forewarn where courses are noticeably under- (or indeed over-) maintained. It is also surely right that if a club has more than one course, each should have its own character. Although Lagos gives you the sight of an olive tree and *Olivos* a shot over water, their names are generally effective descriptions of their character.

*Go to Mijas in May if you want the jacaranda treatment: delicious colours – as here behind medium p3:2, seen from the left close to sunset.*

The main superiority in design of Lagos over *Olivos* is that it was conceived on a slightly grander scale (with bunkering to match) over better ground, with the design quality maintained almost throughout (possibly only the relatively tame finish preventing a higher rating), whereas, after a very promising start, *Olivos* is on a slightly tighter scale with two weaker corners (i.e. 4-5 and 11-15). But, yes, *Olivos* is in some ways much better – especially in its appearance: remodelled in 2001 with 419 Bermuda (fairways) and Pencross (greens), new irrigation and infrastructure (Cabell Robinson, with Michael Lovett and the Mijas team), it has a sheen with which Lagos currently cannot glow. How would Lagos appear, given the same pampering?

# LOS NARANJOS ↗

Trent Jones Snr   1977   €€          **H:** M 25, L 35, J 25/35

✉ **Los Naranjos Golf Club, Apdo. 64, 29660 Nueva Andalucía, Marbella, Málaga**

☎ **+34 952 815 206**

✎ golf@losnaranjos.com   www.losnaranjos.com

🚗 ✈ Málaga: r out of airport exit road onto A7 for Cádiz; r at km229 for AP7 Benalmádena/Algeciras; end of Marbella bypass (km178) take r split onto A7; exit junction 176 (Istán) after tunnel; l at rbt; over bridge; straight over (i.e. do not veer left); 2nd r, up hill, at next rbt; straight over next rbt; over hill past Aloha Golf; straight over mini-rbt; r fork over hill; exit r out of Aloha Golf along Avda. del Prado for 500m; straight over at rbt; after 700m l at rbt into club.

|    | m    | p  |    | m    | p  |
|----|------|----|----|------|----|
| 1  | 334  | 4  | 10 | 415  | 4  |
| 2  | 545  | 5  | 11 | 364  | 4  |
| 3  | 362  | 4  | 12 | 167  | 3  |
| 4  | 190  | 3  | 13 | 373  | 4  |
| 5  | 448  | 5  | 14 | 520  | 5  |
| 6  | 414  | 4  | 15 | 322  | 4  |
| 7  | 345  | 4  | 16 | 357  | 4  |
| 8  | 207  | 3  | 17 | 173  | 3  |
| 9  | 398  | 4  | 18 | 524  | 5  |
|    | 3243 | 36 |    | 3214 | 36 |
|    |      |    |    | 6457 | 72 |

Challenging, rewarding and testingly-bunkered layout with 2 loops of different character: 1-9 more undulating; 10-18 tree-lined, amidst orange groves and palms. Some water carries. A classic Costa del Sol course, close to higher rating.

*Medium p3:11 – 'Palm Sundae' at St Clement's? 3 large vanilla bunkers, spectacularly lined by cathedral column palm trees surround the large, sloping green.*

*Only just short of gold, the fairway vista of long p5:18 shows off the splendid clubhouse and La Concha ('the shell'), the mountain behind – worth seeing at sunset. This is a tough right to left slightly uphill p5 and can prove fatal, if you need to win the hole: the stream seen here runs down into rather more water to the left...*

Los Naranjos is full of flavour, pith, zest – and the odd pip! It has two distinct flavours, as the two 9s are as different as the oranges and lemons of St Clement. The front 9, across the road from the striking Neo-Andalusian clubhouse, is set on rolling ground, intertwined with streams, whilst the back 9 runs seawards over flatter orange groves. Differences also in flora: trees, flowers and shrubs – out; oranges and palms – back. But all is not sweetness and flavour (remember how 'Oranges and Lemons' ends?): a full-length course, Los Naranjos' pith includes demanding holes of each par category (six of the ten p4s exceed 360m, three of the four p5s are over 500m, and two p3s over 200… well, yards). And, yes, that chopper could come out at 18 (see photo caption)! The

*Left to right medium short p4:1 requires a drive (from a tee at approximately the same level as the green) into a fairway sloping towards those bunkers…*

zest comes in excitement and drama: mostly at the more undulating holes (e.g. downhill 2nd over a brook at long p4:6). As for pips, wait until you have to save par: here it can be more difficult than you think. Orange juice can sometimes be bitter, but it's always refreshing!

# NEGURI ↗

Arana   1960   €€€          **H:** M 28, L 36, J 28/36

✉ Real Sociedad de Golf de Neguri, Campo La Galea, Apdo. de Correos 9, 48990 Algorta-Getxo, Vizcaya

☎ +34 944 910 200

✎ rsgn@rsgolfneguri.com   [No website]

🚗 ✈ Bilbao: exit airport r (effectively turning l) onto N633 (westbound); after 5km r at rbt onto BI737; after 2.5km r sliproad onto BI637; after 3.5km r at junction, staying on BI637; after 3km l at rbt onto BI634; straight over next rbt, 150m after which r onto C. Maidagan; after 1km l onto C. Peña de Santa Marina; after 400m l onto C. Kaioa; 1st r onto Arranoa Kalea; 1st l onto Ctra. Faro; after 350m r onto C. Juan Vallejo Real de Asúa; club 1km on l.

| m | p |  | m | p |  |
|---|---|---|---|---|---|
| 1 | 433 | 4 | 10 | 520 | 5 |
| 2 | 168 | 3 | 11 | 292 | 4 |
| 3 | 401 | 4 | 12 | 371 | 4 |
| 4 | 299 | 4 | 13 | 517 | 5 |
| 5 | 481 | 5 | 14 | 192 | 3 |
| 6 | 194 | 3 | 15 | 335 | 4 |
| 7 | 406 | 4 | 16 | 354 | 4 |
| 8 | 335 | 4 | 17 | 158 | 3 |
| 9 | 322 | 4 | 18 | 502 | 5 |
|  | 3039 | 35 |  | 3241 | 37 |
|  |  |  |  | 6280 | 72 |

Mixture of cliff top and tree-lined holes with traditional British feel on gently rolling land – a site destined for golf. Towering pines on back 9 give majestic feel. Understated difficulty, including greens. Sea views.

*Long p4:10 is a right to left dogleg, lined with magnificent pines, which become increasingly dense as the fairway rises gently to a reasonably generous green, bunkered on the right.*

*Neguri's opener is a very long, tree-lined p4 slightly downhill towards the sea: when you stand on the tee, look for the ship and aim for the bow!! The flag is just visible on the right through the trees.*

Javier Arana, himself a renowned player, only designed golf courses in Spain – a misfortune for the rest of the world. However, the character of some of his courses (most notably *El Saler*) suggests that he was not unfamiliar with golf outside his homeland. Neguri provides good evidence: whilst the setting and terrain of its seaside holes (2-7) are more reminiscent of British cliff top courses, their style (particularly around the greensites, some of which have some pronounced slopes) owes much to traditional links design. The remaining holes continue the story: they are more inland, several lined with towering pines, producing a character that could easily be found at inland British, or other more northern European, courses. Don't let this give you a false sense of security: Arana knew what he was doing – Neguri is by no means short, and more challenging than it may first seem, especially from the back tees – even if you are lucky enough not to have to contend with the breezes of Biscay. (Neguri is a private club, but accepts visitors during the week by arrangement.)

*This view over a brow down to the left to right sloping green of short p4:4 shows the way the linksy feel of the clifftop opening holes mixes with the local surroundings. (The sea is to the right, with similar vistas as from 1.)*

# EL PRAT (YELLOW) ↗

**Norman   2003   €€€**                    **H:** M 28, L 36, J 28/36

✉ **Real Club de El Prat, Plans de Bonvillar 17, 08227 Terrassa,
Barcelona**

☎ **+34 937 281 000**

✎ **rcgep@rcgep.com   www.realclubdegolfelprat.com**

🚗 ✈ **Barcelona: C32, B10, B23, AP7 for Girona, l onto C58 away
from Barcelona; exit 16; left at lights onto service road marked
Mercavallès (not onto N150); r after 500m; club entrance l after 2km.**

| | m | p | | m | p |
|---|---|---|---|---|---|
| 1 | 393 | 4 | 10 | 418 | 4 |
| 2 | 166 | 3 | 11 | 525 | 5 |
| 3 | 345 | 4 | 12 | 190 | 3 |
| 4 | 493 | 5 | 13 | 404 | 4 |
| 5 | 348 | 4 | 14 | 428 | 4 |
| 6 | 187 | 3 | 15 | 426 | 4 |
| 7 | 392 | 4 | 16 | 494 | 5 |
| 8 | 408 | 4 | 17 | 146 | 3 |
| 9 | 498 | 5 | 18 | 426 | 4 |
| | 3230 | 36 | | 3457 | 36 |
| | | | | 6687 | 72 |

A memorable course, whose
bunkers may come to haunt
you. Superbly sculpted, the
relatively open ground feel is
made more interesting by
occasional routing through and
alongside tall pine trees.
Respect potentially dangerous
greensites and occasional water.

In the past 30 years, many unimaginative new golf courses have been built on
former agricultural land, more often than not on a low budget. El Prat (Yellow)
is a notable exception. Whilst, in good designers' hands, natural golfing sites
will render even better results, this highly shaped course makes the land feel
like it has been this way for a long time. Apart from the holes illustrated in the
photos, enjoy: the challenge of how to plot your way past the long bunker at
medium p4:3; finding and staying on the green at p3:6, especially in the wind
(we would guess the designer has played a round or two in Scotland…?); the
mid-fairway bunkering at longish p4:8; the archaeology at p5:9 (avoid it!) and
the, by then welcome, shade of the woods at dogleg p5:16…

*A view of 13 from the 12th
tee foreshortens this longish
p4 but shows another
bunkering challenge. Our
focus was on the tee, but
yours must be on playing
safely down fairway (to the
left side of this view), with
a potentially very long
carry over bunkers if the
pin is back left (there's
room for a very slight lay
up front right).*

The classic design and magical setting of lavishly bunkered downhill p3:12 wins instant gold. In imperial measurements it's comfortably over 200yds, so don't be lulled by its beauty on either tee or green – nor even in the sand, which just begs you to visit...

These two sunset shots of p4:5 from front and rear well illustrate the dangers at El Prat (Yellow) – not a particularly long two-shotter by modern standards, yet even a perfect drive leaves you with an enforced carry over bunkers to a raised green, which looks innocent enough from the front. But the shadows of the greenside saplings show up the run-off area behind the green. To score well here, your short game needs to be hot.

# RÍO REAL ↗

Arana 1965 €€          **H:** M 28, L 36, J 28/36

✉ Río Real Golf, Urb. Río Real, Ctra. de Cádiz km185, 29600 Marbella, Málaga

☎ +34 952 765 733

✒ reservas@rioreal.com    www.rioreal.com

🚗 ✈ Málaga: r out of airport exit road onto A7 for Cádiz; r at km229 for AP7 Benalmádena/Algeciras; exit 214 for A7 for Fuengirola/Algeciras (not AP7 autopista); r up small slip road 300m after km186; follow road for approx 1km, l at rbt; club on l at hairpin bend after 300m (if you miss slip road, r at Torre Real and follow signs after 1km).

| | m | p | | | m | p |
|---|---|---|---|---|---|---|
| 1 | 317 | 4 | | 10 | 330 | 4 |
| 2 | 357 | 4 | | 11 | 336 | 4 |
| 3 | 140 | 3 | | 12 | 156 | 3 |
| 4 | 392 | 4 | | 13 | 511 | 5 |
| 5 | 387 | 4 | | 14 | 168 | 3 |
| 6 | 164 | 3 | | 15 | 418 | 4 |
| 7 | 443 | 5 | | 16 | 502 | 5 |
| 8 | 398 | 4 | | 17 | 321 | 4 |
| 9 | 457 | 5 | | 18 | 369 | 4 |
| | 3055 | 36 | | | 3011 | 36 |
| | | | | | 6066 | 72 |

Marbella's oldest course and one of its most charming (though modern noise of A7's traverse cannot have been foreseen). Compact layout, often lined with majestic palms, with testing, slightly raised, amply-bunkered greensites. Successful early dash for beach matched by a few weaker moments. Several crossings of Río Real, all at different angles.

*The contrast between tee and green at right to left longish p4:4 could not be greater: at the tee all other sound is drowned by traffic noise; another kind of drowning waves at you, greenside. But there's another contrast which shows the test of the hole: which way is the wind blowing? (Yes, but look at the flag!)*

*Shortish, well-bunkered p4:17 is attractive to view and potentially deadly to play, especially if you need to win the hole to survive. The raised green can be difficult to hold: often better to lay up short of the bunkers from the tee, to leave yourself a full wedge. The hole almost won gold for the combination of strategic qualities with the aesthetic majesty of the surrounding palms – even with the traffic noise on the tee.*

If there is a classic Costa del Sol course, this may appear to be it – such are land values that the property left for golf is often secondary. This all too often results in compromises in design – and/or buggies-only-mountain-goat terrain. Endowed with the art of compression, Río Real is a refreshingly verdant, entertaining course, which meanders around and across the 'Royal River' down from clubhouse to beach (4th green), back and around. At first sight, it does indeed seem tightly shoe-horned into the land between road, river and housing. In fact, it is the other way round: the course came first, as the layout is one of the oldest on the Costa del Sol, developed in conjunction with the Los Monteros estate, an early hotel and villa urbanización, just east of Marbella,

*Medium p3:12 is an attractive recent addition, with water in front, left and behind the sloping green.*

first frequented by royalty and the jet set in the 1960s. It must then have seemed just around the corner from Los Monteros. Actually, it is 2km away. Such has been the growth in development that the two are islands of peaceful maturity in the swirling sea of new buildings, with the A7 between them. Did we say 'tight'? At medium p3:6 your ball longs for a high-drawn tee shot, so it can down a quick cocktail on an overhanging balcony en route for the green. Miss the green left, and it gets wet another way! A course to be embibed.

# SAN ROQUE (NEW) ↗

Perry Dye & Ballesteros   2003   €€€   **H:** M 28, L 36, J 28/36

Buggy included in green fee

📧 The San Roque Club, N340 km127, San Roque 11360, Cádiz

☎ +34 956 613 030

✎ aperea@sanroqueclub.com   www.sanroqueclub.com

🚗 ✈ Gibraltar: A383 from La Línea; r onto A7 (after 9km); 1st exit (127) and follow signs to club.

| | m | p | | | m | p |
|---|---|---|---|---|---|---|
| 1 | 408 | 4 | | 10 | 341 | 4 |
| 2 | 483 | 5 | | 11 | 565 | 5 |
| 3 | 339 | 4 | | 12 | 312 | 4 |
| 4 | 177 | 3 | | 13 | 167 | 3 |
| 5 | 347 | 4 | | 14 | 416 | 4 |
| 6 | 331 | 4 | | 15 | 418 | 4 |
| 7 | 524 | 5 | | 16 | 457 | 5 |
| 8 | 206 | 3 | | 17 | 197 | 3 |
| 9 | 395 | 4 | | 18 | 414 | 4 |
| | 3210 | 36 | | | 3287 | 36 |
| | | | | | 6497 | 72 |

Undulating, precise, often dramatic, grand-scale parkland layout. Generally large greens (treacherous when slick) are often protected by spectacular mounds and some sharply focused nests of bunkers. Several good shorter par 4s. Some lateral water.

San Roque's two courses are almost identical in length, but don't be lulled by the more open, parkland feel greeting you on New's 1st tee: this course is a serious challenge, even before your short game is tested (which it will be). After a demanding start, you

*Shortish p4:3, played down into, and up out of, a bunkered valley to a semi-blind heavily trapped green (longer than it seems from the fairway), with distant mountain views, is the first of several spectacular holes.*

**Above** *16, a shortish, strategic p5, requires either a long 2nd across a valley and bunkers to a layered green, or a very precise lay-up between bunkers and trees to open up the pin on a potentially dangerously sloping multi-level green.*

**Below** *p4:5 is a strategic hole with a stunning greensite. Club choice at the tee is determined by your attitude to the long left-hand approach bunker, especially as the fairway slopes towards it. Yet the longer you give yourself for your second, the more difficult to stop on a green which slopes towards the chasm behind. Go right, and the penalty is a nest of dramatic bunkers...*

may wish to eschew Seve's own tee for spectacular downhill p3:4, across a chasm: severe death awaits anything short or left. Routed over and around a promontory, with several deep grassy expanses, the course is exposed to the wind, but its position also yields good views of the upper Sotogrande estate and occasionally through to the sea. With maturity, and despite some weaknesses (e.g. the up and down routing dictated by the site, two rather unsatisfactory semi-blind tee shots through mounding at parallel 7 & 14 and inappropriately too many ball-hiding flower beds for a golf course), a higher rating could achievable…

# SANTANA ↗

**Robinson  2003  €€**                    **H:** M 26, L 34, J 26/34

✉ Santana Golf & Country Club, Ctra. La Cala – Entrerríos s/n,
29649 Mijas Costa, Málaga

☎ +34 902 517 700

✎ teetimes@santanagolf.com  www.santanagolf.com

🚗 ✈ Málaga: r out of airport exit road onto A7 for Cádiz; r at
km229 for AP7 Benalmádena/Algeciras; exit 214 for A7 for
Fuengirola/Algeciras (not AP7 autopista); r at exit La Cala de Mijas
(km202); r at rbt below A7 for la Cala; r at rbt after 2.5km; club
1.5km on l.

|    | m    | p  |    | m    | p  |
|----|------|----|----|------|----|
| 1  | 321  | 4  | 10 | 468  | 5  |
| 2  | 160  | 3  | 11 | 291  | 4  |
| 3  | 385  | 4  | 12 | 174  | 3  |
| 4  | 556  | 5  | 13 | 355  | 4  |
| 5  | 321  | 4  | 14 | 295  | 4  |
| 6  | 335  | 4  | 15 | 520  | 5  |
| 7  | 192  | 3  | 16 | 150  | 3  |
| 8  | 602  | 5  | 17 | 335  | 4  |
| 9  | 351  | 4  | 18 | 392  | 4  |
|    | 3223 | 36 |    | 2980 | 36 |
|    |      |    |    | 6203 | 72 |

Excellent, easily walkable,
attractive, partly tree-lined
course on gently rolling well-
sculpted former farmland.
Generally large, undulating
greens, often flanked by
expansive bunkering, will
challenge your handicap.
Some water carries.

*Robinson bunkered long p5:4 for today's longer hitters. Dream of driving some 270m,
carrying the fairway bunkers on the direct line, leaving only 250m to the green
(including a 190m carry over a stream). For now, the remaining 99.9% of us can drive
left of the bunkers (carefully avoiding the clumps of avocados), and then go right of the
next fairway bunker to leave a longish third to the dangerously sloping green. A strategic
and aesthetic winner, which also caters for the even higher-tech future...*

*A view from the saddle half way along p5:15, whence you may hope to play your second. An excellent strategic hole: risk the carry over the bunkers and you shorten the hole enough get there in two. But beware the tricky greensite.*

Ask a Spaniard about avocados and you will probably be referred to the nearest legal practice. Hopefully, as far as the course at Santana is concerned, the lawyers have gone, as its development was completed in late 2003 and it effectively opened for business at the beginning of 2004. But avocados abound indeed: the course was built on a former pear farm whose trees often line holes, and in places come into play. Indeed, in season, there is a danger you could be distracted into premature thoughts of accompaniments to that margarita at the 19th by the sight of ripe green pears lying on the glistening white brilliance of the crushed marble bunkers – do this and you'll be in the guacamole, rather than vice versa later. Santana is rustic, pretty, but potentially very dangerous. Recovery from within the trees is difficult, the bunkering heavy, and there are four artificial lakes and a water course to contend with – even before you reach the often lavishly shaped greens, none of which could be described as flat. Robinson has said that there was no other site for a golf course from Sotogrande to Málaga as good or as easy as this one – nor was it surrounded by houses. He has done a good job, and, whilst its potential is perhaps not quite as high as *La Reserva* (a contemporary work with which it bears comparison), it should mature into one of his very best.

**Below** *We didn't think of going as far as red-carding longish p4:18, but the artificiality of the water hazard (right) meant that it could never be rated better than yellow: the water appears to be higher than the fairway and just doesn't look right.*

# SANT CUGAT ↗

Colt   1917   €€€                    **H:** M 28, L 36, J 28/36

✉  Club de Golf Sant Cugat, C/Villa s/n, 08190 Sant Cugat del
    Vallès, Barcelona

☎  +34 936 743 908

✎  golfsc@teleline.es    www.golfsantcugat.com

🚗 ✈ Barcelona: AP7 towards Girona; exit 24 for Sant Cugat
BP1417, following signs for Centro Ciutat; over rbt exit
immediately after filling station down to Sant Cugat centre; r at
lights to Centre Ciutat; r under railway, l for Centro Ciutat, l at rbt,
back under railway; 2nd r leads to club.

| | m | p | | m | p |
|---|---|---|---|---|---|
| 1 | 325 | 4 | 10 | 323 | 4 |
| 2 | 319 | 4 | 11 | 330 | 4 |
| 3 | 448 | 5 | 12 | 271 | 4 |
| 4 | 300 | 4 | 13 | 171 | 3 |
| 5 | 304 | 4 | 14 | 293 | 4 |
| 6 | 250 | 4 | 15 | 340 | 4 |
| 7 | 365 | 4 | 16 | 298 | 4 |
| 8 | 344 | 4 | 17 | 185 | 3 |
| 9 | 271 | 4 | 18 | 517 | 5 |
| | 2926 | 37 | | 2728 | 35 |
| | | | | 5654 | 72 |

Don't let its old-fashioned
eccentricities put you off
playing one of the oldest
courses in Spain, enhanced by
3 new holes: excellent
bunkering, sloping greens,
geometrical doglegs, trees.
Here, style outclasses length...

*A view of 1 from the fairway – why gold for a seemingly innocuous 325m p4? When
there, go beyond it and you will see the bunkered rear of a superb raised greensite,
constructed with simple efficiency by removing earth from the approach. This creates
dead ground at the front, which, as shown here, gives you the impression of a much
more straightforward hole than it actually is – until you get close to the green. This
genre's epitome is The Jockey Club, Buenos Aires (by MacKenzie, an associate of Colt).*

*Virgin golf: a preview of the dramatic looking new 9th hole (by Vidaor) at Sant Cugat, an uphill medium p4, a few days from opening when we visited.*

You may be surprised at our rating of what at first sight seems a scrappy course, very short by modern standards, squashed between suburban Barcelonan houses. But golf doesn't have to be about 300m titanium-charged drives: play that game here and you may well get into a lot of trouble. The course designers of the early 20th century knew what they were doing, and the money is still in the short game. Here, your wedge approach to a craftily bunkered sloping green requires just as much respect as a 5-iron might on the latest tiger course. Liberally sprinkle in nearing 100 years of tree maturity… you get the point?! (Sant Cugat's history is not untypical of the way the game first spread into Iberia: a group of British and American engineers came to Catalunya as part of the process of installing full electric power to the region. One of them, a Mr Fraser Lawton, would ask the same question whenever he was considering a new project: "Is there golf?". The seed of what was originally Barcelona, then New Barcelona, and finally Sant Cugat Golf Club (1934) was sown. Enter Mr Colt…)

*The 2004 remodelling removed three p3s from the course (the old 3rd having been a gold candidate – its green was just beyond the 1st green). Hence p3:17 is now Sant Cugat's second, last and toughest short hole – the message is simple: it's longer than it looks, and don't go right.*

# SEVILLA ↗

Olazábal  1991  €€                    **H:** M 28, L 36, J 28/36

✉  Real Club de Golf de Sevilla, Autovía Sevilla-Utrera km3.2,
   41500 Alcala de Guadaira, Sevilla

☎  +34 954 124 301

✉  reservas@sevillagolf.com    www.sevillagolf.com

🚗 ✈ Sevilla: A4/E5 towards Sevilla; l at junction after 3km staying
on E5, becomes SE30 Sevilla ring road; exit 6b onto A376 for Utrera;
at exit 4 for Montequinto (km1.8) r into side lane parallel with A376;
r at lights, l at rbt; l under A376 after 400m; fork l at rbt into club
entrance road, r after 100m; straight over rbt after 800m into club.

|    | m    | p  |    | m    | p  |
|----|------|----|----|------|----|
| 1  | 364  | 4  | 10 | 386  | 4  |
| 2  | 413  | 4  | 11 | 181  | 3  |
| 3  | 154  | 3  | 12 | 347  | 4  |
| 4  | 399  | 4  | 13 | 473  | 5  |
| 5  | 470  | 5  | 14 | 392  | 4  |
| 6  | 413  | 4  | 15 | 400  | 4  |
| 7  | 211  | 3  | 16 | 478  | 5  |
| 8  | 347  | 4  | 17 | 207  | 3  |
| 9  | 499  | 5  | 18 | 395  | 4  |
|    | 3270 | 36 |    | 3259 | 36 |
|    |      |    |    | 6529 | 72 |

Two loops of 9 make up one of
the most consistent designs in
Spain – understated, open,
gently sloping parkland layout
with sometimes raised, heavily
bunkered greensites and many
tiered greens, often set at angle
to play. Some water carries.
Testing finish, made more so
for 2004 World Cup.

**Below** *A recapitulation of the main themes in the longish p4
finale: mild right to left dogleg, water, fairway undulations, tiered
green, defended by bunkers and mounds.*

On arrival in Seville, you may be tempted to have your beard fine-tuned for the love of three oranges. Do that if you wish, but leave time to play the Olazábal course just south of the city centre. Sevilla might initially seem like another modern design on relatively flat ground, with moulding and mounding through the green. But take a closer look: it is very much a technical, rather than visually spectacular, golf course, testing your short game in particular – no surprise, given its designer. The greens are small, and tend to curve around bunkers and mounds, giving potentially very demanding pin positions, which in turn put a premium on placing tee shots, so recoveries must be spot on to save par. Sevilla's high score sings out like a theme and variations. The theme is artificial design,

*The green of p4:2 – the first variation: longer than 1, slight left to right dogleg around bunker on direct line from tee, with a tougher greensite, turning around bunker and more pronounced mounding. Pin position back right – sforzando!*

sculpted into relatively flat ground, with distinctive, well-defended small greens and some links reminiscences. It is stated clearly at straightish p4:1 as shown in the photo below. 2: variation 1 – see photo above. 3: p3, raised tee, introduce water, continue theme of angled, bunkered green. 4: p4, slightly more pronounced dogleg, longer with harsher bunkering. 5: first p5 variation – palm trees, seen on earlier holes, now define green. Etc., etc… Musicians may also relate more to the sounds of birdsong here than the incessant, if only occasionally operatic, croaking of frogs. Encore!

*The theme of Sevilla is presented at medium p4:1 – a reasonably open driving hole, undulations crafted into bunkered fairway, mildly two-tiered green angled across line of play, set slightly above encircling bunkers.*

# SON ANTEM (WEST) ↗

Segalés   2001   €€                    **H:** M 27, L 35, J 27/35

✉ Son Antem Golf Resort & Spa, Ctra. Llucmajor km3.4, 07620
Llucmajor, Mallorca

☎ +34 971 129 200

✎ mhrs.pmigs.golf.reservation@marriott.com
www.marriotthotels.com\pmigs

🚗 ✈ Palma de Mallorca: exit airport I onto PM19, becomes
PM602; resort approx 12km from airport on r (before Llucmajor).

| | m | p | | m | p |
|---|---|---|---|---|---|
| 1 | 364 | 4 | 10 | 393 | 4 |
| 2 | 186 | 3 | 11 | 153 | 3 |
| 3 | 482 | 5 | 12 | 367 | 4 |
| 4 | 381 | 4 | 13 | 471 | 5 |
| 5 | 377 | 4 | 14 | 374 | 4 |
| 6 | 297 | 4 | 15 | 384 | 4 |
| 7 | 483 | 5 | 16 | 495 | 5 |
| 8 | 139 | 3 | 17 | 190 | 3 |
| 9 | 357 | 4 | 18 | 400 | 4 |
| | 3066 | 36 | | 3227 | 36 |
| | | | | 6273 | 72 |

Understated, fairly flat and long, testing, slightly artificial but engaging hotel course with multi-tiered bunkered greens, set in natural Mallorquin surrounds. Self-contained, and peaceful, routing of 2 loops of 9 prevents future development except at extremities, encouraging wildlife. Some water.

**12 red:** the blindness of the bunker in a swale just in front of the green is too unfair.

*This view of medium p5:3 shows how the course has been blended into the surrounding landscape. The mounding and fairway undulations are mostly understated – it is only where the routing takes us to more open ground (e.g. p4:15 and p3:17) where it becomes a feature that more obviously affects play.*

*Strategy is tested throughout: at medium p4:9 you may plan to keep as many hazards out of play as possible, but taking on the water is almost inevitable.*

Son Antem was the first facility on Mallorca to boast year-round swimming in thermal water, setting standards which no doubt will become Mallorca's par. But standards are also set at Son Antem (West). Unless you are a fan of perfectly manicured American-style courses massaged between rows of holiday villas, be reassured: here the pampering is left behind at the spa; on the course you get the full treatment.

*The approach bunkers at long p4:15, a right to left dogleg played through mounds, are normally more threatening than the November sky…*

The West is long and often quite aggressively bunkered, with several multi-tiered greens, requiring careful tee shot placement if you want to slap the ball by the flag. Yet the understated undulations in most fairways can make it difficult to achieve that objective, putting a premium on your short game. Go off fairway, and you will soon be greeted by difficult rocky Mallorquin scrub, bushes and trees. If it's hydrotherapy you're after, take the waters on 9, 14 or 18. Just as the spa is artificial (thermal water is piped into the pool from a nearby source), so this is a modern course juxtaposed into natural Mallorquin surrounds, which makes the occasional mounded holes seem out of place, but the very nature of Mallorca (much of it is a flat rock with minimal topsoil) might otherwise have rendered the course too featureless. Wildlife abound, adding to the therapy.

# TORREQUEBRADA ↗

Gancedo   1978   €€                      **H:** M 28, L 36, J 28/36

✉   Golf Torrequebrada, Ctra. de Cádiz km220, 29630
    Benalmádena Costa, Málaga

☎   +34 952 442 742

✎   bookings@golftorrequebrada.com
    www.golftorrequebrada.com

🚗 ✈ Málaga: r out of airport exit road onto A7 for Cádiz; r at
km229 for AP7 Benalmádena/Algeciras; exit 222 Arroyo de la Miel; l
under AP7 and r at next rbt downhill; r at junction before filling station,
down hill; straight over next junction (after 500m); straight over rbt
after 700m; down to rbt with boat, whence r; uphill for 1km; l at filling
station (Campsa); follow bends in road down hill for 1km to club on r.

| | m | p | | m | p |
|---|---|---|---|---|---|
| 1 | 435 | 5 | 10 | 382 | 4 |
| 2 | 337 | 4 | 11 | 164 | 3 |
| 3 | 90 | 3 | 12 | 469 | 5 |
| 4 | 329 | 4 | 13 | 147 | 3 |
| 5 | 345 | 4 | 14 | 462 | 5 |
| 6 | 487 | 5 | 15 | 321 | 4 |
| 7 | 313 | 4 | 16 | 388 | 4 |
| 8 | 361 | 4 | 17 | 354 | 4 |
| 9 | 148 | 3 | 18 | 320 | 4 |
| | 2845 | 36 | | 3007 | 36 |
| | | | | 5852 | 72 |

**Well-designed, hilly, mature Costa del Sol course which presents some entertaining variations within a consistent theme. Uphill, downhill, over water, round corners, over dips (sometimes hidden), over bunkers, undulating greens – a long-standing return destination for many.**

*The dip in front, and the raised, sloping putting surface, of the bunkered green at medium p4:4 are typical of this course.*

As you may learn from this book, José ("Pepe") Gancedo is the most adventurous of Spain's golf course designers. Who else could have created the amazing layout at *Monte Mayor* – a little quirky it may be, but its character and beauty are arresting? Who else could have designed *Golf del Sur*, where the black bunkers give the often disarming feel of a photographic negative? Who else could have breathed new life into a course such as *La Herrería* (and hopefully one day he will be invited to upgrade its back 9)? On the other hand, *Parque da Floresta*, Portugal, is a little disappointing. 5 times Spanish amateur champion, he was still in his 30s when he laid out Torrequebrada, and at

*Maturity of trees and housing development have blocked many of Torrequebrada's former vistas, but the sea is never far away and some views remain, as this one over initially downhill left to right dogleg medium p5:6, which rises (as do many here) to a sloping green (bunkered also, mainly behind the trees, on the right).*

the time could little have known how successful and highly regarded it would become. Step back in time and imagine the late 1970s construction of a hilly course using a now typical Costa del Sol routing through defiles: at the time it was perhaps more adventurous than it now seems. No hole is flat, only one (p3s excepted) is completely straight (and perhaps a couple, 8 and 10, turn rather too much). Downhill-left-to-right-around-and-across-water-with-multi-sloping-green longish p4:16 must have struck fear into everyone at the course's opening. Gancedo has pushed the golf design envelope ever since: long may he do so.

*Don't be seduced by the surroundings of medium p3:11: the tree in front of the bunker foreshortens the hole and the green has three different levels, which makes successful recovery from sand all the more difficult.*

# VILLAMARTÍN ↗

Putman 1972 €          **H:** M 28, L 36, J 28/36

✉ Golf Villamartín, Urb. Golf Villamartín, Ctra. Alicante –
Cartagena km50, 03189 Orihuela, Alicante

☎ +34 966 765 170

✎ Book by phone   [No website]

🚗 ✈ Alicante: N338 – A7 – AP7 exit 763 (N.B. no. may change)
for La Zenia; at rbt follow signs for Villamartín; up hill for 3km;
club on l.

| | m | p | | m | p |
|---|---|---|---|---|---|
| 1 | 485 | 5 | 10 | 320 | 4 |
| 2 | 360 | 4 | 11 | 450 | 5 |
| 3 | 345 | 4 | 12 | 385 | 4 |
| 4 | 336 | 4 | 13 | 185 | 3 |
| 5 | 465 | 5 | 14 | 520 | 5 |
| 6 | 188 | 3 | 15 | 320 | 4 |
| 7 | 308 | 4 | 16 | 375 | 4 |
| 8 | 333 | 4 | 17 | 220 | 3 |
| 9 | 152 | 3 | 18 | 385 | 4 |
| | 2972 | 36 | | 3160 | 36 |
| | | | | 6132 | 72 |

Primarily strategic, undulating,
in some ways refreshingly old-
fashioned, Mediterranean
parkland course, whose design
quality somewhat exceeds its
2004 condition. A few
intriguing doglegs and some
spectacular shots required,
often over valleys, and once
over water. Go for it!

*We think you will get a better idea of the challenge presented by this very long, but
excellent, p3 with a view from behind the two-tiered green, which is banked steeply
down to the player's right. Villamartín's 17th is a truly memorable hole, from
whichever of the tees you play: although we don't normally speak in old money, from
the back this hole measures over 240 yards, downhill admittedly, but you can see that
it takes no prisoners (there's even another bunker, out of shot, between those visible).*

*Trees in the fairway, as well as all round the green, at shortish left-to-right-dogleg-over-a-brow-and-down-the-hill p4:7, probably the best hole on the front 9. Play it with modesty rather than a risky, corner-cutting driver, we suggest....*

Californian golf designer, and successful amateur golfer, Robert Putman is perhaps best known in Iberia for his designs for *La Manga (North)* and *(South)*, but both have been remodelled over the years. Putman designed Villamartín, just up the road (relatively speaking), at the same time as *La Manga* and this course remains basically in its original form. The quality of his design and the way his routing made efficient use of the natural terrain (which, with interesting undulations, is notably better than at *La Manga*) speaks for itself. As you play the course, you can't help noticing the more spectacular use of the land (particularly 7, 14 and 17 as featured in the photos). But the tone is also set in the less obvious holes, starting with p5:1 – over rolling ground, before the olives close in around the rising greensite. On ground like this you cannot avoid uphill holes, but Putman

mainly dealt with them in tee shots (especially at 3 and 8, where the unfolding view of bunkered greens refreshes you as you go over the hill brows). Perhaps a weaker moment with parallel 11 and 12, but, even after the glory of 17, you cannot but admire the way 18 dodges olive trees and bunkers before you reach the sand-defended final green in front of the clubhouse. If staying at *La Manga*, play here too.

**Below** *Yes, this view is on the line of play for the 3rd shot uphill over a ditch below the bunker at long p5:14 – not Villamartín's only tree-surrounded green.*

# ALCAIDESA

Alliss & Clark   1990   €€

✉  Alcaidesa Links Golf Course, Ctra. N340 km124.6, 11315 La
Línea, Cádiz

☎  +34 956 791 040

✎  golf@alcaidesa.com   www.alcaidesa.com

🚗 ✈ Gibraltar: A383 from La Línea; after 9km under A7 r onto
service road; 1st r over A7 into Alcaidesa estate; signposts to
clubhouse (approx 2km, down near sea).

| | m | p | | m | p |
|---|---|---|---|---|---|
| 1 | 346 | 4 | 10 | 400 | 4 |
| 2 | 202 | 3 | 11 | 472 | 5 |
| 3 | 344 | 4 | 12 | 360 | 4 |
| 4 | 264 | 4 | 13 | 467 | 5 |
| 5 | 300 | 4 | 14 | 140 | 3 |
| 6 | 475 | 5 | 15 | 465 | 5 |
| 7 | 152 | 3 | 16 | 180 | 3 |
| 8 | 445 | 5 | 17 | 278 | 4 |
| 9 | 148 | 3 | 18 | 328 | 4 |
| | 2676 | 35 | | 3090 | 37 |
| | | | | 5766 | 72 |

Despite links branding, an undulating cliff/hill-top course, whose greatest quality is its stunning views over Gibraltar. Combination of small greens and wind can result in high scores. Tougher than its card suggests, with a few demanding carries, some over water.

*13, a sporting p5 with a downhill drive to a wide fairway, whence a potentially satisfying, reachable-in-2, carry over a ditch to a small bunkered green (on the right). Once you have driven, dwell on the wonderful vista left of the 3rd green (left of 13th) to Gibraltar and Morocco beyond.*

# ALHAURÍN

Ballesteros 1994 €    **H:** M 28, L 34, J 36

✉ Alhaurín Golf, Ctra. MA426 km15, 29120 Alhaurín el Grande, Málaga

☎ +34 952 595 970

✎ reservasgolf@alhauringolf.com    www.alhauringolf.com

🚗 ✈ Málaga: r out of airport exit road onto A7 for Cádiz; r at first junction (exit at km230 Coín); onto A366 to Alhaurín El Grande; l at rbt with cross onto A387 up hill; l at 1st junction going down hill at km1.5; l at rbt after km4 for Mijas; r into club at A387 km5.5.

|    | m    | p  |    | m    | p  |
|----|------|----|----|------|----|
| 1  | 486  | 5  | 10 | 429  | 4  |
| 2  | 352  | 4  | 11 | 196  | 3  |
| 3  | 167  | 3  | 12 | 370  | 4  |
| 4  | 361  | 4  | 13 | 124  | 3  |
| 5  | 117  | 3  | 14 | 511  | 5  |
| 6  | 510  | 5  | 15 | 353  | 4  |
| 7  | 333  | 4  | 16 | 284  | 4  |
| 8  | 378  | 4  | 17 | 521  | 5  |
| 9  | 404  | 4  | 18 | 325  | 4  |
|    | 3108 | 36 |    | 3113 | 36 |
|    |      |    |    | 6221 | 72 |

An often challenging hill-side hotel course whose eccentricities are no real match for its superb mountain/distant coastline vistas. Testing greens often raised and bunkered. Some water. To say this is a difficult site for golf may be a kindness, yet many enjoy it.

N.B. There are several p3 facilities here.

*This view of longish p5:14 illustrates the mountain backdrops which adorn many of the holes at Alhaurín. After a drive across water, you will probably have a blind shot over a gentle hill-brow down to the green. Not worth the risk of trying it in two – most of us wouldn't reach it anyway.*

# ALMENARA

Thomas  1998  €€

**H:** M 28, L 36, J 28/36

✉ Almenara Golf-Hotel & Spa, Avda. Almenara s/n, Sotogrande,
11310 San Roque, Cádiz

☎ +34 956 582 000

✎ nhalmenaragolf@nh-hotels.com    www.nhalmenara.com

🚗 ✈ Gibraltar: A383 from La Línea; r onto A7 (after 8km); exit
130 for Sotogrande/Valderrama; 1st r at rbt; after 500m r at rbt over
motorway; through security gates and follow signs (approx 2km).

| Pinos | | | Lagos | | | Alcornoques | | |
|---|---|---|---|---|---|---|---|---|
| | m | p | | m | p | | m | p |
| 1 | 513 | 5 | 1 | 376 | 4 | 1 | 381 | 4 |
| 2 | 381 | 4 | 2 | 170 | 3 | 2 | 173 | 4 |
| 3 | 374 | 4 | 3 | 381 | 4 | 3 | 459 | 5 |
| 4 | 197 | 3 | 4 | 452 | 5 | 4 | 435 | 4 |
| 5 | 330 | 4 | 5 | 419 | 4 | 5 | 136 | 3 |
| 6 | 382 | 4 | 6 | 345 | 4 | 6 | 351 | 4 |
| 7 | 170 | 3 | 7 | 183 | 3 | 7 | 323 | 4 |
| 8 | 474 | 5 | 8 | 456 | 5 | 8 | 367 | 4 |
| 9 | 311 | 4 | 9 | 338 | 4 | 9 | 464 | 5 |
| | 3132 | 36 | | 3120 | 36 | | 3089 | 36 |
| PL | 6252 | 72 | PA | 6221 | 72 | LA | 6209 | 72 |

**Lagos 5 red:** the corner of this sadistic left to right dogleg is too far from the tee, and the uphill second shot too long, for it to be fair – and then a (in other circumstances excellent) 3-tier green! **Alcornoques 9 red:** too much of a closing uphill slog.

Hilly, but popular, hotel course with some great views, challenging
holes and plenty of water. Classic Thomas mounding, bunkering
and largish greens abound in mainly pine-lined residential setting.
For 18, omit Alcornoques; for only 9, play Pinos.

*Reflect on the qualities of Lagos 7, a classic tee-water-green p3 whose beauty should
not deceive you into a lack of concentration: it plays every inch of its length and,
even safely over the water, the green's subtleties will make you work hard for a par.*

# ALOHA

Arana   1975   €€€                          **H:** M 24, L 28, J 24/28

✉  Club de Golf Aloha, Urb. Aloha, Nueva Andalucía, 29660
   Marbella, Málaga

☎  +34 952 812 388

✎  office@clubdegolfaloha.com   www.clubdegolfaloha.com

🚗 ✈ Málaga: r out of airport exit road onto A7 for Cádiz; r at
km229 for AP7 Benalmádena/Algeciras; end of Marbella bypass
(km178) take r split onto A7; exit junction 176 (Istán) after tunnel; l at
rbt; over bridge; straight over (i.e. do not veer left); 2nd r, up hill, at
next rbt; straight over next rbt; club 200m on l at top of hill.

| | m | p | | m | p |
|---|---|---|---|---|---|
| 1 | 545 | 5 | 10 | 513 | 5 |
| 2 | 331 | 4 | 11 | 353 | 4 |
| 3 | 315 | 4 | 12 | 377 | 4 |
| 4 | 207 | 3 | 13 | 196 | 3 |
| 5 | 467 | 5 | 14 | 337 | 4 |
| 6 | 375 | 4 | 15 | 365 | 4 |
| 7 | 319 | 4 | 16 | 481 | 5 |
| 8 | 178 | 3 | 17 | 210 | 3 |
| 9 | 314 | 4 | 18 | 410 | 4 |
| | 3051 | 36 | | 3242 | 36 |
| | | | | 6293 | 72 |

Classy Marbella club, enjoyable and in very pleasant surrounds: 2 loops of 9, rolling fairways, testing greens, several shortish p4s, 3 long p3s, water, mountain views… Javier Arana's last course – not his best for design (e.g. too many adverse cambers) but he died before its completion (finished off by Canáles). Just misses ↗ rating (achievable on this site).

**N.B.** There is also 9 hole short course (636m).

*10 is one of the best holes at Aloha: a longish p5 with a fairway split lengthways, viewed here down the left-hand, lower level. As you can see, with the greenside bunkers, it is a bold move to go for it in 2.*

# LAS AMÉRICAS

Jacobs 1998 €€                    **H:** M 28, L 36, J 36

✉ Golf Las Américas, 38660 Playa de las Américas, Arona, Tenerife

☎ +34 922 752 005

✎ info@golf-tenerife.com    www.golf-tenerife.com

🚗 ✈ Tenerife Sur: TF1 towards Playa de las Américas; km72 exit 28; l over bridge over highway; l at rbt; follow road to Hotel Compostela Golf 3; club at end of street.

| | m | p | | m | p |
|---|---|---|---|---|---|
| 1 | 449 | 5 | 10 | 434 | 4 |
| 2 | 381 | 4 | 11 | 166 | 3 |
| 3 | 390 | 4 | 12 | 320 | 4 |
| 4 | 255 | 4 | 13 | 140 | 3 |
| 5 | 194 | 3 | 14 | 258 | 4 |
| 6 | 431 | 4 | 15 | 410 | 4 |
| 7 | 456 | 5 | 16 | 449 | 5 |
| 8 | 168 | 3 | 17 | 314 | 4 |
| 9 | 355 | 4 | 18 | 469 | 5 |
| | 3079 | 36 | | 2960 | 36 |
| | | | | 6039 | 72 |

More difficult than its length suggests, a popular course with 2 loops, both climbing to land behind clubhouse in urban resort surroundings with sea views, trees, water and some testing sloping/tiered greens. 3 good doglegs round swale, sand and water.

*13 is one of the most attractive holes at Las Américas: a tee-water-green p3, backed by palm trees, with mountains beyond. Take care on the green, which slopes towards the water. (There's another lake to the right and a bunker left.)*

# ANDRATX

Kidd 1999 €€

H: M 28, L 36, J 45

Buggy included
in green fee

✉ Golf de Andratx, Carrer Cromlec Nr 1, 01760 Camp de Mar, Mallorca

☎ +34 971 236 280

✎ info@golfdeandratx.com  www.golfdeandratx.com

🚗 ✈ Mallorca: PM19 – PM20 – PM1 – C719 for Port d'Andratx; approx 1.5km after 2nd tunnel, l onto C710a for Peguera; after 1km r onto PM101 for Camp de Mar; 500m to club/hotel.

| | m | p | | | m | p |
|---|---|---|---|---|---|---|
| 1 | 352 | 4 | | 10 | 484 | 5 |
| 2 | 161 | 3 | | 11 | 426 | 4 |
| 3 | 310 | 4 | | 12 | 346 | 4 |
| 4 | 161 | 3 | | 13 | 371 | 4 |
| 5 | 485 | 5 | | 14 | 279 | 4 |
| 6 | 609 | 5 | | 15 | 186 | 3 |
| 7 | 242 | 4 | | 16 | 315 | 4 |
| 8 | 405 | 4 | | 17 | 344 | 4 |
| 9 | 158 | 3 | | 18 | 455 | 5 |
| | 2883 | 35 | | | 3206 | 37 |
| | | | | | 6089 | 72 |

Love it or hate it? Charismatic, demanding, 3-dimensional hotel course with spectacular views, and challenging, yet potentially very satisfying, shot-making opportunities. Maybe not for everyday play, but it sure is different. Mandatory buggy absolutely essential. (We love it *and* we hate it!)

*We were tempted to gild long downhill p4:8 but the golfing challenge is not quite equal to the amazing views from the tee; the lake on the left and the slopes of the green made it a very near miss.*

# LOS ARQUEROS

Ballesteros   1991   €€          **H:** M 28, L 36, J 36

✉  Los Arqueros Golf & Country Club, Ctra. Ronda km166.5,
    29679 Benahavís, Málaga

☎  +34 952 784 712

✎  caddiemaster@es.taylorwoodrow.com
    www.es.taylorwoodrow.com

🚗 ✈ Málaga: r out of airport exit road onto A7 for Cádiz; r at
km229 for AP7 Benalmádena/Algeciras; end of Marbella bypass
(km178) take l split to stay on AP7 autopista to exit 172 for Ronda;
almost U-turn at rbt onto A376 for Ronda; course approx 3km up
hill on l (500m after km45).

| | m | p | | m | p |
|---|---|---|---|---|---|
| 1 | 341 | 4 | 10 | 328 | 4 |
| 2 | 148 | 3 | 11 | 145 | 3 |
| 3 | 361 | 4 | 12 | 327 | 4 |
| 4 | 336 | 4 | 13 | 456 | 5 |
| 5 | 151 | 3 | 14 | 284 | 4 |
| 6 | 513 | 5 | 15 | 377 | 4 |
| 7 | 301 | 4 | 16 | 151 | 3 |
| 8 | 480 | 5 | 17 | 351 | 4 |
| 9 | 275 | 4 | 18 | 338 | 4 |
| | 2906 | 36 | | 2757 | 35 |
| | | | | 5663 | 71 |

Two loops of 9 descend from
clubhouse amidst substantial
residential estate (front 9,
enclosed in bowl, more severely
affected). Uphill, downhill,
doglegs, water and several well-
bunkered greensites. Some holes
more eccentric than others.

*Country folk will be more at home on the relatively rustic back 9 at Los Arqueros.*
*Short p5:13 is its most dramatic hole: after driving down from a high tee, consider*
*cutting the corner to reach the green in two. Seve's challenge is evident: he would*
*surely take it on. Note the well-placed front right greenside bunker.*

# ATALAYA (NEW)

Krings   1993   €€                    **H:** M 28, L 36, J 28/36

✉  Atalaya Golf & Country Club, Ctra. Benahavís km0.7, 29688 Estepona, Málaga

☎  +34 952 882 812

✎  atalayagolf@selected-hotels.com   www.selected-hotels.com

🚗 ✈ Málaga: r out of airport exit road onto A7 for Cádiz; r at km229 for AP7 Benalmádena/Algeciras; end of Marbella bypass (km178) take r split onto A7 past San Pedro; km169.1 r onto MA547 for Benahavís (exit immediately after bridge over Río Guadalmina); club entrance approx 700m on l.

|    | m    | p  |    | m    | p  |
|----|------|----|----|------|----|
| 1  | 302  | 4  | 10 | 274  | 4  |
| 2  | 464  | 5  | 11 | 271  | 4  |
| 3  | 284  | 4  | 12 | 188  | 3  |
| 4  | 147  | 3  | 13 | 167  | 3  |
| 5  | 258  | 4  | 14 | 474  | 5  |
| 6  | 440  | 5  | 15 | 240  | 4  |
| 7  | 248  | 4  | 16 | 155  | 3  |
| 8  | 310  | 4  | 17 | 436  | 5  |
| 9  | 122  | 3  | 18 | 545  | 5  |
|    | 2575 | 36 |    | 2750 | 36 |
|    |      |    |    | 5325 | 72 |

Undulating, often narrow and occasionally tree-lined holiday course with some good sea views. More difficult than its 6 short p4s, 5 p3s and 5 p5s suggest; thoughtful irons off the tee are rewarded. Higher parts exposed to wind. Some water carries. Putt carefully...

**3 red:** uphill from tee, with reachable blind water on left and out of bounds right of narrow fairway. Too unfair.

*Long p3.12 is the first of two consecutive short holes which bring us back to the lower part of the course. Particularly with such a large drop to the green, you will need to judge the wind carefully on the tee.*

# BENALUP

Rolin 2001 €

**H:** M 28, L 32, J 36

✉ Benalup Hotel Golf & Country Club, Calle La Torre s/n, 11190 Benalup-Casas Viejas, Cádiz

☎ +34 956 424 928

✎ info@benalupgolf.com   www.benalupgolf.com

🚗 ✈ Gibraltar: follow signs for Algeciras onto A7; at exit 110 r onto A381 (due to become AP7) for Los Barrios; at (what should become) approx km65 exit onto CA212 for Benalup; follow into Benalup (24km) to top of hill (becomes CA211); after 10km post, l at rbt onto CAP211; l after approx 500m, across rbt and along avenue; at end of avenue straight on, down hill (l fork); round to r at bottom; club entrance 400m on r.

| | m | p | | m | p |
|---|---|---|---|---|---|
| 1 | 361 | 4 | 10 | 139 | 3 |
| 2 | 194 | 3 | 11 | 310 | 4 |
| 3 | 339 | 4 | 12 | 166 | 3 |
| 4 | 334 | 4 | 13 | 528 | 5 |
| 5 | 481 | 5 | 14 | 310 | 4 |
| 6 | 293 | 4 | 15 | 454 | 5 |
| 7 | 404 | 4 | 16 | 353 | 4 |
| 8 | 167 | 3 | 17 | 327 | 4 |
| 9 | 458 | 5 | 18 | 455 | 5 |
| | 3031 | 36 | | 3042 | 37 |
| | | | | 6073 | 73 |

An efficient layout on gently rolling ground, partially tree-lined, with some wonderful rustic views, especially on the back 9. Artificial lakes and fairly light bunkering defend generally raised sloping greens. (Excellent lunch included in green fee.)

**5 red:** taking the direct route down 4th fairway (which has not been made impossible by trees/obstructions), it plays as a medium length p4; also, 2nd water hazard on left is blind uphill from conventional fairway.

*11 swings dogleg left to right up round a single tree in the fairway, but you will also be tested by the elevated green – a fine example of a good uphill p4, with some of the best views on the course (to distant Moroccan mountains on a clear day).*

# CABOPINO

Ligues   2000   €€

**H:** M 28, L 36, J 36

Buggy included
in green fee

✉ Cabopino Golf Marbella, Artola Alta s/n – Apdo. 2119, 29600
Marbella, Málaga

☎ +34 952 850 282

✎ reservas@cabopinogolf.com   www.cabopinogolf.com

🚗 ✈ Málaga: A7 towards Marbella; r at Cabopino exit, km195 (km
sign missing); r at end of slip road; l up hill after 200m; after 200m
straight on up hill; range on r: follow road up hill (beware mid-road
pylons), and round to l to club. *(Important note: on the way up, opposite
range on r, note 12th green on l – you won't see it from the fairway; once
over top of hill, note 14th green back l – you may not see that one from the
fairway, either; also note water in front of green. Don't confuse 14th green with
15th, which is the p3 over water, with the tee on l, just by the road.)*

|    | m    | p  |    | m    | p  |
|----|------|----|----|------|----|
| 1  | 309  | 4  | 10 | 327  | 4  |
| 2  | 275  | 4  | 11 | 336  | 4  |
| 3  | 288  | 4  | 12 | 391  | 5  |
| 4  | 243  | 4  | 13 | 134  | 3  |
| 5  | 378  | 4  | 14 | 456  | 5  |
| 6  | 264  | 4  | 15 | 135  | 3  |
| 7  | 152  | 3  | 16 | 305  | 4  |
| 8  | 277  | 4  | 17 | 268  | 4  |
| 9  | 327  | 4  | 18 | 305  | 4  |
|    | 2513 | 35 |    | 2657 | 36 |
|    |      |    |    | 5170 | 71 |

Short, often hilly, challenging
course, probably too tight for
serious golf (with a few
spectacular shots to compensate).
Good greensites reward accurate
iron play. You may find more
balls than you lose… or the other
way round. Can play a bit easier
2nd time round.

**5 (token) red:** fairway too narrow for a hole of its length, with the slope making it worse.
**6 red:** routing problem: too uphill, with house development encroaching the dogleg.
**12 red:** not clear where the hole goes for 2nd shot on a very reachable-in-2 p5.
**14 red:** reachable-in-2 p5 with second shot uphill blind over water – too unfair.

*3 is the mother of all downhill short p4s. The carry is 255m from the very back (but it also
feels like the green is 100m below the tee): too long for most to reach in one, but still
worth the sheer exhilaration of going for that shot-of-the-holiday, if you are a big hitter.*

Costa del Sol **109**

# La Cala (North)

Robinson   1993   €€                    **H:** M 28, L 36, J 28/36

✉ La Cala Resort, Apdo. de Correos 106, La Cala de Mijas, 29649 Mijas Costa, Málaga

☎ +34 952 669 033

✎ lacala@lacala.com   www.lacala.com

🚗 ✈ Málaga: r out of airport exit road onto A7 for Cádiz; r at km229 for AP7 Benalmádena/Algeciras; exit 214 for A7 for Fuengirola/Algeciras (not AP7 autopista); exit at Cala de Mijas, km201.5; r at rbt below A7; l at rbt after 2.5km; follow signposted road to La Cala.

| | m | p | | m | p |
|---|---|---|---|---|---|
| 1 | 446 | 5 | 10 | 345 | 4 |
| 2 | 325 | 4 | 11 | 217 | 3 |
| 3 | 298 | 4 | 12 | 366 | 4 |
| 4 | 180 | 3 | 13 | 391 | 4 |
| 5 | 324 | 4 | 14 | 332 | 4 |
| 6 | 469 | 5 | 15 | 500 | 5 |
| 7 | 417 | 4 | 16 | 123 | 3 |
| 8 | 118 | 3 | 17 | 355 | 4 |
| 9 | 473 | 5 | 18 | 508 | 5 |
| | 3050 | 37 | | 3137 | 36 |
| | | | | 6187 | 73 |

An extremely hilly site in attractive mountain scenery yields a mixed batch of holes: what comes down has also to go up, unfortunately. Nevertheless, there are some good holes both up- and downhill, often with difficult, small greensites and challenging bunkering.

*Twisting, sharply downhill shortish p5:9 plays much shorter than its length. The final turn is up to its tiny green: don't go left!*

# LA CALA (SOUTH)

Robinson    1991    €€            **H:** M 28, L 36, J 36

✉ La Cala Resort, Apdo. de Correos 106, La Cala de Mijas, 29649 Mijas Costa, Málaga

☎ +34 952 669 033

✎ lacala@lacala.com    www.lacala.com

🚗 ✈ Málaga: r out of airport exit road onto A7 for Cádiz; r at km229 for AP7 Benalmádena/Algeciras; exit 214 for A7 for Fuengirola/Algeciras (not AP7 autopista); exit at Cala de Mijas, km201.5; r at rbt below A7; l at rbt after 2.5km; follow signposted road to La Cala.

| | m | p | | m | p |
|---|---|---|---|---|---|
| 1 | 319 | 4 | 10 | 482 | 5 |
| 2 | 267 | 4 | 11 | 170 | 3 |
| 3 | 145 | 3 | 12 | 359 | 4 |
| 4 | 336 | 4 | 13 | 377 | 4 |
| 5 | 489 | 5 | 14 | 292 | 4 |
| 6 | 349 | 4 | 15 | 360 | 4 |
| 7 | 168 | 3 | 16 | 435 | 5 |
| 8 | 407 | 4 | 17 | 166 | 3 |
| 9 | 449 | 5 | 18 | 355 | 4 |
| | 2929 | 36 | | 2996 | 36 |
| | | | | 5925 | 72 |

This slightly cheeky hillside course is more characterful than the North, and also narrower: you may lose balls, but the walk is marginally less arduous. The slopes around the mainly small greensites are often as hazardous as the spectacular bunkering.

*Medium p3:17 stands out from an otherwise rather weak finish: this view from the back tee shows a little of its class – compulsory carry over chasm and bunkers (bail out left possible) and a treacherous triangular green. (But there are 62 steps up to, and back down from, the back tee!)*

# LA CALA (ACADEMY)

Robinson 1993 €

✉ La Cala Resort, Apdo. de Correos 106, La Cala de Mijas, 29649 Mijas Costa, Málaga

☎ +34 952 669 037

✎ lacala@imgworld.com   www.leadbetter.com

🚗 ✈ Málaga: r out of airport exit road onto A7 for Cádiz; r at km229 for AP7 Benalmádena/Algeciras; exit 214 for A7 for Fuengirola/Algeciras (not AP7 autopista); exit at Cala de Mijas, km201.5; r at rbt below A7; l at rbt after 2.5km; follow signposted road to La Cala and signs to Academy at top of hill.

|   | m | p |
|---|-----|----|
| 1 | 104 | 3 |
| 2 | 135 | 3 |
| 3 | 115 | 3 |
| 4 | 145 | 3 |
| 5 | 80  | 3 |
| 6 | 110 | 3 |
|   | 689 | 18 |

In our view the best p3 design on the Costa del Sol: on an exposed hilltop, with sea views, 6 holes run around La Cala's academy, with tricky, often bunkered greensites. Uphill, downhill, chasms, banks, run-offs, multi-tiered greens, wind at most angles... what more?

*The plan for 3, downhill over a chasm to a tiered promontory green with a striking backdrop, shows bunkering around most of it. If there used to be bunkers, there are none today – run-off banking instead. More subtle   and who said that short grass wasn't a hazard? Hold the green in one, and you still have to putt... Instant gold.*

# La Cañada

Trent Jones Snr/Thomas   1982/2002   €   **H:** M 28, L 36, J 28/36

✉ La Cañada Club de Golf, Ctra. de Guadiaro km1, 11311 Guadiaro-San Roque, Cádiz

☎ +34 956 794 100

✎ cgolflacanada@telefonica.net   www.lacanadagolf.com

🚗 ✈ Gibraltar: A383 from La Línea; after 9km r onto A7; exit at km130 for Guadiaro, underneath A7 and r at rbt; course less than 1km on l.

| | m | p | | m | p |
|---|---|---|---|---|---|
| 1 | 366 | 4 | 10 | 499 | 5 |
| 2 | 142 | 3 | 11 | 125 | 3 |
| 3 | 468 | 5 | 12 | 385 | 4 |
| 4 | 121 | 3 | 13 | 518 | 5 |
| 5 | 489 | 5 | 14 | 364 | 4 |
| 6 | 297 | 4 | 15 | 137 | 3 |
| 7 | 370 | 4 | 16 | 340 | 4 |
| 8 | 322 | 4 | 17 | 145 | 3 |
| 9 | 390 | 4 | 18 | 363 | 4 |
| | 2965 | 36 | | 2876 | 35 |
| | | | | 5841 | 71 |

A tale of two courses: Trent Jones' original, rustic, understated (except 18!) hillier back 9 with good bunkering and greensites, outclass Thomas' new tighter front 9 on inferior terrain nearer the road. Both are fun in their own way and good value, given their location.

*La Cañada's sting is undoubtedly in its tail. Although it looks like another penal example of Trent Jones Snr's style of golf design, medium p4:18 is partially heroic (and therefore strategic): succeed with the long direct line carry across the ravine (which gives the course its name) and you will feel like a champion, but you can play safe to the right, bringing a potential hanging lie and the fairway bunkers into play. The raised greensite gives you a final test... A near miss for gold.*

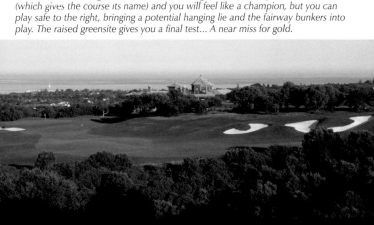

# CASTILLO DE GORRAIZ

**Robinson 1995** €  **H:** M 28, L 36, J 28/36

✉ Club de Golf Castillo de Gorraiz, Urb. Castillo de Gorraiz, 31620 Valle de Egüés, Navarra

☎ +34 948 337 073

✎ administracion@golfgorraiz.com  www.golfgorraiz.com

🚗 ✈ Iruña/Pamplona: N121; r on N135 past A15; becomes NA32; after Olaz r onto NA150; at rbt up the hill into estate; signs to club (basically round to r, up the hill). (Bilbao: A8 to San Sebastián; A15, A16 to Pamplona airport, etc.)

|   | m | p |   |   | m | p |
|---|---|---|---|---|---|---|
| 1 | 331 | 4 | | 10 | 501 | 5 |
| 2 | 495 | 5 | | 11 | 404 | 4 |
| 3 | 355 | 4 | | 12 | 165 | 3 |
| 4 | 160 | 3 | | 13 | 349 | 4 |
| 5 | 360 | 4 | | 14 | 507 | 5 |
| 6 | 406 | 4 | | 15 | 376 | 4 |
| 7 | 325 | 4 | | 16 | 172 | 3 |
| 8 | 201 | 3 | | 17 | 361 | 4 |
| 9 | 446 | 5 | | 18 | 408 | 4 |
| | 3079 | 36 | | | 3243 | 36 |
| | | | | | 6322 | 72 |

Tough, well-designed, sometimes hilly residential course with unusually shaped greens and several dramatic holes, mostly with Robinson's characteristic, visually attractive, off-fairway bunkering. Far reaching urban and mountain views.

**Routing problems, mainly – 6 red:** too long, too uphill, too much of a slog! **18 red:** killer finishing hole – basically flat for ¾ of its considerable length, then straight up to an almost unreachable-in-two green. Neither fair, nor fun.

*The ground falls away steeply from the tee of long p3:8, the second of Castillo de Gorraiz's quality selection of short holes, making it seem shorter than it actually is. Into the wind, we needed a full 1-iron to reach a pin position at the back of the deep and typically irregularly-shaped green.*

# La Dama de Noche

Canáles   1992   €          **H:** M 28, L 48, J 36

✉ Golf La Dama de Noche, Camino de Angel s/n, 29600 Marbella, Málaga

☎ +34 952 818 150

✎ reservas@golfdamadenoche.com
www.golfdamadenoche.com

>27 7/8
<13

✔

🚗 ✈ Málaga: r out of airport exit road onto A7 for Cádiz; r at km229 for AP7 Benalmádena/Algeciras; end of Marbella bypass (km178) take r split onto A7; 1st exit (176 for Istán); l at rbt; over bridge, veer l; course 700m on l.

|   | m | p |
|---|---|---|
| 1 | 285 | 4 |
| 2 | 351 | 4 |
| 3 | 309 | 4 |
| 4 | 141 | 3 |
| 5 | 499 | 5 |
| 6 | 275 | 4 |
| 7 | 440 | 5 |
| 8 | 301 | 4 |
| 9 | 127 | 3 |
|   | 2728 | 36 |

**N.B. The 8th hole has an alternative green, played as 286m.**

Flat, full-length 9 hole course really only notable for being floodlit every Thursday evening. Compact, mainly tree-lined layout with one double green, some water and modest bunkering. Hard on the A7, she is rarely quiet, and comes into her own at night…

**6 red:** right to left dogleg short p4 over river. If the original idea was for the green to be driveable, growth has made it invisible from the tee (a good thing, given that a hook on that line might endanger traffic). 6 is now probably best played as a short iron followed by a medium short iron. It just doesn't work. (It's also the only hole on the other side of the road, with unceasing traffic noise, to boot.)

*Both short holes at La Dama de Noche have lakes, but the one at the 4th is directly between tee and green. This is one of the course's better holes, with the outline of La Concha, the mountain behind, just visible at dusk. The water runs behind and back right of the green as well.*

# DESERT SPRINGS

McEvoy   2001   €€                    **H:** M 28, L 36, J 28/36

✉  Desert Springs Golf Club, 04618 Vilaricos, Cuevas del
   Almanzora, Almería

☎  +34 950 467 104

✒  desertsprings@almanzora.com   www.almanzora.com

🚗 ✈ Almería: AL12, becomes A7, towards Murcia; exit 534 r
onto C3327; bypassing Vera, l onto A352; r for Palomares; r into
club after Las Cunas.

| | m | p | | m | p |
|---|---|---|---|---|---|
| 1 | 514 | 5 | 10 | 371 | 4 |
| 2 | 165 | 3 | 11 | 400 | 4 |
| 3 | 480 | 5 | 12 | 173 | 3 |
| 4 | 399 | 4 | 13 | 468 | 5 |
| 5 | 331 | 4 | 14 | 147 | 3 |
| 6 | 276 | 4 | 15 | 386 | 4 |
| 7 | 385 | 4 | 16 | 333 | 4 |
| 8 | 206 | 3 | 17 | 316 | 4 |
| 9 | 465 | 5 | 18 | 358 | 4 |
| | 3221 | 37 | | 2952 | 35 |
| | | | | 6173 | 72 |

Themed Wild West desert
resort course, to be respected
more for entertainingly 'going
for it' than for its design –
blander than its surrounds. Off
fairway, be prepared to play out
of hardpan, cacti, dry water
courses... Sloping greens. Yihaa!

*In addition to the typically undulating mounded green and white sanded bunkers,
this view of medium long p4:10 shows the desert elements: (not always) dry river
beds, cacti, hardpan, boulders. Your second at this slightly right to left hole has to
carry the water course, which is a little further from the green than it looks.*

# La Duquesa

Trent Jones Snr   1989   €€          **H:** M 28, L 36, J 28/36

✉ Golf & Country Club La Duquesa, Urb. El Hacho, Ctra. de Cádiz km143.5, 29691 Manilva, Málaga

☎ +34 952 890 425

✎ gduquesa@arrakis.es   www.golfladuquesa.com

🚗 ✈ Málaga: r out of airport exit road onto A7 for Cádiz; r at km229 for AP7 Benalmádena/Algeciras; end of Marbella bypass (km178) take l split to stay on AP7 autopista to Estepona bypass; take A7 from exit 153; course is just past Manilva 900m on r after km144.

| | m | p | | m | p |
|---|---|---|---|---|---|
| 1 | 512 | 5 | 10 | 338 | 4 |
| 2 | 174 | 3 | 11 | 342 | 4 |
| 3 | 332 | 4 | 12 | 135 | 3 |
| 4 | 327 | 4 | 13 | 381 | 4 |
| 5 | 508 | 5 | 14 | 187 | 3 |
| 6 | 171 | 3 | 15 | 379 | 4 |
| 7 | 356 | 4 | 16 | 497 | 5 |
| 8 | 129 | 3 | 17 | 321 | 4 |
| 9 | 517 | 5 | 18 | 536 | 5 |
| | 3026 | 36 | | 3116 | 36 |
| | | | | 6142 | 72 |

Two well-conceived, fairly open loops of 9 ascend into hills from seaside clubhouse, with often testingly-bunkered and raised greensites. Some spectacular holes amidst some lesser ones, and the course is generally much better than appears from the road. Extensive sea and mountain views.

*This photo of spectacular shortish p3:8 also shows p5s 1 (right) and 9 (left). The original order of playing the front and back 9s has been reversed: 8 is as potentially terrifying as it may be invitingly downhill – but was even more so when it was the penultimate hole: think of the matchplay implications… And, once on the green, you have to contend with slopes all around.*

# ESTEPONA

Lopez   1989   €                    **H:** M 28, L 36, J 36

✉ Estepona Golf, Arroyo Vaquero, Ctra. de Cádiz km150, Apdo. 532, 29680 Estepona, Málaga

☎ +34 952 113 081

✎ proshop@esteponagolf.com   www.esteponagolf.com

🚗 ✈ Málaga: r out of airport exit road onto A7 for Cádiz; r at km229 for AP7 Benalmádena/Algeciras; end of Marbella bypass (km178) take l split to stay on AP7 autopista to Estepona bypass; take A7 from exit 153; r 100m after km150; follow signs (approx 1km to club).

| | m | p | | m | p |
|---|---|---|---|---|---|
| 1 | 390 | 4 | 10 | 267 | 4 |
| 2 | 360 | 4 | 11 | 475 | 5 |
| 3 | 568 | 5 | 12 | 313 | 4 |
| 4 | 290 | 4 | 13 | 345 | 4 |
| 5 | 157 | 3 | 14 | 190 | 3 |
| 6 | 449 | 5 | 15 | 335 | 4 |
| 7 | 174 | 3 | 16 | 185 | 3 |
| 8 | 360 | 4 | 17 | 512 | 5 |
| 9 | 327 | 4 | 18 | 304 | 4 |
| | 3075 | 36 | | 2926 | 36 |
| | | | | 6001 | 72 |

The investment here has been in consistently good greensites, which adorn this scenic, open, welcoming, pleasantly unsophisticated, sometimes hilly pay-&-play layout. Wide fairways and minimal bunkering elsewhere make p5s seem rather long until you get to the green. Except 9, wysiwyg!

**9 red:** almost right-angle left to right dogleg with no indication as to whether safe to attempt to cut corner; bunker on outside of corner acceptable to stop balls from getting lost. From design viewpoint hazards best placed on inside of dogleg, but, with terrain and position of corner relative to tee, even that wouldn't really work – it's just all wrong. (Good greensite.)

*Slight left to right dogleg p4:10 is a bit of a teaser: from the high tee the green looks very tempting (well, it is just about on – to long-hitting madmen, at any rate). This photo also illustrates the investment-in-greensite emphasis of the course's design: a four-leafed clover in this case, with gentle slopes (and swans) which require respect.*

# LOS FLAMINGOS

Garrido   2001   €€                    **H:** M 24, L 34, J 24/34

✉ Flamingos Golf Club, Ctra. de Cádiz km166, 29679
Benahavís, Marbella, Málaga

☎ +34 952 889 157

✎ info@flamingos-golf.com   www.flamingos-golf.com

🚗 ✈ Málaga: r out of airport exit road onto A7 for Cádiz; r at
km229 for AP7 Benalmádena/Algeciras; end of Marbella bypass
(km178) take r split onto A7; past San Pedro towards Estepona, r
200m after km166 and follow signs up hill to club.

| | m | p | | m | p |
|---|---|---|---|---|---|
| 1 | 454 | 5 | 10 | 371 | 4 |
| 2 | 188 | 3 | 11 | 484 | 5 |
| 3 | 362 | 4 | 12 | 165 | 3 |
| 4 | 142 | 3 | 13 | 312 | 4 |
| 5 | 315 | 4 | 14 | 372 | 4 |
| 6 | 464 | 5 | 15 | 462 | 5 |
| 7 | 332 | 4 | 16 | 130 | 3 |
| 8 | 323 | 4 | 17 | 297 | 4 |
| 9 | 330 | 4 | 18 | 404 | 4 |
| | 2910 | 36 | | 2997 | 36 |
| | | | | 5907 | 72 |

Occasionally challenging,
sometimes understated, but
not particularly long, hotel
course with interesting, at
times eccentrically undulating,
greens and excellent sea views
from higher tees. Several
shortish par 4s. 1st 9 fairly
tight; 2nd 9 more open. Should
improve with maturity.

N.B. There is also a 9 hole p3 course (1123m), due to be extended to 18, par 60, in 2005.

*Archaeologists seeking to demonstrate that golf began when Roman soldiers hit stones
with clubs will find proof as they leave the 2nd green, behind which 3 columns stand
sentinel in memoriam – surely the only remains of a Roman grandstand extant in
Iberia? It presumably also overlooked the tee of well-bunkered medium p4:3 (below).
As with many holes at Los Flamingos, the 3rd fairway undulates – indeed, here the
ground often moves rather more than is initially apparent from the tees. Sadly, since
this photo was taken, development has ruined this view.*

# GUADALHORCE

Kuronen  1990  €

✉ Guadalhorce Club de Golf, Ctra. Cártama km7, Apdo.
Correos 48, 29590 Campanillas, Málaga

☎ +34 952 179 378

✎ inma@guadalhorce.com  www.guadalhorce.com

🚗 ✈ Málaga: exit airport over bridge towards Málaga onto A7;
r onto A7 for Motril/Antequera; exit 236A and then 236B onto
A357 for Cártama; exit 64 onto MA401 towards Mercamálaga for
approx 800m; fork back r onto track; club on l across railway (TGV
currently under construction – allow for small diversion).

|   | m | p |   |   | m | p |
|---|---|---|---|---|---|---|
| 1 | 329 | 4 |   | 10 | 520 | 5 |
| 2 | 120 | 3 |   | 11 | 185 | 3 |
| 3 | 358 | 4 |   | 12 | 362 | 4 |
| 4 | 457 | 5 |   | 13 | 356 | 4 |
| 5 | 146 | 3 |   | 14 | 313 | 4 |
| 6 | 354 | 4 |   | 15 | 408 | 4 |
| 7 | 470 | 5 |   | 16 | 480 | 5 |
| 8 | 416 | 4 |   | 17 | 164 | 3 |
| 9 | 369 | 4 |   | 18 | 387 | 4 |
|   | 3019 | 36 |   |   | 3175 | 36 |
|   |   |   |   |   | 6194 | 72 |

N.B. There is also a 9 hole p3 course.

Better than first meets the eye,
a fairly open parkland course
with a little water. Land for
back 9 is as flat as front 9 isn't.
Some interesting greensites
(including 2 doubles), strategic
bunkering and water.
Remarkably rustic, given
proximity of Málaga airport –
flightpath noise does not
unduly detract.

*This view of the folding
fairway of medium
p4:6 is from its gun-
platform tee, whence
the land immediately
falls away. With
today's equipment this
hole may be no more
than a drive and a
pitch for some players,
but the raised green,
which turns right-angle
left beyond a ridge
behind the flag
position shown to
form a double green
with the 8th, has no
sympathy for anything
but an accurate shot.*

# GUADALMINA (NORTE)

**Nardi 1965 €€**                    **H:** M 27, L 35, J 27/35

✉ Guadalmina Club de Golf, Urb. Guadalmina Alta, 29678 San Pedro de Alcántara, Málaga

☎ +34 952 886 522

✎ Please book by phone   www.guadalminagolf.org

🚗 ✈ Málaga: r out of airport exit road onto A7 for Cádiz; r at km229 for AP7 Benalmádena/Algeciras; end of Marbella bypass (km178) take r split onto A7; through San Pedro de Alcántara; r 200m after 'Marbella' bridge; l after 700m (just before greens thru trees on r); immediately r into club car park.

|   | m | p |   |   | m | p |
|---|---|---|---|---|---|---|
| 1 | 269 | 4 |   | 10 | 539 | 5 |
| 2 | 148 | 3 |   | 11 | 133 | 3 |
| 3 | 348 | 4 |   | 12 | 445 | 5 |
| 4 | 446 | 5 |   | 13 | 290 | 4 |
| 5 | 535 | 5 |   | 14 | 188 | 3 |
| 6 | 174 | 3 |   | 15 | 344 | 4 |
| 7 | 328 | 4 |   | 16 | 369 | 4 |
| 8 | 306 | 4 |   | 17 | 273 | 4 |
| 9 | 312 | 4 |   | 18 | 319 | 4 |
|   | 2866 | 36 |   |   | 2900 | 36 |
|   |   |   |   |   | 5766 | 72 |

More suburban and less demanding than Guadalmina (Sur), a worthy second course, despite perhaps one too many short p4s. Some holes quite tight, but minimal rough and easy walking. Several water hazards.

N.B. questionable, possibly temporary, lengthening of 13 in 2004 ignored.

*The fairway of p4:16 is not quite as narrow as it seems from the tee. This is the longest, and one of the best, p4s on the course, with a challenging 2nd shot up to a hill-brow green.*

# La Herrería

Gómez   1976   €€€ (€ weekdays)     **H:** M 28, L 36, J 28/36

✉ La Herrería Club de Golf, Ctra. de Robledo de Chavela s/n, 28200 San Lorenzo de El Escorial, Madrid

☎ +34 918 905 111

✗ Please book by phone     www.golflaherreria.com

🚗 ✈ Madrid: AP6 for Segovia; l at exit 47 onto M600 to San Lorenzo de El Escorial; M505 for Robledo de Chavela; course approx 1km beyond San Lorenzo de El Escorial on l.

|   | m | p |   | m | p |
|---|-----|----|----|-----|----|
| 1 | 413 | 4 | 10 | 167 | 3 |
| 2 | 428 | 4 | 11 | 489 | 5 |
| 3 | 194 | 3 | 12 | 367 | 4 |
| 4 | 346 | 4 | 13 | 183 | 3 |
| 5 | 371 | 4 | 14 | 324 | 4 |
| 6 | 314 | 4 | 15 | 467 | 5 |
| 7 | 144 | 3 | 16 | 322 | 4 |
| 8 | 502 | 5 | 17 | 360 | 4 |
| 9 | 353 | 4 | 18 | 347 | 4 |
|   | 3065 | 35 |   | 3026 | 36 |
|   |  |  |   | 6091 | 71 |

Accessible, woodland, fairly hilly course, requiring some occasional challenging shots. Front 9 recently upgraded with new, undulating, well-bunkered greens; back 9 rather more simplistic, but with the best views of nearby famous historic El Escorial monastery. Welcoming pay-&-play visitors, the most accessible quality course near Madrid. Combine with must-see monastery visit.

*Pepe Gancedo's upgrading of the front 9 has produced some excellent greensites, but this view of shortish p5:15 shows the quality of the site, enhanced by a faint December mist. Even with its original greensite, this hole is challenging: it is all a matter of where to place your tee shot, to enable you to play your second without being disadvantaged by the tree in the middle of the fairway. Similar problems on 16…*

# ISLA CANELA

Cadarineu   1993   €€                    **H:** M 28, L 36, J 28/36

✉ Isla Canela Golf, Ctra. de la Playa s/n, 21409 Ayamonte, Huelva

☎ +34 959 477 263

✎ golf@islacanela.es   www.islacanela.es

🚗 ✈ Faro: N125-10 airport exit road for Faro; r after 3km for A22; after 7km r onto A22 for Spain (becomes A49); r at first exit in Spain to Ayamonte; through town and over bridge towards Isla Canela beach; club entrance approx 1km after bridge on l.

|   | m | p |   | m | p |
|---|---|---|---|---|---|
| 1 | 179 | 3 | 10 | 347 | 4 |
| 2 | 489 | 5 | 11 | 157 | 3 |
| 3 | 394 | 4 | 12 | 349 | 4 |
| 4 | 355 | 4 | 13 | 473 | 5 |
| 5 | 173 | 3 | 14 | 413 | 4 |
| 6 | 333 | 4 | 15 | 328 | 4 |
| 7 | 470 | 5 | 16 | 169 | 3 |
| 8 | 372 | 4 | 17 | 522 | 5 |
| 9 | 336 | 4 | 18 | 389 | 4 |
|   | 3101 | 36 |   | 3147 | 36 |
|   |   |   |   | 6248 | 72 |

Spanish frontier town course – an 'honorary Algarve' inclusion. Flat layout on former marshland with predominantly two-tiered greens, playable by all standards but more suited to high handicappers. Plenty of water. Puts most Algarve courses into context.

*Isla Canela's p5 13th has an obelisk mid-fairway, but the tree and bunker front right of the two-tiered green are more likely to cause you trouble (note the bunker on the left of the green, just in case you were thinking it would be better to play longer – and there's another one beyond right). This hole may be reachable in two, but a chip from a judicious lay up may be preferable to an involuntary bunker shot.*

# ISLANTILLA

Canáles & Pecasens   1992   €€          **H:** M 28, L 36, J 28/36

✉ Islantilla Golf Club, Ctra. La Antilla, Isla Cristina s/n, Apdo.
212, 21410 Huelva

☎ +34 959 486 039

✎ direccion@golfislantilla.com   www.islantillagolfresort.com

🚗 ✈ Faro: N125-10 airport exit road for Faro; r after 3km for
A22; after 7km r onto A22 to Spain (becomes A49); r at exit 117 for
Lepe; r towards Ayamonte; l after 800m La Redondela; after 6.5km l
for La Antilla; after 3.2km l at 3rd rbt; club 500m on r opposite hotel.

| Blue | | | Yellow | | | Green | | |
|---|---|---|---|---|---|---|---|---|
| | m | p | | m | p | | m | p |
| 1 | 335 | 4 | 1 | 484 | 5 | 1 | 350 | 4 |
| 2 | 190 | 3 | 2 | 204 | 3 | 2 | 151 | 3 |
| 3 | 299 | 4 | 3 | 445 | 5 | 3 | 484 | 5 |
| 4 | 423 | 4 | 4 | 171 | 3 | 4 | 312 | 4 |
| 5 | 401 | 4 | 5 | 482 | 5 | 5 | 360 | 4 |
| 6 | 341 | 4 | 6 | 119 | 3 | 6 | 146 | 3 |
| 7 | 508 | 5 | 7 | 354 | 4 | 7 | 398 | 4 |
| 8 | 155 | 3 | 8 | 328 | 4 | 8 | 502 | 5 |
| 9 | 355 | 4 | 9 | 362 | 4 | 9 | 432 | 4 |
| | 3007 | 35 | | 2949 | 36 | | 3135 | 36 |
| BY | 5956 | 71 | BG | 6142 | 71 | YG | 6084 | 72 |

Three undulating,
pine-lined,
sometimes a little
over-residential,
loops of 9 with
occasional sea
views, sloping
greens and water.
Good holes, bad
holes, moderate
holes, including
some rather
eccentric par 5s.
Location makes it
an 'honorary
Algarve' course.

**Two unfair holes – Y1 red:** a medium downhill p5, in theory
reachable in two by longer hitters, but the green is completely
blind over a bluff, with a ditch in front. As a double dogleg,
played in three, there is insufficient notice of the greensite to
make a proper judgment for your second. **Y3 red:** ridiculous left
to right banana short p5 – the drive is rather dangerously towards
the road, the fairway has a reverse camber, and the green is
tucked away blind uphill over a bunker and surrounded by trees.

# IZKI

**Ballesteros 1994 €**

**H:** M 28, L 36, J 48

✉ Izki Golf, C. Arriba s/n, 01119 Urturi, Alava

☎ +34 945 378 262

✎ izkigolf@izkigolf.com   www.izkigolf.com

🚗 ✈ Vitoria/Gasteiz: – through city and exit south on A2124 to Ventas de Armentia; l onto BU471; l for Urturi after approx 17km (before Bernedo); signs to course in village.

| | m | p | | m | p |
|---|---|---|---|---|---|
| 1 | 335 | 4 | 10 | 348 | 4 |
| 2 | 393 | 4 | 11 | 392 | 4 |
| 3 | 513 | 5 | 12 | 492 | 5 |
| 4 | 443 | 4 | 13 | 319 | 4 |
| 5 | 371 | 4 | 14 | 175 | 3 |
| 6 | 165 | 3 | 15 | 410 | 4 |
| 7 | 387 | 4 | 16 | 452 | 5 |
| 8 | 477 | 5 | 17 | 189 | 3 |
| 9 | 203 | 3 | 18 | 512 | 5 |
| | 3287 | 36 | | 3289 | 37 |
| | | | | 6576 | 73 |

One of Seve's better designs: undulating, remote public course with raised, sometimes elusive greensites and stunning views of surrounding nature. Occasionally dramatic holes with gullies and trees. Toughish set of par 3s. Peaceful. Worth the detour.

**Below** *The sloping green of left to right dogleg medium p4:5, played from a high tee, is raised above fairway level, which, combined with the greenside bunker (menacing with the pin left), makes this a challenging hole. It doesn't help to overshoot, either: thin your recovery, and you are back on the fairway or in sand.*

**Opposite** *A mound inside the corner of right to left dogleg medium p4:8 on Islantilla's Yellow 9 throws drives towards the right-hand bunker in view here. From our camera position you would be well placed to carry the lake in front of the green with a short iron, but from the bunker this would be a huge gamble. Normally played as the 17th, this all makes it a good matchplay hole.*

Northern Spain **125**

# LAURO

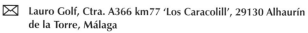

Nardi/Benitez  1992/2002  €          H: M 28, L 36, J 28/36

✉ Lauro Golf, Ctra. A366 km77 'Los Caracolill', 29130 Alhaurín de la Torre, Málaga

☎ +34 952 412 767

✎ info@laurogolf.com    www.laurogolf.com

🚗 ✈ Málaga: r out of airport exit road onto A7 for Cádiz; r at first junction (exit at km230 Coín) onto A366 for Coín; course approx 5km after Alhaurín de la Torre, 500m on r after km76.

>27 7/8
<13

| | A | | | B | | | C | |
|---|---|---|---|---|---|---|---|---|
| | m | p | | m | p | | m | p |
| 1 | 303 | 4 | 10 | 311 | 4 | 19 | 470 | 5 |
| 2 | 131 | 3 | 11 | 119 | 3 | 20 | 331 | 4 |
| 3 | 325 | 4 | 12 | 313 | 4 | 21 | 195 | 3 |
| 4 | 183 | 3 | 13 | 573 | 5 | 22 | 349 | 4 |
| 5 | 461 | 5 | 14 | 179 | 3 | 23 | 385 | 4 |
| 6 | 395 | 4 | 15 | 343 | 4 | 24 | 311 | 4 |
| 7 | 580 | 5 | 16 | 415 | 4 | 25 | 308 | 4 |
| 8 | 303 | 4 | 17 | 485 | 5 | 26 | 168 | 3 |
| 9 | 322 | 4 | 18 | 329 | 4 | 27 | 513 | 5 |
| | 3003 | 36 | | 3067 | 36 | | 3000 | 36 |
| AB 6070 | | 72 | AC 6003 | | 72 | BC 6067 | | 72 |

*Lauro's downhill shortish p4:A3 is where the course begins to get going: you're almost tempted to think that it is driveable (well, it is – just – with modern equipment), but look carefully at the greensite – there's a swale in front and bunkers all around...*

Rustic feel and mountain views (especially from newer, tighter 19-27) are the best features of this gently undulating olive-lined complex, whose holes are named after famous bullfighters and bandits. A few good holes and greensites. Watery finish to each loop.

# LERMA

Gancedo  1992  €

H: M 28, L 36, J 28/36

✉ Golf Lerma, Autovía Madrid – Burgos km195, 09340 Lerma, Burgos

☎ +34 947 171 214

✎ reservas@golflerma.com  www.golflerma.com

🚗 ✈ Madrid: M10; r onto A1 towards Burgos; club is at km195 on l; follow signs.

| | m | p | | m | p |
|---|---|---|---|---|---|
| 1 | 527 | 5 | 10 | 499 | 5 |
| 2 | 410 | 4 | 11 | 381 | 4 |
| 3 | 366 | 4 | 12 | 202 | 3 |
| 4 | 317 | 4 | 13 | 364 | 4 |
| 5 | 155 | 3 | 14 | 341 | 4 |
| 6 | 352 | 4 | 15 | 187 | 3 |
| 7 | 290 | 4 | 16 | 385 | 4 |
| 8 | 471 | 5 | 17 | 534 | 5 |
| 9 | 187 | 3 | 18 | 295 | 4 |
| | 3075 | 36 | | 3188 | 36 |
| | | | | 6263 | 72 |

Rather bland on first sight, but comes alive once you understand the potential permutations of the many pin positions on large, bunkered, testing greens, especially in wind. A few unusual features (e.g. tree on edge of 15th green). Some water carries.

*Uphill shortish p4:4, a good risk and reward hole, is much more difficult than its length suggests. The green is 100% fronted by a deep bunker. The foreground (right-hand) bunker runs from 150m to 180m off the tee; another bunker, 50m long, runs along the left side of the fairway from 200m off the tee. The choices are: driver over right-hand bunker to the widest part of the fairway; 3 wood left of the right-hand bunker to narrower ground short of left bunker; iron short of bunkers. Then carry that deep bunker...*

# MARBELLA CLUB

Thomas   1999   €€€          **H:** M 24, L 26, J 28/36

✉ Marbella Club Golf Resort, Ctra. de Benahavís km3.7, 29679
Benahavís, Málaga

☎ +34 952 889 101

✎ lmoya.golf@marbellaclub.com   www.marbellaclub.com

🚗 ✈ Málaga: r out of airport exit road onto A7 for Cádiz; r at
km229 for AP7 Benalmádena/Algeciras; end of Marbella bypass
(km178) take r split onto A7; through San Pedro de Alcántara; at
km169.1 r onto Benahavís road (exit immediately on r after Río
Guadalmina bridge); l after 3.7km (800m after tunnel under AP7);
follow signs for 4km; r at t junction; r into club.

| | m | p | | m | p |
|---|---|---|---|---|---|
| 1 | 374 | 4 | 10 | 323 | 4 |
| 2 | 130 | 3 | 11 | 350 | 4 |
| 3 | 376 | 4 | 12 | 146 | 3 |
| 4 | 175 | 3 | 13 | 485 | 5 |
| 5 | 372 | 4 | 14 | 316 | 4 |
| 6 | 511 | 5 | 15 | 193 | 3 |
| 7 | 467 | 5 | 16 | 350 | 4 |
| 8 | 465 | 5 | 17 | 388 | 4 |
| 9 | 363 | 4 | 18 | 495 | 5 |
| | 3233 | 37 | | 3046 | 36 |
| | | | | 6279 | 73 |

Functional, often peaceful and rustic, mostly well-bunkered hilly course with generally good greensites. Some water. Mountain and sea views, interrupted only occasionally by residential development. 2 loops of 9 returning to clubhouse almost at lowest point: The Grand Old Duke of York would have been happy here!

*This view from the tee of long p3:15 is deceptive in several ways: the hole is longer than it looks, the green has more slopes than at first appears, and we have cropped out both the bunker below left of the putting surface and the relatively benign grassy approach. But have no illusions when you play it: this is a tough hole, particularly with a wind from right to left.*

# MASÍA BACH

Olazábal   1990   €€€

**H:** M 28, L 36, J 36

✉ Club Golf Masía Bach, Ctra. Martorell-Capellades km19.5,
08635 Sant Esteve Sesrovires, Barcelona

☎ +34 937 728 800

✎ info@golfmasiabach.com   www.info.masiabach.com

🚗 ✈ Barcelona: C31 – C32c – B10 – A2 – AP7 towards
Tarragona; exit 25 for Martorell; r immediately after toll on B224
for Capellades; club 500m on r after km20.

|   | m | p |   |   | m | p |
|---|---|---|---|---|---|---|
| 1 | 514 | 5 |   | 10 | 502 | 5 |
| 2 | 160 | 3 |   | 11 | 338 | 4 |
| 3 | 383 | 4 |   | 12 | 376 | 4 |
| 4 | 376 | 4 |   | 13 | 522 | 5 |
| 5 | 174 | 3 |   | 14 | 150 | 3 |
| 6 | 402 | 4 |   | 15 | 344 | 4 |
| 7 | 515 | 5 |   | 16 | 153 | 3 |
| 8 | 342 | 4 |   | 17 | 389 | 4 |
| 9 | 283 | 4 |   | 18 | 348 | 4 |
|   | 3149 | 36 |   |   | 3122 | 36 |
|   |   |   |   |   | 6271 | 72 |

Hilly, generally tree-lined course with views to the spectacular Montserrat mountain. The often raised greens are well bunkered, testing short game and putting. Ravines, lakes and undulations add to the fun.

**N.B. There is also a 9 hole course (1789m).**

*Medium p4:11 is a yellow hole, but the tones of the extraordinary outlines of Montserrat ('saw mountain') behind, near sunset, would be easier fodder for an alchemist, than to gild (let alone green) an uphill, semi-blind two-shotter…*

# MEDITERRÁNEO

Espinosa   1978   €                                         **H:** M 28, L 36, J 28/36

✉   Club de Campo del Mediterráneo, Urb. La Coma, 12190
Borriol, Castellón

☎   +34 964 321 227

✎   club@ccmediterraneo.com   www.ccmediterraneo.com

🚗 ✈ Valencia: AP7 towards Barcelona; exit 46 (Castellón
Norte) towards Castellón; r after 700m at sign; follow road over
hill, keeping left at fork – club in valley beyond.

| | m | p | | m | p |
|---|---|---|---|---|---|
| 1 | 345 | 4 | 10 | 320 | 4 |
| 2 | 208 | 3 | 11 | 307 | 4 |
| 3 | 380 | 4 | 12 | 204 | 3 |
| 4 | 530 | 5 | 13 | 545 | 5 |
| 5 | 353 | 4 | 14 | 320 | 4 |
| 6 | 178 | 3 | 15 | 362 | 4 |
| 7 | 310 | 4 | 16 | 182 | 3 |
| 8 | 506 | 5 | 17 | 481 | 5 |
| 9 | 376 | 4 | 18 | 332 | 4 |
| | 3186 | 36 | | 3053 | 36 |
| | | | | 6239 | 72 |

The epitome of a Mediterranean parkland course on gentle slopes of a secluded valley abundant with olives, carobs, etc. Mixture of a few quite demanding, and some more subtle, holes. Stronger on rather more undulating back 9. Better than first impression. Some water.

*Uphill shortish p4:10 at Mediterráneo shows the character of the course, and some of its teeth: note the mixture and location of the trees (the olive to the left of the flag protects the upper tier of the green), the sloping fairways and the yawning greenside bunker.*

# MIJAS (OLIVOS)

Trent Jones Snr  1983  €€          **H:** M 28, L 36, J 28/36

✉ Mijas Golf International, Ctra. Vieja de Coín km3.5, 29650 Mijas Costa, Málaga

☎ +34 952 476 843

✎ Please book tee times by phone   www.mijasgolf.org

🚗 ✈ Málaga: r out of airport exit road onto A7 for Cádiz; r at km229 for AP7 Benalmádena/Algeciras; exit 214 for A7 for Fuengirola/Algeciras (not AP7 autopista); r at exit 700m after km210 (Coín); r at rbt onto MA426; course on r after 2.5km.

|    | m    | p  |    | m    | p  |
|----|------|----|----|------|----|
| 1  | 308  | 4  | 10 | 511  | 5  |
| 2  | 397  | 4  | 11 | 336  | 4  |
| 3  | 161  | 3  | 12 | 368  | 4  |
| 4  | 320  | 4  | 13 | 300  | 4  |
| 5  | 398  | 4  | 14 | 163  | 3  |
| 6  | 167  | 3  | 15 | 433  | 4  |
| 7  | 350  | 4  | 16 | 135  | 3  |
| 8  | 211  | 3  | 17 | 360  | 4  |
| 9  | 489  | 5  | 18 | 433  | 5  |
|    | 2801 | 34 |    | 3039 | 36 |
|    |      |    |    | 5840 | 70 |

Popular parkland course, recently upgraded (by Robinson). Challenge only slightly less demanding than Mijas (Lagos), but Olivos is tighter, shorter and, in places, hillier. Good bunkering, testing greens and some water carries.

*The dazzling, demanding simplicity of shortish p4:1 almost provides Olivos with a golden start: to drive the bunkers on line is 229m from the back, but then are you too close for a controlled pitch? Or an iron left – beware: more bunkers? Either way, control on the cascading green is essential. No prizes for being short!*

# MIRAFLORES

Nardi   1989   €                    **H:** M 28, L 36, J 28/36

✉ Miraflores Golf, Ctra. de Cádiz km198, Urb. Riviera del Sol, 29647 Mijas Costa, Málaga

☎ +34 952 931 960

✎ Please book by phone

🚗 ✈ Málaga: r out of airport exit road onto A7 for Cádiz; r at km229 for AP7 Benalmádena/Algeciras; exit 214 for A7 for Fuengirola/Algeciras (not AP7 autopista); r at exit Riviera (km198.5); r at rbt up Avda. del Golf over hill; r at bottom 100m after range into C. Zafiro; r after 200m all the way up hill to club.

| | m | p | | | m | p |
|---|---|---|---|---|---|---|
| 1 | 251 | 4 | | 10 | 273 | 4 |
| 2 | 408 | 5 | | 11 | 109 | 3 |
| 3 | 349 | 4 | | 12 | 480 | 5 |
| 4 | 203 | 3 | | 13 | 130 | 3 |
| 5 | 315 | 4 | | 14 | 418 | 5 |
| 6 | 454 | 5 | | 15 | 121 | 3 |
| 7 | 163 | 3 | | 16 | 292 | 4 |
| 8 | 293 | 4 | | 17 | 308 | 4 |
| 9 | 304 | 4 | | 18 | 242 | 4 |
| | 2740 | 36 | | | 2373 | 35 |
| | | | | | 5113 | 71 |

Shortish, sometimes hilly course, whose interesting greensites undeservedly fail to make up for the horrific density of the surrounding housing development, between which the course first runs in valleys leading to more open area on back 9. More challenging than card suggests.

**15 red:** 'The Water Jump'?! – the water 'feature' around the green of this short p3 is very artificial and the hole in general (bridges included) is out of style with the rest of the course.

*This view from the tee of short p4:8 shows how tough it is (even before you reach the steeply tiered green): there is a lay up area below (whence a semi-blind shot), but however you choose to play your tee shot, you have to put your brain as well your game into gear…*

# MONTE MAYOR

Gancedo   1989   €€                    **H:** M 28, L 36, J 28/36

Buggy included in green fee

✉ Monte Mayor Golf Club, Ctra. de Benahavís km3.7, 29769 Benahavís, Málaga

☎ +34 952 937 111

✎ reservations@montemayorgolf.com
www.montemayorgolf.com

🚗 ✈ Málaga: r out of airport exit road onto A7 for Cádiz; r at km229 for AP7 Benalmádena/Algeciras; end of Marbella bypass (km178) take r split onto A7; through San Pedro de Alcántara; at km169.1 r onto Benahavís road (exit immediately on r after Río Guadalmina bridge); l after 3.7km (800m after tunnel under AP7); follow signs for 4km; r at T-junction; go 500m past Marbella Club, round hill; r into club drive (approx 1km).

|   | m | p |   |   | m | p |
|---|-----|---|---|---|-----|---|
| 1 | 481 | 5 | | 10 | 391 | 4 |
| 2 | 362 | 4 | | 11 | 256 | 4 |
| 3 | 193 | 3 | | 12 | 337 | 4 |
| 4 | 425 | 5 | | 13 | 291 | 4 |
| 5 | 108 | 3 | | 14 | 334 | 4 |
| 6 | 359 | 4 | | 15 | 337 | 4 |
| 7 | 352 | 4 | | 16 | 479 | 5 |
| 8 | 311 | 4 | | 17 | 312 | 4 |
| 9 | 175 | 3 | | 18 | 149 | 3 |
| | 2766 | 35 | | | 2886 | 36 |
| | | | | | 5652 | 71 |

A unique layout on which a game resembling golf may be played. Set in a beautiful mountain valley, up which the course winds and returns, with jungle marked as water hazard immediately off fairway. Some spectacular holes and spectacular shots to several interesting greensites. A must-play-at-least-once course. All credit to Gancedo and his contractors.

*Short p5:4 is a wonderful strategic challenge. Having driven to our camera position, you must choose whether to go for the green in one or two more shots (if one, probably a fairway wood for most of us). The penalty for failure is all too obvious.*

# MONTECASTILLO

Nicklaus   1993   €€€                    **H:** M 28, L 36, J 36

✉ Montecastillo Hotel & Golf Resort, Ctra. de Arcos km9.6,
11406 Jerez de la Frontera, Cádiz

☎ +34 956 151 200

✎ deportes@montecastillo.com   www.montecastillo.com

🚗 ✈ Jerez: exit airport; l onto (old) NIV; after approx 2km l
through Guadalcacin del Caudillo; l onto A382 for Arcos de la
Frontera after approx 1.5km; r 400m after km6 for Arcos motor
race circuit and Montecastillo; l into hotel entrance immediately
after racetrack Aceso 1.

| | m | p | | m | p |
|---|---|---|---|---|---|
| 1 | 354 | 4 | 10 | 375 | 4 |
| 2 | 202 | 3 | 11 | 214 | 3 |
| 3 | 516 | 5 | 12 | 477 | 5 |
| 4 | 348 | 4 | 13 | 388 | 4 |
| 5 | 380 | 4 | 14 | 157 | 3 |
| 6 | 378 | 4 | 15 | 424 | 4 |
| 7 | 395 | 4 | 16 | 473 | 5 |
| 8 | 174 | 3 | 17 | 342 | 4 |
| 9 | 473 | 5 | 18 | 386 | 4 |
| | 3220 | 36 | | 3236 | 36 |
| | | | | 6456 | 72 |

Set over sometimes hilly land,
an out and back layout with
generally large undulating
greens and grand-scale, though
not always completely relevant,
bunkering. Some water carries.
Bar a few memorable holes, a
course that fails to match well-
used-by-Tour pedigree. Adjoins
Arcos motor race track.

*Medium p3:14 is the highlight of the back 9: its anticipatory view of tough uphill
p4:15 (white green in background, being sanded) may whet your appetite, but
concentrate on avoiding the bunkers at this excellent short hole, whose sloping
green has the potential for some very awkward pin positions. Try not to overshoot
in your bid to avoid the hazards short left: the sand visible back right is only the tip
of a 'sandberg' – the largest bunker here runs all round the back of the green.*

# MONTENMEDIO

Maldonado 1996 €€    **H:** M 28, L 36, J 36

✉ Montenmedio Golf & Country Club, Ctra. A48 km42.5, 11150 Vejer de la Frontera, Barbate, Cádiz

☎ +34 956 451 216

✎ reservas@monteenmedio.com    www.monteenmedio.com

🚗 ✈ Gibraltar: take road from La Línea to A7 at San Roque; A7 (becomes A48) past Algeciras for Cádiz; club on l 400m after km43.

| | m | p | | m | p |
|---|---|---|---|---|---|
| 1 | 343 | 4 | 10 | 371 | 4 |
| 2 | 281 | 4 | 11 | 437 | 5 |
| 3 | 427 | 5 | 12 | 530 | 5 |
| 4 | 359 | 4 | 13 | 183 | 3 |
| 5 | 497 | 5 | 14 | 407 | 4 |
| 6 | 323 | 4 | 15 | 324 | 4 |
| 7 | 121 | 3 | 16 | 185 | 3 |
| 8 | 285 | 4 | 17 | 366 | 4 |
| 9 | 326 | 4 | 18 | 166 | 3 |
| | 2962 | 37 | | 2969 | 35 |
| | | | | 5931 | 72 |

A missed design opportunity, perhaps, on a great natural site, but this is one of the more rustic and relaxing Iberian courses. Birds (and sculptures) abound amidst pines and wild olives, and several quite demanding holes make a good score no pushover…

*18 is a relatively straightforward p3, protected by bunkers front right and left, and run-off areas to the back. This misty morning flight, and the trees behind, exemplify Montenmedio's rustic qualities.*

# LA MORALEJA (1)

Nicklaus & Muirhead   1975   €€€     **H:** M 27.9, L 35.9, J 28/36

✉ La Moraleja 1, C. Marquesa Viuda de Aldama 50, 28109 Madrid

☎ +34 916 500 700

✎ *no email nor website*

🚗 ✈ Madrid: M10; r onto A1; exit 12a Fuencarral; then exit 12b Colmenar onto Ctra. Irún; after 1.4km r onto Paseo del Conde de los Gaitanes, past Pl de la Moraleja; after 1.2km becomes Paseo de La Marquesa Viuda de Aldama; after 1.3km straight over mini-rbt (crossing Camino Ancho); after 150m r into C. Marquesa Viuda de Aldama.

| | m | p | | m | p |
|---|---|---|---|---|---|
| 1 | 342 | 4 | 10 | 387 | 4 |
| 2 | 182 | 3 | 11 | 384 | 4 |
| 3 | 282 | 4 | 12 | 483 | 5 |
| 4 | 193 | 3 | 13 | 299 | 4 |
| 5 | 342 | 4 | 14 | 285 | 4 |
| 6 | 460 | 5 | 15 | 168 | 3 |
| 7 | 416 | 4 | 16 | 288 | 4 |
| 8 | 367 | 4 | 17 | 159 | 3 |
| 9 | 475 | 5 | 18 | 446 | 5 |
| | 3059 | 36 | | 2899 | 36 |
| | | | | 5958 | 72 |

Tree-lined, occasionally tight, often heavily-bunkered, out and back residential course, at times with charm and character, over undulating ground with several testing short-medium par 4s and smallish greens. Some water carries. (Very difficult to find clubhouse!)

*La Moraleja (1)'s downhill medium p5:12 sweeps from left to right around these trees before the green twists the hole back left behind a pond. Bunkers lie beyond the putting surface.*

# LA MORALEJA (2)

**Golden Bear   1990   €€€**          **H:** M 27.9, L 35.9, J 28/36

✉  La Moraleja 2, Camino Ancho 17, 28109 Madrid

☎  +34 916 585 380

✗  *no email nor website*

🚗 ✈ Madrid: M10; r onto A1; exit 12a Fuencarral; then exit 12b Colmenar onto Ctra. Irún; after 1.4km r onto Paseo del Conde de los Gaitanes, past Pl de la Moraleja; after 1.2km becomes Paseo de La Marquesa Viuda de Aldama; after 1.3km, r at mini-rbt onto Calle Camino Ancho; after approx 1.2km (i.e. after Camino Viejo jctn.), r into Camino Ancho.

| | m | p | | | m | p |
|---|---|---|---|---|---|---|
| 1 | 371 | 4 | | 10 | 318 | 4 |
| 2 | 392 | 4 | | 11 | 499 | 5 |
| 3 | 328 | 4 | | 12 | 397 | 4 |
| 4 | 158 | 3 | | 13 | 143 | 3 |
| 5 | 380 | 4 | | 14 | 377 | 4 |
| 6 | 526 | 5 | | 15 | 400 | 4 |
| 7 | 212 | 3 | | 16 | 488 | 5 |
| 8 | 491 | 5 | | 17 | 165 | 3 |
| 9 | 377 | 4 | | 18 | 381 | 4 |
| | 3235 | 36 | | | 3168 | 36 |
| | | | | | 6403 | 72 |

Demanding, fairly open, American-style layout emanating from (difficult to find) hillside clubhouse, with occasionally watery holes on plain below. Generally excellent greensites on what is otherwise a more masculine, but blander, course than its eponymous sister.

*The slightly Star Wars background to La Moraleja (2)'s longish p4 9th is provided by the construction of Madrid's new airport terminals. Fortunately the course is not on the flightpath, but bunkers are on yours if you go right with your second into a long, thin double green shared, round to the right, with 18.*

# NOVO SANCTI PETRI (A)

Ballesteros   1990   €€          **H:** M 36, L 36, J 36

✉ Club de Golf Novo Sancti Petri, Urb. Novo Sancti Petri, 11130 Chiclana de la Frontera, Cádiz

☎ +34 956 494 005

✎ reservas@golf-novosancti.es   www.golf-novosancti.es

🚗 ✈ Jerez: exit airport; l onto (old) NIV; after approx 2km l through Guadalcacin del Caudillo; l 200m before A382 over rbt; r onto AP4; l onto (old) NIV after 23km; then onto A48 (under construction – currently ends at exit 10, becoming N340; N.B. there may be a future exit near km16); 700m after (current) N340 km16 r for Urb. Novo Sancti Petri; after 4km, l at rbt (up and over hill); after approx 1km r at rbt; after approx 1km straight over rbt; after approx 1km l at rbt; club 500m on l.

| | m | p | | m | p |
|---|---|---|---|---|---|
| 1 | 409 | 4 | 10 | 405 | 4 |
| 2 | 468 | 5 | 11 | 453 | 5 |
| 3 | 409 | 4 | 12 | 314 | 4 |
| 4 | 318 | 4 | 13 | 528 | 5 |
| 5 | 358 | 4 | 14 | 351 | 4 |
| 6 | 324 | 4 | 15 | 166 | 3 |
| 7 | 208 | 3 | 16 | 416 | 4 |
| 8 | 535 | 5 | 17 | 421 | 4 |
| 9 | 187 | 3 | 18 | 206 | 3 |
| | 3216 | 36 | | 3260 | 36 |
| | | | | 6476 | 72 |

Two different loops of 9, formerly Mar and Pinos, which well describe their character: 1st 9 over relatively exposed, slightly undulating ground close to beach; 2nd 9 flatter and more in inland forest. Some small greens and water carries. Residential development frequently abuts.

*A photo taken a little from the left, rather than straight down the line of play, but one relevant to your second shot to medium p4:6 showing the true extent of the raised green's exposure to sea and wind. In such conditions take a par thankfully, and hope to match it at the next hole – just a 208m p3…*

# NOVO SANCTI PETRI (B)

Ballesteros   1990/2001   €€                    **H:** M 36, L 36, J 36

✉ Club de Golf Novo Sancti Petri, Urb. Novo Sancti Petri, 11130 Chiclana de la Frontera, Cádiz

☎ +34 956 494 005

✎ reservas@golf-novosancti.es   www.golf-novosancti.es

🚗 ✈ Jerez: exit airport; l onto (old) NIV; after approx 2km l through Guadalcacin del Caudillo; l 200m before A382 over rbt; r onto AP4; l onto (old) NIV after 23km; then onto A48 (under construction – currently ends at exit 10, becoming N340; N.B. there may be a future exit near km16); 700m after (current) N340 km16 r for Urb. Novo Sancti Petri; after 4km, l at rbt (up and over hill); after approx 1km r at rbt; after approx 1km straight over rbt; after approx 1km l at rbt; club 500m on l.

| | m | p | | m | p |
|---|---|---|---|---|---|
| 1 | 387 | 4 | 10 | 147 | 3 |
| 2 | 406 | 4 | 11 | 502 | 5 |
| 3 | 489 | 5 | 12 | 177 | 3 |
| 4 | 180 | 3 | 13 | 462 | 5 |
| 5 | 457 | 5 | 14 | 416 | 4 |
| 6 | 164 | 3 | 15 | 369 | 4 |
| 7 | 286 | 4 | 16 | 194 | 3 |
| 8 | 125 | 3 | 17 | 481 | 5 |
| 9 | 501 | 5 | 18 | 328 | 4 |
| | 2995 | 36 | | 3076 | 36 |
| | | | | 6071 | 72 |

Partially pine-lined otherwise mainly parkland course on gently rolling ground with brief, open, sea-view corner exposed to wind – comprises original Centro 9 with a new 9 inserted mid-round (5-13). Newer holes' slight inconsistency with older ones should fade with maturity. Some interesting greens.

*The best overall sea view at Novo Sancti Petri comes with the second shot at medium p5:11 on the B course. With a drive to a bunkered ridge, whence this view, the hole seems simple enough, but the green will only hold a well-executed shot and the wind effectively makes it a smaller target than it seems (it's not flat, either!).*

# EL PARAÍSO

Player   1973   €€                                    **H:** M 28, L 36, J 36

✉ El Paraíso Golf Club, Urb. El Paraíso, Ctra. de Cádiz km167, Estepona, Málaga

☎ +34 952 883 835

✎ info@elparaisogolfclub.com   www.elparaisogolfclub.com

🚗 ✈ Málaga: r out of airport exit road onto A7 for Cádiz; r at km229 for AP7 Benalmádena/Algeciras; end of Marbella bypass (km178) take r split onto A7; through San Pedro de Alcántara; r 200m after km167; across mini-rbt and follow signs to club.

| | m | p | | m | p |
|---|---|---|---|---|---|
| 1 | 292 | 4 | 10 | 331 | 4 |
| 2 | 353 | 4 | 11 | 395 | 4 |
| 3 | 432 | 4 | 12 | 339 | 4 |
| 4 | 367 | 4 | 13 | 399 | 4 |
| 5 | 178 | 3 | 14 | 138 | 3 |
| 6 | 442 | 5 | 15 | 514 | 5 |
| 7 | 157 | 3 | 16 | 488 | 5 |
| 8 | 342 | 4 | 17 | 198 | 3 |
| 9 | 381 | 4 | 18 | 385 | 4 |
| | 2944 | 35 | | 3187 | 36 |
| | | | | 6131 | 71 |

Graceful parkland course with a rustic run of holes through valley on front 9. Two less attractive uphill holes rewarded by subsequent tee shots. Some slightly raised greens. Bunkering a little more aggressive than it seems. Cortijo 19th reflects environs.

*Downhill medium p4:8 is the best hole at El Paraíso: attractive to see, with the white of the fairway bunker making a dazzling contrast to the green fairway, and attractive to play – successfully negotiating the fairway bunker, and then the greenside sand, is very satisfying.*

# LA QUINTA

Piñero/Garrido   1989   €€          **H:** M 28, L 36, J 48

✉ La Quinta Golf & Country Club, Urb. La Quinta Golf, Nueva Andalucía, 29660 Marbella, Málaga

☎ +34 952 762 390

✎ reserves@laquintagolf.com   www.laquintagolf.com

🚗 ✈ Málaga: r out of airport exit road onto A7 for Cádiz; r at km229 for AP7 Benalmádena/Algeciras; AP7 past Marbella to exit for San Pedro de Alcántara/Ronda (km172); l at rbt (i.e. not to Ronda), wiggle up round to r, l over motorway bridge; club after about 700m at top of hill.

| | A | | | B | | | C | |
|---|---|---|---|---|---|---|---|---|
| | m | p | | m | p | | m | p |
| 1 | 469 | 5 | 1 | 297 | 4 | 1 | 261 | 4 |
| 2 | 341 | 4 | 2 | 147 | 3 | 2 | 196 | 3 |
| 3 | 410 | 4 | 3 | 332 | 4 | 3 | 386 | 4 |
| 4 | 150 | 3 | 4 | 364 | 4 | 4 | 342 | 4 |
| 5 | 412 | 4 | 5 | 368 | 4 | 5 | 450 | 5 |
| 6 | 210 | 3 | 6 | 420 | 5 | 6 | 432 | 4 |
| 7 | 291 | 4 | 7 | 163 | 3 | 7 | 518 | 5 |
| 8 | 151 | 3 | 8 | 357 | 4 | 8 | 114 | 3 |
| 9 | 450 | 5 | 9 | 270 | 4 | 9 | 332 | 4 |
| | 2884 | 35 | | 2718 | 35 | | 3031 | 36 |
| AB | 5602 | 70 | AC | 5915 | 71 | BC | 5749 | 71 |

Popular hotel course with three evenly balanced, reasonably hilly loops of 9. Good bunkering, doglegs and water defend often raised greensites, but rather overlooked by villas and at one end built on top of the motorway. B improved by Piñero (2003).

*Piñero has made significant improvements in his 2003 upgrading of the B 9, as is evident at medium p4:4: longer, with a lower tee and higher fairway, this hole is a roller-coaster-dipper no more, but a milder left to right dogleg whose green is much more visible from a fairway bunkered on the right. An attractive hole (for golf) – but no enhancement will remove the overlooking houses.*

# SALOBRE (SOUTH)

Fauré  2000  €€

**H:** M 28, L 36, J 28/36

Buggy included
in green fee

✉ Salobre Golf & Resort, Autopista Gran Canaria 1 km53,
35100 Maspalomas, Gran Canaria

☎ +34 928 010 103

✎ reservation@salobregolfresort.com
www.salobregolfresort.com

🚗 ✈ Gran Canaria: GC1 past Maspalomas/Playa Inglés; r at
exit 53 Salobre Golf; up hill round to r, follow signs to clubhouse.

| | m | p | | m | p |
|---|---|---|---|---|---|
| 1 | 496 | 5 | 10 | 383 | 4 |
| 2 | 285 | 4 | 11 | 402 | 4 |
| 3 | 114 | 3 | 12 | 450 | 5 |
| 4 | 336 | 4 | 13 | 344 | 4 |
| 5 | 384 | 4 | 14 | 187 | 3 |
| 6 | 150 | 3 | 15 | 357 | 4 |
| 7 | 362 | 4 | 16 | 397 | 4 |
| 8 | 201 | 3 | 17 | 206 | 3 |
| 9 | 529 | 5 | 18 | 529 | 5 |
| | 2857 | 35 | | 3255 | 36 |
| | | | | 6112 | 71 |

Modern resort layout demanding some spectacular shots (but also several uphill), with tricky tiered greens and lakes, set in palm-lined oasis amidst lava crags. Perhaps a little under-bunkered. Distant sea views. (North Course due to open in 2005.)

*Salobre (South)'s downhill medium p4:13 is one of its most dramatic holes: from the tee (whence this view) it seems that one could easily reach the green, but it is further than it looks and the ground dips a little in front. With some awkward pin positions, par is no pushover. (More downhill drama at p3:14...)*

# SAN ROQUE (OLD)

Thomas & Jacklin   1990   €€€        **H:** M 28, L 36, J 28/36

Buggy included in green fee

✉  The San Roque Club, N340 km127, San Roque 11360, Cádiz

☎  +34 956 613 030

✎  aperea@sanroqueclub.com   www.sanroqueclub.com

🚗 ✈ Gibraltar: A383 from La Línea; r onto A7 (after 9km); 1st exit (127) and follow signs to club.

>27 / 7/8
<13

| | m | p | | m | p |
|---|---|---|---|---|---|
| 1 | 367 | 4 | 10 | 483 | 5 |
| 2 | 420 | 4 | 11 | 405 | 4 |
| 3 | 155 | 3 | 12 | 370 | 4 |
| 4 | 347 | 4 | 13 | 412 | 4 |
| 5 | 481 | 5 | 14 | 171 | 3 |
| 6 | 411 | 4 | 15 | 327 | 4 |
| 7 | 193 | 3 | 16 | 189 | 3 |
| 8 | 404 | 4 | 17 | 519 | 5 |
| 9 | 449 | 5 | 18 | 391 | 4 |
| | 3227 | 36 | | 3267 | 36 |
| | | | | 6494 | 72 |

*The challenge of medium p4:1 makes one respect the importance of warming up at the adjoining practice range, whilst the long, tree-in-middle right-hand bunker sets the style. Sadly, the original tree in the bunker is dead – long live the tree!*

Popular cork/olive tree-lined hotel course on two sides of a hill, adjoining mostly under-developed housing plots. Large sloping greens and grand-scale bunkering. Seriously classy start makes blander middle section feel a bit disappointing, before tough finish. (Judicious enhancement of weaker sections could easily render higher rating.)

# SAN SEBASTIÁN

Hirigoyen   1968   €€€                    **H:** M 28, L 36, J 28/36

✉   Real Golf Club de San Sebastián, Chalet Bordo Gain Apdo. 6,
      20280 Hondarribia, Guipúzcoa – Pais Vasco

☎   +34 943 616 845

✎   rgcss@golfsansebastian.com    [no website]

🚗 ✈ Donostia-San Sebastián: exit airport l for Irún; r at lights
just over bridge at end of airport perimeter, towards San Sebastián;
after 2km at junction with N1 (may become A1) r at rbt into club.

|    | m    | p  |    |    | m    | p  |
|----|------|----|----|----|------|----|
| 1  | 338  | 4  |    | 10 | 266  | 4  |
| 2  | 381  | 4  |    | 11 | 373  | 4  |
| 3  | 458  | 5  |    | 12 | 132  | 3  |
| 4  | 150  | 3  |    | 13 | 427  | 4  |
| 5  | 404  | 4  |    | 14 | 335  | 4  |
| 6  | 253  | 4  |    | 15 | 356  | 4  |
| 7  | 429  | 4  |    | 16 | 502  | 5  |
| 8  | 168  | 3  |    | 17 | 379  | 4  |
| 9  | 440  | 5  |    | 18 | 171  | 3  |
|    | 3021 | 36 |    |    | 2941 | 35 |
|    |      |    |    |    | 5962 | 71 |

Testing, often well-bunkered,
greensites abound on this fairly
hilly, mostly tree-lined course
with wonderful views of the
Basque mountains. Not
particularly long, but it will try
your short game. The lower,
closing holes are a bit
disappointing.

*Long p4:5, with distant vistas of the Basque Pyrenees (see pages 16-17), really
invites you to go for it: with the downhill drive you will need as much length as
you can get, as your second has to be carried all the way to the deceptively
bunkered sloping green, which is further than it looks.*

# SANTA CLARA

**Buggy included in green fee**

Canáles & Busquet  1998  €€€  **H:** M 30, L 38, J 38 – Minimum age: 14

✉ **Santa Clara Golf Club, Ctra. de Cádiz km187.5, 29600
Marbella, Málaga**

☎ **+34 952 850 111**

✐ reservas@santaclara-golf.com   www.gruposantaclara.com

🚗 ✈ **Málaga: r out of airport exit road onto A7 for Cádiz; r at
km229 for AP7 Benalmádena/Algeciras; exit 214 for A7 for
Fuengirola/Algeciras (not AP7 autopista); r for Marbella Golf at
km188 (immediately after El Rosario exit); over 1st rbt parallel with
A7; r at 2nd rbt; 2nd exit at 3rd rbt; club entrance on l after barrier.**

>27 🌡 7/8
<13

|    | m    | p  |    | m    | p  |
|----|------|----|----|------|----|
| 1  | 340  | 4  | 10 | 462  | 5  |
| 2  | 195  | 3  | 11 | 289  | 4  |
| 3  | 240  | 4  | 12 | 420  | 4  |
| 4  | 332  | 4  | 13 | 208  | 3  |
| 5  | 320  | 4  | 14 | 547  | 5  |
| 6  | 197  | 3  | 15 | 173  | 3  |
| 7  | 323  | 4  | 16 | 292  | 4  |
| 8  | 506  | 5  | 17 | 319  | 4  |
| 9  | 351  | 4  | 18 | 364  | 4  |
|    | 2804 | 35 |    | 3074 | 36 |
|    |      |    |    | 5878 | 71 |

Well-maintained, popular resort
course in two loops of 9 with
minimal rough, occasionally
good bunkering, some water
carries, one steep climb and a
good collection of short holes.
Danger: be careful to ensure
that the proximity of some
fairways (especially 4-6) doesn't
also make this your last resort.

**7 red:** routing problem – unimaginative uphill hole.

*One of the best holes at Santa Clara, success at long p3:2 requires concentration –
from the back tee, the direct route to any pin position right of centre is over the
stream and front greenside bunker. True to resort course principles, bail-out space
is provided on the right, but subtle contours at the front of the green demand a
precise pitch if you come up short.*

# SANTA MARÍA

Garrido/IH   1991/96   €€               **H:** M 28, L 36, J 28/36

✉ Santa María Golf & Country Club, Urb. Elviria, Ctra. de Cádiz
km192, 29600 Marbella, Málaga

☎ +34 952 831 036

✎ caddymaster@santamariagolfclub.com
www.santamariagolfclub.com

🚗 ✈ Málaga: r out of airport exit road onto A7 for Cádiz; r at
km229 for AP7 Benalmádena/Algeciras; exit 214 for A7 for Fuengirola/
Algeciras (not AP7 autopista); r at exit Elviria (km192); straight over
rbt onto Avda. de España; 1st r at next rbt into Avda. Santa María; l at
rbt over hill, staying on Avda. Santa María; 200m to club.

|    | m    | p  |    | m    | p  |
|----|------|----|----|------|----|
| 1  | 338  | 4  | 10 | 150  | 3  |
| 2  | 477  | 5  | 11 | 302  | 4  |
| 3  | 370  | 4  | 12 | 157  | 3  |
| 4  | 252  | 4  | 13 | 481  | 5  |
| 5  | 294  | 4  | 14 | 380  | 4  |
| 6  | 309  | 4  | 15 | 166  | 3  |
| 7  | 205  | 3  | 16 | 372  | 4  |
| 8  | 478  | 5  | 17 | 151  | 3  |
| 9  | 324  | 4  | 18 | 380  | 4  |
|    | 3047 | 37 |    | 2539 | 33 |
|    |      |    |    | 5586 | 70 |

Opening out from original
rather narrow 9 holes in valley
to newer 9 (designed in-house)
inserted above motorway, this
hilly, panoramic but
unsophisticated holiday track is
popular, pleasant and
accessible. Some good bunkering.
Par 3s better than the rest.

**11 red:** right to left downhill dogleg around hillside with water straight ahead. You can't see round
corner: trying to drive green over hill is foolhardy. You can't see much of fairway from back tee
anyway – only the water. So you are forced to play a mediumish iron and then a shortish iron.
Doesn't quite work, though we accept for shorter-hitting higher handicappers it may not seem so bad.

# Son Antem (East)

Segalés   1994   €€                              **H:** M 54, L 54, J 54

✉ Son Antem Golf Resort & Spa, Ctra. Llucmajor km3.4, 07620
   Llucmajor, Mallorca

☎ +34 971 129 200

✒ mhrs.pmigs.golf.reservation@marriott.com
   www.marriotthotels.com\pmigs

🚗 ✈ Palma de Mallorca: exit airport l onto PM19, becomes
PM602; resort approx 12km from airport on r (before Llucmajor).

|   | m | p |   | m | p |
|---|---|---|---|---|---|
| 1 | 468 | 5 | 10 | 504 | 5 |
| 2 | 122 | 3 | 11 | 368 | 4 |
| 3 | 315 | 4 | 12 | 325 | 4 |
| 4 | 324 | 4 | 13 | 176 | 3 |
| 5 | 191 | 3 | 14 | 402 | 4 |
| 6 | 356 | 4 | 15 | 389 | 4 |
| 7 | 539 | 5 | 16 | 165 | 3 |
| 8 | 363 | 4 | 17 | 391 | 4 |
| 9 | 408 | 4 | 18 | 521 | 5 |
|   | 3086 | 36 |   | 3241 | 36 |
|   |   |   |   | 6327 | 72 |

Two longish, reasonably
bunkered, often tree-lined
loops of 9 emanate from hotel
on fairly level ground, initially
flanked by timeshare villas,
with back 9 foray into peaceful
former Mallorquin hunting
ground. Water and game
abound. (Preferred to Son
Antem (West) by some.)

**Below** *Mild left to right dogleg longish p4:14 comes towards the end of Son Antem East's
rustic odyssey. This understated hole mainly uses trees instead of bunkers as hazards.*

**Opposite** *Morning shadows make medium p4:1 look rather seductive. But what
the camera doesn't show is that your first shot of the day will have to carry water
to a fairway that you always thought was nearer – until you mistimed it!*

# SON MUNTANER

Rosskneckt  2001  €€€          **H:** M 28, L 36, J 28/36

✉ Son Muntaner Golf, Finca Son Muntaner, Ctra. Son Vida s/n, 07013 Palma de Mallorca

☎ +34 971 783 030

✉ info@golfsonmuntaner.com   www.golfsonmuntaner.com

🚗 ✈ Palma de Mallorca: exit airport r onto PM19; after 6km r onto PM20 (Palma ring road); after 6.5km r for Son Rapinya; straight over rbt after 400m; l after approx 800m at sign for Son Muntaner Golf.

|   | m | p |   |   | m | p |
|---|------|---|---|----|------|----|
| 1 | 377 | 4 |   | 10 | 387 | 4 |
| 2 | 491 | 5 |   | 11 | 192 | 3 |
| 3 | 355 | 4 |   | 12 | 365 | 4 |
| 4 | 409 | 4 |   | 13 | 133 | 3 |
| 5 | 204 | 3 |   | 14 | 316 | 4 |
| 6 | 419 | 4 |   | 15 | 525 | 5 |
| 7 | 137 | 3 |   | 16 | 444 | 5 |
| 8 | 507 | 5 |   | 17 | 332 | 4 |
| 9 | 392 | 4 |   | 18 | 362 | 4 |
|   | 3291 | 36 |  |    | 3056 | 36 |
|   |      |   |   |    | 6347 | 72 |

Often secluded, peaceful, modern, reasonably open and, in places, well-bunkered Mediterranean parkland course in two loops of 9 over rolling terrain in lush setting. Many hourglass-shaped sloping greens. Walls: are you capable of carrying ha-ha at 10?!

*The green at medium short trees-in-fairway p4:12 is not as benign as it looks from here: set across the line of play it is guarded by bunkers, a depression front left and a bunker back right.*

# Son Vida

F Hawtree   1964   €€          **H:** M 28, L 36, J 28/36

✉ **Son Vida Golf, Urb. Son Vida, 07013 Palma de Mallorca, Mallorca**
☎ **+34 971 791 210**
✎ **info@sonvidagolf.com   www.sonvidagolf.com**

🚗 ✈ Palma de Mallorca: exit airport r onto PM19; after 6km r
onto PM20 (Palma ring road); after 6.5km r for Son Rapinya; straight
over rbt after 400m; after 1km l onto Carrer Capocorb; club on r.

>27 | 7/8
<13

Practice facilities shared with *Son Muntaner.*

| | m | p | | m | p |
|---|---|---|---|---|---|
| 1 | 264 | 4 | 10 | 265 | 4 |
| 2 | 193 | 3 | 11 | 482 | 5 |
| 3 | 364 | 4 | 12 | 140 | 3 |
| 4 | 139 | 3 | 13 | 501 | 5 |
| 5 | 361 | 4 | 14 | 331 | 4 |
| 6 | 450 | 5 | 15 | 368 | 4 |
| 7 | 300 | 4 | 16 | 126 | 3 |
| 8 | 130 | 3 | 17 | 400 | 4 |
| 9 | 317 | 4 | 18 | 470 | 5 |
| | 2518 | 34 | | 3083 | 37 |
| | | | | 5601 | 71 |

The oldest course in Mallorca.
Popular layout with more
character than length: 1-12 twist
up, down and around mature,
often narrow tree-lined valleys
amidst upmarket villas; last 6
(upgraded by Rosskneckt, 2001)
in wider plain. Three downhill
p3s and some water carries.
Surprise view of Palma from 6.

*The first 12 holes at Son Vida seem to twist as much as this trunk close to the
green of longish p3:2, which appears to have been shortened from a p4 because
pressure from adjoining house development meant it had to twist too much for
safety. Hence the relatively long walk to the tee.*

# TERRAMAR

Fazio   1993   €€                    **H:** M 28, L 28, J 28/36

✉ Club de Golf Terramar, Camí de la Carrerada s/n, Apdo. de
   Correos 6, 08870 Sitges, Barcelona

☎ +34 938 940 580

✎ terramar.golf@teleline.es   www.golfterramar.com

🚗 ✈ Barcelona: C31c – C32 towards Vilanova/Tarragona; exit
27 for Sitges; into town centre, to sea front; r immediately before
Hotel Terramar; r into C Joseph D Foix; fork r into Av Navarra; l
into Av Salvador Casacuberia; l at T-junction; follow road (railway
comes in on r) to club.

|    | m    | p  |    | m    | p  |
|----|------|----|----|------|----|
| 1  | 361  | 4  | 10 | 166  | 3  |
| 2  | 338  | 4  | 11 | 367  | 4  |
| 3  | 174  | 3  | 12 | 311  | 4  |
| 4  | 472  | 5  | 13 | 324  | 4  |
| 5  | 294  | 4  | 14 | 171  | 3  |
| 6  | 326  | 4  | 15 | 348  | 4  |
| 7  | 183  | 3  | 16 | 513  | 5  |
| 8  | 385  | 4  | 17 | 452  | 5  |
| 9  | 475  | 5  | 18 | 394  | 4  |
|    | 3008 | 36 |    | 3046 | 36 |
|    |      |    |    | 6054 | 72 |

Fairly flat, often pine-lined
course by the sea with some
well-conceived holes, though
most are inland of the railway.
Reasonably large, occasionally
raised greens are defended by
bunkers and some lakes.

*The closing hole at Terramar is a long left to right dogleg p:4, turning around pines
which line the hole almost all the way to the slightly raised bunkered green. Never
more than 200m from the sea, the wind can be a significant factor here,
particularly with the influence of the trees.*

# VALLE DEL ESTE

Canáles   2002   €€                    **H:** M 36, L 36, J 36/36

✉  Valle del Este Golf Club, Urb. Valle del Este Resort, 04620
Vera, Almería

☎  +34 950 398 743

✎  clubdegolf@valledeleste.es    www.valledeleste.es

🚗 ✈ Almería: AL12, becomes A7 towards Murcia; r onto A352
at exit 529; r at 1st rbt; r at 2nd rbt (effectively making all but a U-
turn) and follow road parallel to A7 to club entrance on l after 500m.

| | m | p | | | m | p |
|---|---|---|---|---|---|---|
| 1 | 382 | 4 | | 10 | 428 | 5 |
| 2 | 183 | 3 | | 11 | 320 | 4 |
| 3 | 345 | 4 | | 12 | 152 | 3 |
| 4 | 470 | 5 | | 13 | 340 | 4 |
| 5 | 285 | 4 | | 14 | 136 | 3 |
| 6 | 147 | 3 | | 15 | 390 | 4 |
| 7 | 344 | 4 | | 16 | 353 | 4 |
| 8 | 297 | 4 | | 17 | 322 | 4 |
| 9 | 486 | 5 | | 18 | 316 | 4 |
| | 2939 | 36 | | | 2757 | 35 |
| | | | | | 5696 | 71 |

Different desert style to, and
more three-dimensional as a
golf course than, nearby Desert
Springs. Often wide fairways,
large bunkers and lava waste
well exploit natural features of
undulating terrain. Some water.
Development is beginning to
encroach…

**9 red:** buildings are too close to inside corner of dogleg, preventing original corner-cutting
shot to get home in two.

*Compare the general features in this view of excellent medium p3:12 with our
picture of* Desert Springs *(page 116) and you will immediately see the stylistic
differences between Andalucía's two desert courses. (Be happy with a 3 here!)*

# LA ZAGALETA

Benz  1994  members only          **H:** M 28, L 36, J 36

✉  Club de Campo La Zagaleta, Ctra. Ronda km38, 29679
Benahavís, Málaga

☎  Playable as guest of member only.

🚗 ✈ Málaga: The La Zagaleta estate is on the Ronda road from
San Pedro de Alcántara, some 9km above the San Pedro exit from
the AP7 autopista; entrance is for residents only.

| | m | p | | | m | p |
|---|---|---|---|---|---|---|
| 1 | 330 | 4 | | 10 | 361 | 4 |
| 2 | 161 | 3 | | 11 | 472 | 5 |
| 3 | 365 | 4 | | 12 | 391 | 4 |
| 4 | 542 | 5 | | 13 | 132 | 3 |
| 5 | 193 | 3 | | 14 | 314 | 4 |
| 6 | 482 | 5 | | 15 | 148 | 3 |
| 7 | 281 | 4 | | 16 | 355 | 4 |
| 8 | 457 | 5 | | 17 | 198 | 3 |
| 9 | 356 | 4 | | 18 | 501 | 5 |
| | 3167 | 37 | | | 2872 | 35 |
| | | | | | 6039 | 72 |

Hilly layout with some
spectacular shots (but even
better views), which required
much earth movement to create
rolling fairways and some
interesting greensites. Overall
quality unquestionable, but could
benefit from more character...
Some water. (2nd course under
construction, 2004.)

*Shortish on paper, p5:6 plays much longer, as the tiered green is no less than 20m
higher than the lowest point of the fairway (some 150m short of the putting surface).
This picture gives you an idea of the mountain serenity of the course, and also (in
reverse, against our normal principles) one of the best views of the hole, because the
putting surface is not visible from the fairway. Despite this weakness, 6 earns a green
rating because of the simple but most effective single hazard – the tree in the middle
of the fairway. You cannot play this hole without having to plot your way around it.*

# ZAUDÍN

Player 1992 €€

✉ Club Zaudín, Ctra. Tomares-Mairena km1.5, 41940 Tomares, Sevilla

☎ +34 954 154 159

✎ zaudingolf@teleline.es   www.clubzaudingolf.com

🚗 ✈ Sevilla: A4/E5 towards Sevilla; l at junction after 3km staying on E5, becomes SE30 Sevilla ring road; over suspension bridge; staying on SE30, after subsequent ordinary-style river bridge, l for Mairena at exit 15a; notice salmon pink with green roof Hotel Alcora on top of hill to r; exit r for Tomares, below hotel; once up onto next highway, exit r for hotel (also sign for Zaudín); round up and over highway to rbt (Carrefour); straight over this and next 2 rbts; over next lights; U-turn at next rbt, back to previous lights, whence r and follow road for approx 1km to club entrance.

|   | m | p |   |   | m | p |
|---|-----|---|---|----|-----|---|
| 1 | 326 | 4 |   | 10 | 380 | 4 |
| 2 | 364 | 4 |   | 11 | 200 | 3 |
| 3 | 188 | 3 |   | 12 | 458 | 5 |
| 4 | 492 | 5 |   | 13 | 362 | 4 |
| 5 | 359 | 4 |   | 14 | 353 | 4 |
| 6 | 366 | 4 |   | 15 | 364 | 4 |
| 7 | 365 | 4 |   | 16 | 165 | 3 |
| 8 | 461 | 5 |   | 17 | 398 | 4 |
| 9 | 182 | 3 |   | 18 | 409 | 4 |
|   | 3103 | 36 |  |    | 3089 | 35 |
|   |      |    |  |    | 6192 | 71 |

Gently undulating, generally olive-treed course with occasional palms, that starts and finishes strongly; elsewhere perhaps a few missed opportunities. Two water features well used, requiring potentially spectacular shots. Some good bunkering.

*Sunset reveals some of the contours at medium p4:5, gently downhill over a brow before the water eats away the right of the fairway in front of the undulating green – water is also behind.*

# COSTA DEL SOL SHORT COURSES

## ARTOLA
Mackinlay 1964 €

✉ Hotel Artola, Ctra. de Cádiz km194, 29600
Marbella, Málaga

☎ +34 952 831 390 (No need to reserve)

🚗 ✈ Málaga: r out of airport exit road onto A7 for
Cádiz; r at km229 for AP7 Benalmádena/Algeciras; exit 214
for A7 for Fuengirola/Algeciras (not AP7 autopista); go 200m
past hotel entrance on l at km195; U-turn at Las Chapas exit
back onto A7 back to hotel on r.

(Holes unrated)

| | m | p |
|---|---|---|
| 1 | 56 | 3 |
| 2 | 50 | 3 |
| 3 | 38 | 3 |
| 4 | 62 | 3 |
| 5 | 65 | 3 |
| 6 | 116 | 3 |
| 7 | 113 | 3 |
| 8 | 25 | 3 |
| 9 | 99 | 3 |
| | 624 | 27 |

>27 7/8
<13

## COTO LA SERENA
Morán 1990 €

✉ Coto La Serena, Ctra. de Cádiz km163.5, 29680
Estepona, Málaga

☎ +34 952 804 700  Please book by phone

🚗 ✈ Málaga: r out of airport exit road onto A7 for
Cádiz; r at km229 for AP7 Benalmádena/Algeciras; end of
Marbella bypass (km178) take r split onto A7 past San Pedro;
km163.5 – reception in service road on r; course behind.

| | m | p |
|---|---|---|
| 1 | 99 | 3 |
| 2 | 121 | 3 |
| 3 | 134 | 3 |
| 4 | 81 | 3 |
| 5 | 127 | 3 |
| 6 | 121 | 3 |
| 7 | 86 | 3 |
| 8 | 112 | 3 |
| 9 | 121 | 3 |
| | 963 | 27 |

>27 7/8
<13

## GREENLIFE
IH 2001 €

✉ Greenlife Golf Marbella, Urb. Elviria Hills, Avda.
Las Cumbres s/n, 29600 Marbella, Málaga

☎ +34 952 839 142

✎ golf@greenlife-golf.com   www.greenlife-golf.com

🚗 ✈ Málaga: r out of airport exit road onto A7 for Cádiz;
r at km229 for AP7 Benalmádena/Algeciras; exit 214 for A7 for
Fuengirola/Algeciras (not AP7 autopista); r at exit Elviria
(km192); straight over rbt onto Avda. de España; l at next rbt;
r at hill brow onto Avda. Las Cumbres; r into Greenlife estate
(but straight on for range); l at rbt; l to clubhouse.

| | m | p |
|---|---|---|
| 1 | 140 | 3 |
| 2 | 120 | 3 |
| 3 | 102 | 3 |
| 4 | 151 | 3 |
| 5 | 137 | 3 |
| 6 | 88 | 3 |
| 7 | 133 | 3 |
| 8 | 131 | 3 |
| 9 | 169 | 3 |
| | 1171 | 27 |

>27 7/8
<13

## LA NORIA
Collado 2003 €   **H:** M 36, L 42, J 42 (Min age: 8)

✉ La Noria Golf & Resort, Llano de la Cala s/n, 29649
La Cala de Mijas, Málaga

☎ +34 952 587 653  Please book by phone

🚗 ✈ Málaga: r out of airport exit road onto A7 for
Cádiz; r at km229 for AP7 Benalmádena/Algeciras; exit
214 for A7 for Fuengirola/Algeciras (not AP7 autopista);
exit La Cala de Mijas km201.5; r at rbt below A7, signed
for La Cala; l after 200m into La Noria estate.

| | m | p |
|---|---|---|
| 1 | 153 | 3 |
| 2 | 225 | 4 |
| 3 | 310 | 4 |
| 4 | 338 | 4 |
| 5 | 198 | 4 |
| 6 | 197 | 3 |
| 7 | 438 | 5 |
| 8 | 107 | 3 |
| 9 | 186 | 3 |
| | 2152 | 33 |

>27 7/8
<13

# MONTE PARAÍSO

Piñero 2003 €

✉ Monte Paraíso Golf, Camino do Camoján s/n,
29600 Marbella, Málaga

☎ +34 952 822 781

✎ monteparaisogolf@monteparaiso.com
www.monteparaiso.com

🚗 ✈ Málaga: r out of airport exit road onto A7 for
Cádiz; r at km229 for AP7 to Marbella; exit 184 Casco
Antigua/Avd. del Trapiche; over bridge across AP7/A7;
over rbt; r at lights; fork r at 2nd lights (after approx
500m); 1km, after viaduct, r at rbt into Monte Paraíso.

| | m | p |
|---|---|---|
| 1 | 84 | 3 |
| 2 | 71 | 3 |
| 3 | 130 | 3 |
| 4 | 111 | 3 |
| 5 | 149 | 3 |
| 6 | 98 | 3 |
| 7 | 98 | 3 |
| 8 | 85 | 3 |
| 9 | 126 | 3 |
| | 952 | 27 |

❷ >27 7/8 <13

# LA SIESTA

Canáles 1980 €

✉ Club de Golf La Siesta, Urb. Sitio de Calahonda,
29650 Mijas Costa, Málaga

☎ +34 952 933 362  Please book by phone

🚗 ✈ Málaga: r out of airport exit road onto A7 for
Cádiz; r at km229 for AP7 Benalmádena/Algeciras; exit
214 for A7 for Fuengirola/Algeciras (not AP7 autopista);
exit Calahonda km196; last exit off rbt up Avda. De
España; r after 400m into Calle Don Jose de Orbaneja; l
after 100m marked Club de Golf; club 400m uphill on l.

| | m | p |
|---|---|---|
| 1 | 70 | 3 |
| 2 | 51 | 3 |
| 3 | 70 | 3 |
| 4 | 60 | 3 |
| 5 | 107 | 3 |
| 6 | 129 | 3 |
| 7 | 175 | 3 |
| 8 | 76 | 3 |
| 9 | 134 | 3 |
| | 872 | 27 |

❷ >27 7/8 <13

# EL SOTO

Piñero 2003 €

✉ El Soto, Urb. El Soto de Marbella, Edif. Club Social,
29610 Ojén, Málaga

☎ +34 952 852 124

✎ direccion@elsotoclubdegolf.com
www.elsotoclubdegolf.com

🚗 ✈ Málaga: r out of airport exit road onto A7 for
Cádiz; r at km229 for AP7 Benalmádena/Algeciras; exit
214 for A7 for Fuengirola/Algeciras (not AP7 autopista); r
at exit Elviria (km 192); straight over rbt onto Avda. de
España; 2nd r at next rbt; up hill approx 4km; r at La
Mairena sign and follow road; r at rbt; take upper fork r,
then lower fork l; clubhouse on r after 300m.

| | m | p |
|---|---|---|
| 1 | 60 | 3 |
| 2 | 45 | 3 |
| 3 | 50 | 3 |
| 4 | 35 | 3 |
| 5 | 40 | 3 |
| 6 | 50 | 3 |
| 7 | 60 | 3 |
| 8 | 50 | 3 |
| 9 | 80 | 3 |
| | 470 | 27 |

❷ >27 7/8 <13

The Costa del Sol is well supplied with learners'/practice facilities. **Coto La Serena** (excellent small greensites), **El Soto** (some water), **Greenlife** (2, 5 and 9 are quite challenging; floodlit range up the hill), **Monte Paraíso** (attractive bunkering) and **La Siesta** (quirky but can be kind of fun) are p3 courses. **La Noria** is probably the weakest design on the Costa del Sol. (Further 9 planned on apparently better land – this may improve...? Red 2: – potentially dangerous dogleg p4 of p3 length; 5 – ditto uphill; 4 – p4 almost impossible to reach fairway over water from back tee.) **Artola** is a friendly, family-run hotel, with an inexpensive 9 hole pitch & putt garden course alongside the pool; excellent for young'uns... There are sundry other ranges. N.B. La Cala (Academy) and La Dama de Noche have their own separate courses.

*The dramatic vista (seawards over the 2nd and 3rd holes) from the 1st green of the visually spectacular Machico 9 at Santo da Serra, Madeira.*

# PORTUGAL

Portuguese courses, on average, are better than those in Spain, but there are fewer of them. The Algarve has the highest concentration, but two of the very best layouts in Iberia are within an hour of Lisbon, an increasingly commendable golf destination. Golf in Madeira is perhaps an add-on to a different kind of holiday, whilst Azorean São Miguel, blessed with outstanding natural features, is a wonderful away-from-it-all place to visit, that just happens to have a course to match. As with Spain, be prepared for rain in the peak golf season.

# FURNAS ★★

P M Ross/Cameron & Powell   1939/90   €   **H:** M 28, L 36, J 36

✉ Furnas Golf Course, Achada das Furnas, 9675 Furnas, São Miguel, Açores

☎ +351 296 498 559

✎ verdegolf@virtualazores.com   www.verdegolf.net

🚗 ✈ Ponta Delgada: from airport exit follow signs for Ribeira Grande; after 19km r for Furnas past Porto Formoso and São Brás; after 20km road veers r up hill for Furnas; club on r after 6km.

| | m | p | | m | p |
|---|---|---|---|---|---|
| 1 | 367 | 4 | 10 | 330 | 4 |
| 2 | 160 | 3 | 11 | 167 | 3 |
| 3 | 449 | 5 | 12 | 333 | 4 |
| 4 | 372 | 4 | 13 | 410 | 4 |
| 5 | 470 | 5 | 14 | 447 | 5 |
| 6 | 315 | 4 | 15 | 320 | 4 |
| 7 | 432 | 4 | 16 | 190 | 3 |
| 8 | 157 | 3 | 17 | 425 | 4 |
| 9 | 396 | 4 | 18 | 492 | 5 |
| | 3118 | 36 | | 3114 | 36 |
| | | | | 6232 | 72 |

Raised, bunkered and seemingly frighteningly small undulating greens are the key feature at this gem of a natural golf course, whose rolling fairways are framed by phalanxes of Japanese cedars, mystical in the mists. But it is more forgiving than it looks and a joy for players of all standards. Some water. Joint best course in all Iberia. (The original 9, left by themselves, would have been its only *** course.)

You may wonder if it really is worth flying two hours west from Lisbon into the middle of the Atlantic, followed by rather windy 50 minute drive from Ponta Delgada up into the oft mist-cloaked eastern mountains of São Miguel, just to play one golf course, and one which gives the impression it will frustrate you if your

**Below** *A panorama from behind longish p4:9 (green right, tee distant left, to right of foreground tree) gives the flavour of the Cameron & Powell 9. 9 has the smallest and toughest greensite on the course. Par here is likely to equate to birdie against any field.*

*The fairway of Furnas' right to left dogleg medium p4:4 rolls like surf and then rises up to a typically bunkered green – uphill, but you don't notice it: a good drive leaves you at the same height as the green. The best p4 in Iberia.*

short game is a tad off. Answer: emphatically yes. With its multi-sloping greensites, protected by menacingly-faced bunkers, Furnas has something deliciously wicked (yet fair) about it, and the mysterious feel, provided by the clouds or mist which often swirl through ranks of dimension-creating cedars, has its own magic.

Originally the private course of a multimillionaire, Furnas is playable all year round, but, despite being at Mediterranean latitudes and the reputation of Azorean highs, the island's mid-Atlantic position produces a fickle climate: better not to expect perfect weather – July-September are the best months.

*Medium p3:2 is a superbly natural golf hole: over water, the green lies below cedars in a fold of land which gathers an inaccurate shot onto the putting surface, whilst deflecting all but the most precise shots from being really close to the pin. (See panoramic view, Acknowledgments page.)*

(Given that you have to go that far, we should add that São Miguel, with its volcanic scenery is a delightful place to visit. It isn't known as the 'green island' for nothing: pollution-free, and covered with stone walls dividing green fields, home to cattle that provide a large part of Portugal's milk. Meat. Fish! There are another 27 holes at *Batalha* and possibly two more courses planned nearby...)

# OITAVOS ★★

Hills   2001   €€€                          **H:** M 28, L 36, J 28/36

✉ Quinta da Marinha – Oitavos Golfe, Casa da Quinta, No 25,
Quinta da Marinha, 2760-715 Cascais, Lisbon

☎ +351 214 860 600

✎ oitavosgolfe@quinta-da-marinha.pt
www.quinta-da-marinha.pt

🚗 ✈ Lisbon: exit airport following signs for IC19 Sintra onto 2ª
Circular; follow signs for IC19 and then A5 Cascais (via IC17 CRIL);
onto A5 for Cascais until end – continue off slip road for 400m; r at rbt
(sign); after 400m l at rbt (sign); veer r after 1km (sign for Quinta da
Marinha, but not golf); l after 200m (sign); follow road for 900m, then r (QdM
sign); l after 400m (sign) ignoring sign for golfe to l; l after 600m (sign);
(ignore sign for golfe to l) straight over rbt after 600m; r at next 2 rbts to club.

| | m | p | | | m | p |
|---|---|---|---|---|---|---|
| 1 | 380 | 4 | | 10 | 406 | 4 |
| 2 | 311 | 4 | | 11 | 318 | 4 |
| 3 | 184 | 3 | | 12 | 214 | 3 |
| 4 | 324 | 4 | | 13 | 486 | 5 |
| 5 | 434 | 4 | | 14 | 153 | 3 |
| 6 | 399 | 4 | | 15 | 170 | 3 |
| 7 | 458 | 5 | | 16 | 524 | 5 |
| 8 | 532 | 5 | | 17 | 434 | 4 |
| 9 | 143 | 3 | | 18 | 433 | 4 |
| | 3165 | 36 | | | 3138 | 35 |
| | | | | | 6303 | 71 |

Opening and closing pine
wood golf, eclipsed by
wonderfully neo-Scottish, raw
nature, shared-fairway, hard,
linksy test in exposed sandhills
beyond. Excellent bunkering
and imaginative greens. Wide
sea and mountain views. First
European course to win
Audubon Gold Signature
environmental award.

*A sunset view of 14, the first of Oitavos' consecutive p3s: at 153m over a restored
dune (home to two endangered plant species), it is best to be longer rather than
shorter, though, once over the dune, you can run the ball to the sloping green.*

*Oitavos has a primaeval links feel, enhanced by the occasional pines left amidst the wind strewn dunes. A few frame the Caledonianally eccentric greensite of gold-rated net downhill short p4:11. The fenced path down the right, and the wide bunkered fairway left (whence a pitch up to a green sharply tiered down and away from you), are reminiscent of St Andrews (Old). 11 is also strategic: with a good following wind, you can try to drive it!*

It is encouraging to see a break from the general second half of the 20th century practice of routing a golf course to render two 9 hole loops, each returning to the clubhouse. The concept is admirable, and was one of Dr Alister MacKenzie's 13 principles of golf course design, but the routing and par rating of a golf course must be sensitive to the land, not just to the computer. Oitavos has an out and back layout (the 9th green being the furthest point from the clubhouse). To have routed two loops of 9 (even if environmentally possible) would not have produced so good a result, nor would all the duneland have been within practical reach (note alternative designs on lower clubhouse walls). Hills emphasises the point by including not just consecutive p5s, but consecutive p3s as well. Unusual, yet, if it makes the best use of the land, commendable: 4 excellent holes are the result. (Even The Doctor broke his own rules when the circumstances required, e.g. Cypress Point, one of his greatest masterpieces, is routed out and back, and also has consecutive p3s: unforgettable 15 and 16, both over the Pacific, for which the course is famous.)

*The reverse angle view of 11 shows the fairway shared with shortish right to left dogleg p5:13. The more you play safe on 11, or the more you try to cut the corner on 13 (sometimes reachable in 2), the more you risk bunker trouble...*

# TROIA ★★

Trent Jones Snr   1980   €€                    **H:** M 28, L 36, J 36

✉ Troia Golf Championship Course, Troia, 7570-789 Carvalhal
   – Grândola

☎ +351 265 494 112

✎ troiagolf@sonae.pt   www.troiagolf.com

🚗 ✈ Lisbon: exit airport following signs for Sul and A12, over
Vasco da Gama bridge, for Setúbal, whence follow Troia signs to
ferry boat; take ferry; from Troia EN253-1 towards Comporta; club
approx 1.5km from ferry on r.

| | m | p | | | m | p |
|---|---|---|---|---|---|---|
| 1 | 473 | 5 | | 10 | 313 | 4 |
| 2 | 186 | 3 | | 11 | 165 | 3 |
| 3 | 368 | 4 | | 12 | 346 | 4 |
| 4 | 141 | 3 | | 13 | 411 | 4 |
| 5 | 393 | 4 | | 14 | 475 | 5 |
| 6 | 401 | 4 | | 15 | 398 | 4 |
| 7 | 515 | 5 | | 16 | 405 | 4 |
| 8 | 305 | 4 | | 17 | 160 | 3 |
| 9 | 379 | 4 | | 18 | 486 | 5 |
| | 3161 | 36 | | | 3159 | 36 |
| | | | | | 6320 | 72 |

Beautiful, undulating, rather
linksy fairways woven through a
sandy pine forest, with sea
views when up on dunes. Small
tricky raised greens. Sand of
excellent bunkering dazzles in
white contrast against the
greens and blues of trees, sea
and sky. Difficult from the back.

**Below** *Even in late afternoon sunshine, this view of strategic left to
right dogleg medium p5:7 shows the contrasts of colours created by
the mix of greens, blues and whites – the hole is reachable in two, with
a long, precise, bunker-clearing second; otherwise, lay up to the left.*

*Vilamoura (Old)* and *Furnas* are clear winners at the top of our Iberian league table, but there is little to separate the two candidates for 3rd place in Portugal. *Oitavos* and Troia are both about an hour's drive from Lisbon, one west, the other southeast. You should make time for them both. Whereas *Oitavos* may seem a little stark in the exposed middle of the round (made up for by the quality of the holes), Troia exudes charm all the way round: the golf is unquestionably good, the walk undemanding, the sea views from the dunes alluring, the vistas within the forest often dramatic – and probably would have been, whoever designed the course. But Robert Trent Jones Snr stamped his signature on the land, with some spectacular bunkering (you are warned of what's to come at 1), spicy doglegs, raised

*Troia's p3:4 is short, but very demanding. Hard on the dunes leading to the beach, out of bounds on the left and exposed to the winds, with everything falling away from a green bunkered either side, give it a lot of respect – and enjoy the views (after you have played!).*

and undulating greens (preparing you for the potential nightmares of the 18th green), amidst sandy wastes that often replace rough. This all takes it into another class. No surprise that Troia has played host to the Portuguese Open – Sam Torrance won in 1983, the only player to beat par during the four days of competition. We suggest you first get used to the course before trying it from the tees further back, whence it plays much tighter.

*Low sun at gold-rated p3:2 reveals the heavy bunkering, breaking in front of the green like rollers in the surf (visible beyond the dunes, when you're on the tee). As well as being scenically stunning, this hole is a monster into any wind off the sea: all the bunkers (which foreshorten the hole) must be carried, and the dangerous green is long and thin, set across the line of play. If you birdied the first, an achievement in itself, be happy to stand on the 3rd tee at level par (net or gross – as you wish).*

# VILAMOURA (OLD) ★★

**Pennink   1969   €€€**
**H:** M 24, L 28, J 28

✉ The Old Course, 8125-507 Vilamoura, Algarve
☎ +351 289 310 333
✎ reservas_golfe@lusotur.pt   www.vilamoura.net

🚗 ✈ Faro: N125-10 airport exit road for Faro; r after 3km for A22; after 4km r onto N125 for Almancil; 11km past 1st Almancil sliproad l at lights into Vilamoura estate; l at 2nd rbt (1.3km); straight over next rbt (300m); club on l up hill after 200m.

| | m | p | | m | p |
|---|---|---|---|---|---|
| 1 | 310 | 4 | 10 | 153 | 3 |
| 2 | 435 | 5 | 11 | 390 | 4 |
| 3 | 324 | 4 | 12 | 487 | 5 |
| 4 | 163 | 3 | 13 | 348 | 4 |
| 5 | 485 | 5 | 14 | 440 | 5 |
| 6 | 212 | 3 | 15 | 150 | 3 |
| 7 | 393 | 4 | 16 | 514 | 5 |
| 8 | 419 | 4 | 17 | 353 | 4 |
| 9 | 265 | 4 | 18 | 413 | 4 |
| | 3006 | 36 | | 3248 | 37 |
| | | | | 6254 | 73 |

Majestic, grand-scale, undulating, mature, pine-lined course with a presence that puts it in a class above its neighbours. Shots must be positioned carefully in relation to trees to score well on testing greensites. Joint best course in all Iberia.

*Downhill medium short p4:1 immediately sets both the standard and the scene, and excels as an opener: a lone pine will influence your drive (which could even be for the green), whilst its relatives, short left of the green, particularly the last one (shown here), will affect your second unless you drive to the right. Distant views from the tee fade as you focus on the inviting fairway: ideal for a warm-up – a first hole shouldn't be too hard, should it? Oh taste and see… As you walk off the green with your par, be very happy. We kid you not!*

*Understated, longish p4:18 exemplifies the majestic aesthetics of The Old Course: it runs between towering pines, whose trunks feel architectural, like columns in a temple, while the lightness of the bark stands out against greens, richer and lighter on the fairways, skeletal and darker at treetop level (look back down 5 en route from 18 to 19…).*

What is it that makes Vilamoura (Old) stand out amongst so many quality courses in Iberia, and (with one Azorean exception) over the handful of even better ones? To be at the upper end of our ** bracket requires at least a well-designed golf course, which Vilamoura undoubtedly is (and always was – though the relatively recent make-over has improved its appearance enormously). But it has to have something else. We could point to endless ticked boxes on some checklist of attributes of good golf courses. But this analytical approach would miss the point: at this level we are into the art, not just the science, of golf course design. In a nutshell, here is not just a very good course, but one which feels as if it is naturally part of its own environment, not something imposed upon it. And when that environment (and the vistas offered from within it) are

*The other three of The Old Course's challenging p3s are relatively modest in length, but be thankful that p3:6, is significantly downhill: just 212m downhill, actually. Fortunately the sloping green is relatively large, but you do have to carry the ball all the way, as there's another bunker to the right of the green, and the putting surface rises above its surrounds.*

as consistently harmonious, yet as dramatic (for shot-making and visually), as here, you have something which satisfies senses and intellect, as well as the physical and mental challenge of playing golf. But words are insufficient: better you go experience it for yourself.

# PENINA (CHAMPIONSHIP) ★

Cotton   1966   €€€

**H:** M 28, L 36, J 36

✉ Penina Golf & Resort Hotel, Apdo.146, Penina, 8501-952 Portimão, Algarve

☎ +351 282 420 200

✎ reservations@lemeridien-algarve.com
www.lemeridien-penina.com

🚗 ✈ Faro: N125-10 airport exit road for Faro; r after 3km for A22; after 7km 2nd r sliproad onto A22 for Portimão; exit 4 (km18) for Alvor; r onto N125 for Figueira; hotel 700m on l.

| | m | p | | m | p |
|---|---|---|---|---|---|
| 1 | 407 | 4 | 10 | 498 | 5 |
| 2 | 388 | 4 | 11 | 494 | 5 |
| 3 | 306 | 4 | 12 | 385 | 4 |
| 4 | 353 | 4 | 13 | 185 | 4 |
| 5 | 451 | 5 | 14 | 358 | 4 |
| 6 | 176 | 3 | 15 | 301 | 4 |
| 7 | 310 | 4 | 16 | 192 | 3 |
| 8 | 171 | 3 | 17 | 476 | 5 |
| 9 | 386 | 4 | 18 | 436 | 5 |
| | 2948 | 35 | | 3325 | 38 |
| | | | | 6273 | 73 |

Mature, flat, understated, traditional English, tree-lined hotel course, historic design of Sir Henry Cotton in his days as Algarve's golf pioneer. Sympathetic upgrading has brought much needed improvement.

N.B. There are also two 9 hole courses (2987m and 1851m).

**Below** *Penina has an unusual configuration of holes: the back 9 starts and finishes with consecutive p5s. There is only one p5 on the front 9. Result: an unbalanced par across the two 9s (ultimately, never a problem: good routing is more important than arithmetic). 18 is reachable in 2, in which case it is all about the pin position on the sloping green; otherwise, place your 2nd carefully.*

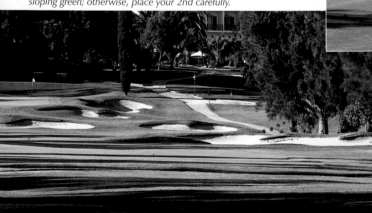

Just as it is difficult to mention *Valderrama*, Spain, without the name of Jaime Ortiz-Patiño, its owner (and head greenkeeper), passing one's lips, the very word 'Penina' evokes memories of Sir Henry Cotton. Some will

*This view of medium long p3:6 shows the raised, sloping green and irregularly shaped bunkers; both are features of the successful recent enhancement.*

say that that Cotton's prowess as a golfer was perhaps rather greater than as a course designer, but that is to miss the point: without Cotton's presence in the area in the 1960s, golf in the Algarve would not have become what it is today – likewise with Patiño and the western Costa del Sol, to say nothing about the standards of greenkeeping on a wider scale. It is difficult to imagine Cotton's vision (and, it has to be said, that of his all important development partners and financiers): the site of Penina used to be a rice field – flat, wet and treeless. With relatively limited resources Cotton moved enough earth to

**Above** *Penina's p3 13th, from the back tee, whence nearly its full length is over water. A tough tee shot to a tough greensite, but it is the fact that Sir Henry also offers less risky routes to the pin that clinches gold. (The flag is at the right of the right-hand bunker, which from this angle marks the left of the green.)*

create what has (with the recent reinvestment) again become one of the better courses in the area. He then proceeded to plant thousands upon thousands of trees. '*Si monumentum requiris, circumspice*' is Sir Christopher Wren's epitaph, inscribed in St Paul's Cathedral, London: if you wish for a memorial to his achievements, you are invited to look around you. Penina is Sir Henry's cathedral: the fairways are its nave, the trees its columns. Go there, and don't just worship the sun: enjoy the communion of golf and nature that he created.

# PRAIA D'EL REY ★

Robinson   1997   €€                    **H:** M 28, L 36, J 36

✉ Praia d'el Rey Golf & Country Club, Vale de Janelas, Apdo.2,
2510-451 Óbidos

☎ +351 262 905 005

✎ golf@praia-del-rey.com   www.praia-del-rey.com

🚗 ✈ Lisbon: from airport exit follow signs for Norte and A8;
A8 to Óbidos exit 13; for Peniche (approx 70km) l at T-junction;
after 2km, under bridge and l for Peniche; after 9km r in Serra d'el
Rey (sign); r after 1.5km (sign); follow road for 4 km to resort.

| | m | p | | m | p |
|---|---|---|---|---|---|
| 1 | 385 | 4 | 10 | 480 | 5 |
| 2 | 463 | 5 | 11 | 183 | 3 |
| 3 | 167 | 3 | 12 | 362 | 4 |
| 4 | 304 | 4 | 13 | 300 | 4 |
| 5 | 441 | 4 | 14 | 150 | 3 |
| 6 | 361 | 4 | 15 | 399 | 4 |
| 7 | 519 | 5 | 16 | 427 | 4 |
| 8 | 168 | 3 | 17 | 570 | 5 |
| 9 | 393 | 4 | 18 | 395 | 4 |
| | 3201 | 36 | | 3266 | 36 |
| | | | | 6467 | 72 |

Demanding but fair course, 2/3rds of which is in stunning duneland hard on the Atlantic, with the rest in pines. Tricky greens. Becoming a little tarnished by residential/hotel development, but play it you must.

Praia d'el Rey is worthy of a king, beach or no beach, simply because of the excellence of its golf course – as a golf course, regardless of what is going on around it. But some readers may be disappointed that we have

**Below** *14 at Praia d'el Rey is a relatively short p3, which comes in the middle of the shoreline run from the 12th to 15th greens. With a green just above the beach, the bunkers are kept below ground to protect the sand from the wind. If you look closely, the shadows reveal two bunkers left and three right of a putting surface which slopes in every direction. Avoid them if you can.*

*Yes, Praia d'el Rey really does feel like the dunes of more northerly links, not least some of those more Himalayan ones whipped up over the years by the Atlantic in southwest England, and the fine morning sea mist makes this view up short p4:4 a little hazy. 4 is played as a slight dogleg, with the tee out of shot and behind right, over a bunker (also out of shot) inside the corner of the dogleg. Thence a pitch up the slopes of the 48m long green, with a distinctive hump just behind the pin position shown. A classic links heroic hole: with a fair wind, the green may even be driveable, but is it worth the risk? Regardless, to cut the corner over the bunker requires a 236m carry from the back tee: if you succeed, it makes you feel you've deserved a birdie, but there's a lot of work left to achieve one...*

not rated it higher. We would have, a few years ago. Unfortunately (for the golf course, that is), the price of success is being paid in the form of property development around the inland parts of the course, and over some areas between clubhouse and sea. Whilst we understand and accept the commercial importance (indeed, without plans for such investment, the course may never have been built), we cannot ignore its negative aesthetic impact. On the plus side, the routing is clever enough to bring us seawards twice, leaving us with two development-free interludes – and these still excel.

**Above** *This view of p4:1 shows the pine-lined character of the more inland holes at Praia d'el Rey. The design puts pressure on you from the start: 1 is a right to left dogleg with trees on the inside of the corner and a couple of bunkers on the outside. The green, which is thin and long (44m), runs down to pot bunkers on the right, hoping to spoil your start.*

# QUINTA DE CIMA ★

Roquemore  2002  €€                    **H:** M 28, L 36, J 36

✉ Quinta de Cima Golf, Quinta da Ria, 8900-057 Vila Nova de Cacela, Algarve

☎ +351 281 950 580

✎ qdria@mail.telepac.pt    www.quintadariagolf.com

🚗 ✈ Faro: N125-10 airport exit road for Faro; r after 3km for A22; after: N125-10 airport exit road for Faro; r after 3km for A22; after 7km r onto A22 for Spain; exit 16 (after km103) for Tavira; across rbt onto N270 for Tavira; after 3km l at Vela ao Venta rbt; follow N125 for Vila Real de Santo António; r after 10.5km for Cacela Velha and sign for golfe; r after 800m into club drive.

| | m | p | | m | p |
|---|---|---|---|---|---|
| 1 | 485 | 5 | 10 | 379 | 4 |
| 2 | 140 | 3 | 11 | 155 | 3 |
| 3 | 314 | 4 | 12 | 457 | 5 |
| 4 | 335 | 4 | 13 | 358 | 4 |
| 5 | 369 | 4 | 14 | 386 | 4 |
| 6 | 495 | 5 | 15 | 386 | 4 |
| 7 | 379 | 4 | 16 | 470 | 5 |
| 8 | 184 | 3 | 17 | 171 | 3 |
| 9 | 378 | 4 | 18 | 415 | 4 |
| | 3079 | 36 | | 3177 | 36 |
| | | | | 6256 | 72 |

A beautiful, understated, olive tree course over gently rolling ground with Mediterranean feel, set up to challenge players of all standards. Abundant bunkering, undulating greens and excellent, limited use of water.

**Below** *This late afternoon shot of Quinta de Cima's medium p4 13th shows the atmosphere created by the mixture of olive trees and sand around the green. Don't underestimate the olive trees: they may make a big aesthetic contribution to the course, but they also often act as three-dimensional hazards.*

Quinta de Cima is the best course built on the Algarve to date in the 21st century. A serious challenge for the good player from the back tees, yet, with wide fairways and only one compulsory carry over water (at demanding tee-water-tricky-green p3:17), it is enjoyable by everyone else – played at less demanding lengths. And the design is wonderfully consistent: the playing characteristics are maintained even at 14 and 15, where we cross onto some slightly different ground (and there the aesthetics will increasingly grow in integrity as

*Medium p5:16 is challenging: water comes into play twice (at least?!) – the stream in the foreground crosses the fairway and will worry shorter hitters over their second; the greenside lake will worry everyone, especially with a pin on the right of the waterwards-sloping putting surface.*

the course and trees mature). Another plus is that, despite plans for an adjoining hotel, the routing prevents the course from being lined with housing: there are no spaces between the fairways for that. Most refreshing. A final word: practise your putting before coming here – wizardry will be required more than once to avoid 3 putting. (*Quinta da Ria*, Cima's peaceful sister course, ain't bad, either!)

*We turn for home at longish p4:15, the first of four strong finishing holes. The fairway runs out to the left, but, by playing it straight over the bunkers, you can shorten the hole. Look closely and you may just discern the monstrous slopes on the green, which rises sharply just beyond the pin.*

# QUINTA DO PERU ★

Roquemore   1994   €€                    **H:** M 28, L 36, J 36

✉  Golfe Quinta do Peru, Alameda da Serra 2, 2975-527 Quinta
    do Conde, Setúbal

☎  +351 212 134 320

✎  play@golfquintadoperu.com   www.golfquintadoperu.com

🚗 ✈ Lisbon: exit airport following signs for IC19 Sintra onto 2ª
Circular (but do not take IC19), then follow signs for A2 for Setúbal
over 25 de Abril bridge; r at exit 2 (km14) for Azeitão onto N10;
immediately r onto sliproad for Azeitão; follow road (N10), skirting
Quinta do Conde (after 8km); r after 11km (at end of Q d Conde –
sign); after 500m l at rbt (sign); after 2km l into Q d Peru estate;
immediately r for club.

| | m | p | | | m | p |
|---|-----|---|---|---|-----|---|
| 1 | 515 | 5 | | 10 | 481 | 5 |
| 2 | 340 | 4 | | 11 | 157 | 3 |
| 3 | 178 | 3 | | 12 | 318 | 4 |
| 4 | 350 | 4 | | 13 | 449 | 5 |
| 5 | 492 | 5 | | 14 | 304 | 4 |
| 6 | 309 | 4 | | 15 | 356 | 4 |
| 7 | 335 | 4 | | 16 | 178 | 3 |
| 8 | 199 | 3 | | 17 | 322 | 4 |
| 9 | 366 | 4 | | 18 | 387 | 4 |
| | 3084 | 36 | | | 2952 | 36 |
| | | | | | 6036 | 72 |

Well-conceived residential
parkland course on rolling
land with grand-scale, often
sloping greens, doglegs and
bunkering. Some good
uphill par 4s and downhill
par 5s. Picturesque, but
tough, pine-lined finish.

*Evening shadows cross the grand-scale bunkering of shortish p4:14 (seen from the
tee). Success at this hole is all about keeping your ball in play: you don't need to
use a driver, and you will certainly prefer not to need to use a sand wedge.*

*The short p5 seems to have become all too rare in modern golf course design, but Quinta do Peru's 13th is a worthy exception. It is downhill, which makes it all the more reachable in two – on paper. That's the good news. A stream crosses the fairway, which then turns increasingly left, with a tree (centre right foreground) exaggerating the corner. Like it or not, it will influence your second – and look at that bunker right in front of the green. Maybe it's better to lay up? Long live strategic golf.*

With the number of members limited to 600, Quinta do Peru is one of the most exclusive clubs in the Lisbon area, matched by the quality of the residences alongside its pleasant, generally tree-lined, fairways. But the course is no turkey: it is easy here to build up a score that, for sure, may be exclusively yours, but won't have any value. Much will depend on how difficult the pin positions are on the day (and there are some you may prefer not to see), and then how aggressive is your game plan. Robert Trent Jones Snr had a dictum that a par should be hard, but a bogey easy. There is nothing such as 'easy' in golf, as we all know, but Roquemore has provided Quinta do Peru with a course that at least seems inviting: the fairways are generally wide, and the bunkers should, if you are not too greedy, cost you only half a stroke (as it were). These factors, plus the many strategic features, just tripped our ★ rating. When you go there, hold something in reserve for the finish: the toughest hole is the last, a long uphill p4 with a tricky green – or just make sure you win over 17 holes.

*Water stares straight at us as we look from the tee down medium p4:15. You may prefer to drive to the left side of the fairway, so your line into the green is angled away from the water, but go too far left and there's another fairway bunker (out of shot). Of course, the green slopes towards the water. Take care, whichever way you play this hole.*

# SAN LORENZO ★

Lee/Roquemore  1988  €€€          **H:** M 28, L 36, J 28/36

✉ San Lorenzo Golf Club, Quinta do Lago, 8135 Almancil, Algarve

☎ +351 289 396 522

✎ san.lorenzo@lemeridien-algarve.com
www.lemeridien-donafilipa.com

🚗 ✈ Faro: N125-10 airport exit road for Faro; r after 3km for A22; after 4km r onto N125 for Almancil; after 3km slip road r for Almancil; after 1.8km (in Almancil) l at lights (small blue signs on l); after 200m l fork for Quinta do Lago reaching "Q" rbt after 2.7km; 3rd exit (l) onto QdL estate road; l at rbt "6" (3.6km); l fork after 400m; l fork after 400m into club.

| | m | p | | m | p |
|---|---|---|---|---|---|
| 1 | 494 | 5 | 10 | 519 | 5 |
| 2 | 162 | 3 | 11 | 350 | 4 |
| 3 | 334 | 4 | 12 | 395 | 4 |
| 4 | 339 | 4 | 13 | 359 | 4 |
| 5 | 129 | 3 | 14 | 157 | 3 |
| 6 | 386 | 4 | 15 | 473 | 5 |
| 7 | 345 | 4 | 16 | 190 | 3 |
| 8 | 525 | 5 | 17 | 344 | 4 |
| 9 | 366 | 4 | 18 | 371 | 4 |
| | 3080 | 36 | | 3158 | 36 |
| | | | | 6238 | 72 |

Grand-scale, often spacious, generally pine-lined, residential course over gently undulating terrain, with both 9 hole loops emerging from trees to watery climaxes. Several doglegs, good bunkers and large, sloping greens.

**18 red:** a beautiful p4 – the fairway is initially out to the right, but crosses the direct line from the tee less than a full wedge from the green, running up to the greenside from the left; everything else is water. The conservative route is, say, a 3 wood to the right fairway, thence a 6-iron to the green. The fairway crossing to the left tempts longer hitters to cut the corner, but the landing area (for a drive with some 240m compulsory carry) is only 15m deep betwixt water. Land on that postage stamp and you will have less than a full wedge to a green surrounded by bunkers and water (wouldn't you prefer to have a full shot to grip such a green?). An attainable strategy, but not worth the risk. The angles just don't work.

*This view, from near the tee of medium p4:13, gives a flavour of the inland side to San Lorenzo: a right to left dogleg, with excellent bunkering and trees on the inside of the corner. Notice how the bunkers have been set into rising ground, which makes them look more natural, particularly in the context of the hole's flowing land.*

*Medium p4:7 is a continuation of the theme begun on the 6th tee and this time we show you the view from on high at low water (to be compared with the greenside view of 6 at high water, below). 7 may be shorter than 6, but the green is heavily bunkered and further out into the water. It deserves respect.*

*Penina* and *Quinta do Lago* were landmarks in the development of the Algarve as one of continental Europe's major golf destinations. The construction of San Lorenzo in the late 1980s took the area to new heights (now joined by back to nature *Quinta de Cima*), the upgrading of *Vilamoura (Old)* aside. Whilst San Lorenzo was built on a slightly grander scale than its predecessors, its site enabled the introduction of close proximity to expanses of water and all its aesthetics. The routing combines two stunning aquatic experiences with some very challenging tests of golf (indeed, to excess, if you accept our perhaps controversial view of 18). Some may have expected an even higher rating, but, at these levels, we would need to see more consistency and integrity of design in what is a blend of inland and water holes. Our use of 'holes' is perhaps the key: ultimately, the whole does not hang together quite as well as the sum of its parts. But it's still good. Very, very good.

*We emerge from the pines at the high tee of longish right to left dogleg p4:6 into quite different territory for three superb holes, all with water right of fairway and close to their greens, as here at 6.*

# AROEIRA (1) ↗

Pennink   1973   €€

H: M 28, L 36, J 36

✉ Clube Golfe Aroeira, Herdade da Aroeira, 2815-207 Charneca de Caparica

☎ +351 212 979 110

✎ golf.reservas@aroeira.com   www.aroeira.com

🚗 ✈ Lisbon: exit airport following signs for IC19 Sintra onto 2ª Circular (but do not take IC19), then follow signs for A2 for Setúbal over 25 de Abril bridge; r at exit 1 IC20 (km6) for Caparica; l at lights at entrance to Caparica (after 6km) onto N377-1 (sign); straight over all junctions and up into forest; r fork after 6.4km (sign); r onto road coming in from l after 1.6km; l after 1.3km (sign); r after 600m (sign), through security and r for 600m to club.

|    | m    | p  |    | m    | p  |
|----|------|----|----|------|----|
| 1  | 484  | 5  | 10 | 486  | 5  |
| 2  | 396  | 4  | 11 | 356  | 4  |
| 3  | 377  | 4  | 12 | 352  | 4  |
| 4  | 158  | 3  | 13 | 381  | 4  |
| 5  | 351  | 4  | 14 | 124  | 3  |
| 6  | 315  | 4  | 15 | 459  | 5  |
| 7  | 372  | 4  | 16 | 137  | 3  |
| 8  | 185  | 3  | 17 | 296  | 4  |
| 9  | 457  | 5  | 18 | 358  | 4  |
|    | 3095 | 36 |    | 2949 | 36 |
|    |      |    |    | 6044 | 72 |

Amply-bunkered, English-style, pine-lined course with flowing fairways, whose difficulty and beauty generally increase as the round develops, especially with greater undulation on the back 9. Subtle greens. Some water and pleasant intra-course vistas add charm.

*p5:15 is just reachable in two if you are a long hitter, but you will need to be straight as there are hazards on either side. This view also shows Aroeira (1)'s rural charm, despite the surrounding houses.*

Sir Henry Cotton's pioneering days in the Algarve in the 1960s set the foundations of the more recent Portuguese golf boom. Frank Pennink was the second main designer off the mark, with the first two courses at *Vilamoura* (1969 and 1975) and *Palmares* in 1975. In 1973 he designed the first 'modern' Lisbon course at Aroeira, which has brought much of the feel of a suburban English residential course to the area in its maturity (though houses are still being built). It has also set fine standards of golf design to follow. Indeed, the south Lisbon suburbs across the bridge have become a quality mini golfing destination in their own right, with the addition of *Quinta do Peru* and nearby *Aroeira (2)* (different clubhouse; quite different golf design; very different residential feel), both of which should also be played. (It is perhaps not surprising to learn that Donald Steel, the designer of the latter, was a trainee and later a partner in Pennink's firm.)

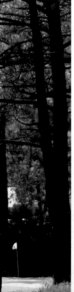

**Left** *Aroeira's p5 9th, seen through some of the pine trees lining the fairway, turns very slightly right. Such trees dominate the layout and, combined with the design's classic inland feel, give it some of the character of, say, a Surrey course. Storm damage removed many trees further from the clubhouse on the front 9, but the design is good enough without them.*

**Above** *The p3s at Aroeira (1) have a reasonable variety in length. At 124m, 15 is the shortest, but you really do have to hit the green (going over the back is hardly better than being short, because you may be left with a tricky recovery shot – back towards the water). Length is not always everything.*

# OPORTO ↗

**Probably IH   1890   €**                     **H:** M 28, L 36, J 36

✉  Oporto Golf Club, Paremos, 4500 Aspenão, Oporto

☎  +351 227 342 008

✎  oportogolfclub@oninet.pt     [no website]

🚗 ✈ Oporto: take A1 towards Lisbon; r onto IC24 to centre of Espinho; l towards Silvade; after about 1km take any side road r and follow railway l to & over level crossing; follow road to golf course; club after two bends on l.

| | m | p | | m | p |
|---|---|---|---|---|---|
| 1 | 315 | 4 | 10 | 322 | 4 |
| 2 | 269 | 4 | 11 | 497 | 5 |
| 3 | 168 | 3 | 12 | 364 | 4 |
| 4 | 390 | 4 | 13 | 336 | 4 |
| 5 | 301 | 4 | 14 | 155 | 3 |
| 6 | 259 | 4 | 15 | 294 | 4 |
| 7 | 399 | 4 | 16 | 114 | 3 |
| 8 | 149 | 3 | 17 | 315 | 4 |
| 9 | 454 | 5 | 18 | 455 | 5 |
| | 2704 | 35 | | 2852 | 36 |
| | | | | 5556 | 71 |

Some subtle undulations enhance this rather Scottish-feel historic links with windswept trees often protecting greensites. The watery ground at the start and finish of both loops is flatter but just as hazardous. Understated and underestimated.

**Above** *Medium-long p4:12 is defended by aerial hazards in the form of three windswept trees on the left and another front right. Depending on wind direction, the flag may be in the lee of the bushes on the right, and therefore deceptive.*

**Below** *With its two-tier green and bunkered all around, p3:3 is played into any wind off the sea, which, at high tide, is only a driver away over the 'flowerpot men' sea wall and just visible behind it, centre shot.*

*p3:8 narrowly missed out on gold (mainly because of the bank behind the green). Not a long one shotter, but directly into any wind off the sea. The classic simplicity of the two-tier green (and the higher level is far from flat), protected by the central pot bunker, speaks for itself: wherever the pin, the bunker will prey on your mind, and two putts from the wrong level of the green will make par feel like birdie.*

Our ✐ rating of a relatively short course by an unknown designer (possibly even some of the first club members, remodelled by PM Ross, 1958) on a fairly flat piece of ground between a railway and the sea a little south of Oporto, may initially surprise you. If that is your reaction, we invite you to recall Alister MacKenzie's 13 principles of golf course design:

1  two 9 hole loops (✔);
2  large proportion of two shot holes and at least 4 one shot holes (✔);
3  minimal walking between greens and tees (✔);
4  undulating ground but no hill climbing (✔);
5  every hole different in character (partial fail, we accept);
6  minimum of blind shots (✔);
7  beautiful surroundings (slight fail) and minimal artificiality (✔);
8  heroic carries and alternative routes (✔);
9  infinite variety of strokes (✔);
10  complete absence of having to look for balls (partial fail);
11  interesting even to a scratch player seeking ways to improve (✔);
12  enjoyable for high handicappers (✔);
13  equally good in winter and summer (✔).

Of course, this layout also has its weaknesses, but we rest our case. Oh, and one final little point: links ain't everything, but the oceanside land over the road (3-8 and 11-14) is the nearest to real linksland we have seen anywhere in Iberia, *El Saler* included.

# PENHA LONGA (ATLANTICO) ↗

Trent Jones Jnr   1994   €€€        **H:** M 28, L 36, J 36

✉ Penha Longa Golf Resort, Estrada da Lagao Azul, Linhó, 2714-511 Sintra

☎ +351 219 249 011

✒ golfres@caesarparkpenhalonga.com
www.penhalonga.com

🚗 ✈ Lisbon: exit airport following signs for IC19 Sintra onto 2ª Circular; follow signs for IC19 (via IC17 CRIL) onto IC19; exit 13 for Cascais (not Cascais via IC16), l-hand lane; l onto N9 for Cascais at rbt after 1km (sign); r after 2.8km for Malveira (sign); l into hotel entrance after 1km.

|   | m | p |   |   | m | p |
|---|---|---|---|---|---|---|
| 1 | 335 | 4 |   | 10 | 382 | 4 |
| 2 | 362 | 4 |   | 11 | 359 | 4 |
| 3 | 324 | 4 |   | 12 | 453 | 5 |
| 4 | 397 | 4 |   | 13 | 322 | 4 |
| 5 | 191 | 3 |   | 14 | 381 | 4 |
| 6 | 455 | 5 |   | 15 | 180 | 3 |
| 7 | 182 | 3 |   | 16 | 402 | 4 |
| 8 | 508 | 5 |   | 17 | 187 | 3 |
| 9 | 374 | 4 |   | 18 | 496 | 5 |
|   | 3128 | 36 |   |   | 3162 | 36 |
|   |   |   |   |   | 6290 | 72 |

A testingly-bunkered, partially tree-lined, challenging but fair layout over hilly ground with distant sea views across both natural and man-made scenery, adjoining the Estoril motor circuit. The elevations require a few spectacular shots. Some water.

N.B. There is also a 9 hole course (2588m). N.B. 8 142 p3

*The aesthetic qualities of long p4:16 played from a high tee down into a valley and then back up to a green, whose putting surface is not visible from the fairway, are not matched sufficiently by its playing qualities to rate higher than yellow. Nevertheless, a par here feels good.*

Penha Longa is set in the grounds of a historic former monastery estate, now the site of an excellent luxurious hotel, with plenty of non-golfing facilities as well – worth a pilgrimage in its own right. But, although it was undoubtedly a testing venue for the Portuguese Open in 1994 and 1995, with only one p4 over 400m from the back, the course can be your prey too, particularly if you avoid the challenging bunkering, and occasional lakes (especially those at 7 and 15, both p3s). After the tree-lined start (and, incidentally, finish) of this out and back layout, we climb to a slightly more open area that unfolds sea views, ancient arches and sadly, a little further, a modern housing development enclosed by the end of the course. On the way back, don't let the Estoril circuit distract you with dreams of winning the Grand Prix: be careful how you drive or you may end up losing the golf!

*Seen from the right of the fairway, the greensite of uphill medium short p4:1 seems embraced by trees, but you will find there is more room than appears. Warm up your short irons before you start: you will prefer to avoid the approach bunkers, which foreshorten the hole.*

**Opposite** *Downhill p5:18 can play shorter than its length suggests: a good drive will use the downslope from the initially higher section of the fairway to run down to a lower part beyond, whence the green is reachable – a particularly good feature for a closing tournament golf hole, as a last minute, trophy-snatching eagle can never be ruled out. However, Penha Longa's excellent bunkering can have the last laugh: the foreground bunker in this view is well short of the green, and you can just see the central greenside one lurking below right of the flag. Easy to reach in three, this hole is nevertheless a fair challenge to all abilities.*

# PINTA

Fream   1992   €€                          **H:** M 27, L 36, J 36

✉ Pinta Course, Pestana Golf Resort Carvoeiro, Apdo.1011,
   Carvoerio, Lagoa 8401-908, Algarve

☎ +351 282 340 900

✐ info@pestanagolf.com   www.pestanagolf.com

🚗 ✈ Faro: N125-10 airport exit road for Faro; r after 3km for A22;
after 7km 2nd sliproad on A22 for Portimão; exit 6 (km39); l onto
N124-1 over A22 for Carvoeiro; after 1.8km l fork for Carvoeiro, leads
to N125; after 800m almost U-turn r at lights (sign Parque Aquatico); l
at rbt after 1km; l at rbt after 1km up to club.

N.B. Please check in at *Gramacho* p. 201. (Pinta's own clubhouse is planned.)

| | m | p | | | m | p |
|---|-----|---|---|----|-----|---|
| 1 | 318 | 4 | | 10 | 382 | 4 |
| 2 | 356 | 4 | | 11 | 163 | 3 |
| 3 | 360 | 4 | | 12 | 488 | 5 |
| 4 | 512 | 5 | | 13 | 336 | 4 |
| 5 | 132 | 4 | | 14 | 480 | 5 |
| 6 | 411 | 4 | | 15 | 179 | 3 |
| 7 | 184 | 3 | | 16 | 323 | 4 |
| 8 | 335 | 4 | | 17 | 202 | 3 |
| 9 | 373 | 4 | | 18 | 581 | 5 |
| | 2981 | 35 | | | 3134 | 36 |
| | | | | | 6115 | 71 |

Engaging and popular olive, almond and carob tree course over rolling country, well-defined with several doglegs, challenging bunkering, testing greens and limited water. Choose tee colour appropriate to your game to get the best out of it.

*Pinta's p4 3rd seen from the tee, across the dogleg: gold, for its strategic quality. There is plenty of room to the right (out of shot), but the design just begs you to cut the corner to the just reachable fairway beyond the bunkers and right of the tree clump (centre). The more you play safe, the more the carry over the greenside bunker will prey on you. Also completely fair: if you try to cut the corner and fail, the penalties are obvious.*

*This view of longish p5:4 shows the corner of the dogleg and the challenge of the bunkering (left greenside bunker also just visible). Place your second to the right to open up the green.*

Rather like excellent *Quinta de Cima*, in that, abundant with olives, it is Mediterranean in feel compared to many of its Algarve peers, Pinta is also more of a serious golfer's course than a holiday course. Both kinds of courses have their place at tourist golf destinations and, with *Gramacho* falling more (but not completely) into the other category (like *Cima's Quinta da Ria*), Carvoeiro is a well-balanced place to play – even before you consider the bounty of layouts nearby. Pinta's reputation as one of the best Algarve courses to be built in the 1990s is borne out by the demand to play it: this is one of the busiest courses in the area and you should allow plenty of time for your round. Our hole ratings suggest that the front 9 is superior: yes, from a design viewpoint, but you will need to keep up your game all the way to the last, a very demanding p5.

*Pinta's p3 15th – evening shadows highlight the undulations of the greensite, showing why your enjoyment may be enhanced by playing from the tee that most suits your standard: from the forward tee (as in this view) you play straight down the green; from the back tee (higher and to the left) you play over trees and the bunker at an angle such that, if you overshoot, will leave you a delicate chip back – bunkerwards...*

# QUINTA DO LAGO (SOUTH) ↗

Mitchell   1974   €€€                    **H:** M 28, L 36, J 36

✉   Quinta do Lago, 8135-024 Almancil, Algarve
☎   +351 289 390 700
✏   golf@quintadolago.com   www.quintadolago.com

🚌   ✈ Faro: N125-10 airport exit road for Faro; r after 3km for
A22; after 4km r onto N125 for Almancil; after 3km slip road r for
Almancil; after 1.8km (in Almancil) l at lights (small blue signs on l);
after 200m l fork for Quinta do Lago reaching 'Q' rbt after 2.7km;
3rd exit (l) onto QdL estate road; r at rbt '4' (2km); r into club.

| | m | p | | | m | p |
|---|---|---|---|---|---|---|
| 1 | 390 | 4 | | 10 | 410 | 4 |
| 2 | 500 | 5 | | 11 | 190 | 3 |
| 3 | 387 | 4 | | 12 | 460 | 5 |
| 4 | 171 | 3 | | 13 | 325 | 4 |
| 5 | 505 | 5 | | 14 | 383 | 4 |
| 6 | 350 | 4 | | 15 | 200 | 3 |
| 7 | 182 | 3 | | 16 | 372 | 4 |
| 8 | 385 | 4 | | 17 | 510 | 5 |
| 9 | 355 | 4 | | 18 | 413 | 4 |
| | 3225 | 36 | | | 3263 | 36 |
| | | | | | 6488 | 72 |

Grand-scale, classy, mature undulating, pine-lined residential course that set new local standards on opening. Generally wide fairways, large sloping greens, attractive bunkering and some water.

Quinta do Lago brought Algarve golf design to a new level after the ground was broken at *Penina* by Sir Henry Cotton. Here was a piece of land with dimension – much more suited to golf than *Penina's* former rice field (but look at what he did with it, before you think of criticising

*This view of Quinta do Lago's p4 13th is demonstrative of the mature and high quality golfing atmosphere of the course. You are encouraged to play towards the bunker on the left, because of water on the right (out of shot), but the best position whence to attack the upslopes of the green is on the right.*

*A view of the highly rated p5:17 from the approach. With its slopes and bunkering, the greensite is a potential match-loser even if you've avoided water off the tee and not strayed to the right, behind those trees, with your second.*

Sir Henry). But it wasn't just the land, it was the scale of the whole concept (and the scale of the investment, we suspect): although 'Quinta' has quite a strong British 'Surrey' feel to it, Mitchell brought American standards to the course's design and infrastructure. This may leave you wondering why we have not rated it higher: we probably would have, 15 years ago, and only minor improvements now might yield a ★. What has happened, which is to Quinta's great credit, is that it has encouraged everyone else to raise their standards – and this is a pattern seen in the British Isles and other parts of Europe, championed, not least, by Jaime Ortiz-Patiño at *Valderrama*. Consumers' expectations have been further encouraged by the standards apparent on our satellite television screens almost every week. So go to Quinta, enjoy it and celebrate: without it and its history, you wouldn't now have such a wonderful choice of courses in Portugal.

*A longish p4 which, being significantly downhill, plays shorter, 1 (seen from just behind the fairway bunker) is a good opening hole: with trees, slopes and moderate bunkering, it immediately introduces the character of the course, which evolves consistently during the round. Better to drive slightly left.*

# VALE DO LOBO (OCEAN) ↗

**Cotton/Roquemore**  1968/2003  €€€  **H:** M 28, L 36, J 28/36

✉ Vale do Lobo Golf Club, 8135-864 Vale do Lobo, Algarve
☎ +351 289 353 465
✎ golf@vdl.pt  www.vdl.pt

🚗 ✈ Faro: N125-10 airport exit road for Faro; r after 3km for A22; after 4km r onto N125 for Almancil; after 3km slip road r for Almancil; after 1.8km (in Almancil) l at lights (small blue signs on l); after 200m r fork for Vale do Lobo; r at T-junction after 1.8km; l into VdL estate after 1.6km; straight over 3 rbts – club on r after 700m.

| | m | p | | m | p |
|---|---|---|---|---|---|
| 1 | 423 | 4 | 10 | 440 | 5 |
| 2 | 287 | 4 | 11 | 400 | 4 |
| 3 | 343 | 4 | 12 | 307 | 4 |
| 4 | 357 | 4 | 13 | 149 | 3 |
| 5 | 195 | 3 | 14 | 344 | 4 |
| 6 | 456 | 5 | 15 | 192 | 3 |
| 7 | 142 | 3 | 16 | 481 | 5 |
| 8 | 402 | 5 | 17 | 146 | 3 |
| 9 | 344 | 4 | 18 | 407 | 5 |
| | 2949 | 36 | | 2866 | 36 |
| | | | | 5815 | 72 |

With newer, slightly more open holes mid front 9, a mixture of inland and pine-strewn holes leading to the Algarve's closest golf to the surf. Undulating ground requiring some testing shots. Several sloping greens. 'Second course' and 'holiday golf' tags would be inappropriate.

**8 red:** too much uphill with nothing to redeem it when you get to the top.

Just as on the Costa del Sol, there is very little golf right on the sea in the Algarve. The 'links' holes at *Palmares* bring you to the beach (but it's the other side of a fence and you

**Below** *Long p4:1 measures longer than 8 and 18, both p5s, but these are significantly uphill. 1 is equally downhill but still presents a tough start to your round. This is one of the holes revamped in the 2003 remodelling, which, despite a mixture of styles, has improved the layout.*

*This view of long p4:11 shows how the design maximises the aesthetic potential of the sea: playing the hole for the first time, you initially think that the green is hard on the beach, but in fact the 15th (see photo below) runs behind it. Think carefully about club selection for your second shot: wind!*

can't see that much), and there are two dramatic clifftop holes (*Pine Cliffs* 6, and the famous *Vale do Lobo (Royal)* 16), but the Ocean course, as with *Guadalmina (Sur)* 11 on the Costa del Sol, puts you in touch with the waves. Is this a big issue? After all, you don't get much of the sea at many historic links, St Andrews included. Yet people are prepared to pay more for a hotel room with a sea view. In golf, it is probably very much a matter of individual preference: indeed, some players positively dislike seaside courses. Nonetheless, in prime location Iberia the land value of seaside property is such as to make golf use of it an extremely scarce luxury. If you want golf right by the sea in Portugal, we recommend *Troia*, *Praia d'el Rey* and *Estela* further north. Vale do Lobo (Ocean) is not without its flaws, not least the mixture of styles, but with the aesthetics of those beach holes just earns a ✈.

*Vale do Lobo (Ocean)'s p3 15th is the pinnacle of the seaside loop at the centre of the back 9 and the closest golf to the Atlantic surf on the Algarve. Despite a weakness in bunker-shaping, the hole is a good match for its wonderful location.*

# VALE DO LOBO (ROYAL) ↗

Cotton/Roquemore   1968/97   €€€      **H:** M 28, L 36, J 28/36

Buggy compulsory
until 10.30am

✉ Vale do Lobo Golf Club, 8135-864 Vale do Lobo, Algarve

☎ +351 289 353 465

✎ golf@vdl.pt   www.vdl.pt

🚗 ✈ Faro: N125-10 airport exit road for Faro; r after 3km for
A22; after 4km r onto N125 for Almancil; after 3km slip road r for
Almancil; after 1.8km (in Almancil) l at lights (small blue signs on l);
after 200m r fork for Vale do Lobo; r at T-junction after 1.8km; l into
VdL estate after 1.6km; straight over 3 rbts – club on r after 700m.

|   | m | p |   |   | m | p |
|---|-----|---|---|----|-----|---|
| 1 | 430 | 5 |   | 10 | 330 | 4 |
| 2 | 290 | 4 |   | 11 | 485 | 5 |
| 3 | 390 | 4 |   | 12 | 335 | 4 |
| 4 | 315 | 4 |   | 13 | 365 | 4 |
| 5 | 470 | 5 |   | 14 | 355 | 4 |
| 6 | 395 | 4 |   | 15 | 295 | 4 |
| 7 | 150 | 3 |   | 16 | 214 | 3 |
| 8 | 385 | 4 |   | 17 | 370 | 4 |
| 9 | 155 | 3 |   | 18 | 330 | 4 |
|   | 2980 | 36 |  |    | 3079 | 36 |
|   |      |    |  |    | 6059 | 72 |

Challenging, residential pine-lined course, with Roquemore's currently more rustic 9 mid-round, before the famous clifftop par 3 and tough finish put pressure on your card. Bunkered sloping greens.

*Medium p5:11 is the penultimate of the 9 Roquemore holes added to the original Yellow Course. It bends sharply right, so the angle for reaching the green leads you towards the water, especially with the pin on the left. If you over-compensate into the bunker right, take great care or you'll still get wet.*

*16 is one of the most photographed holes and toughest long p3s on the planet. It wins gold not just for the spectacle and its demands on your golfing prowess: it is also strategic. If you prefer to chip and hope for one putt, there's lay-up room to the right, though the recent waste area modification has diminished this quality. Coming late in a matchplay round, as it does, your opponent may respect you for that strategy. Then, as long as you don't hold up play, hit another one – just to prove you can get there in one, anyway!*

In recent years Vale do Lobo have made significant investments in upgrading their courses. The completion of the Ocean course revamp in 2003 marks the culmination of this work. At last, approaching 40 years after Sir Henry Cotton first cut ground, Vale do Lobo has two fully equipped modern standard courses. Elements from both layouts combine to make the demanding Championship Course which staged the Portuguese Open in 2003 (Royal 1-6, 12-18 and Ocean 10,11,15,16 and 18). It is a pity that plans for 36 holes were not set down at the start, because the mass of housing development has led, in some places on both courses, to the breach of one of Dr Alister MacKenzie's criteria for good golf course design, namely that there should be minimal walking between green and tee. The Buggy Path Solution may now be rampant over Europe, but many golfers still

*You may prefer to take a 3-wood off the tee at medium left to right dogleg p4:14. It pays to be straight rather than long here: also better to be slightly short right than long left with your midiron second (significantly uphill), because of the severe slope across the green (back left down to front right).*

enjoy one of the game's best attributes, distracted exercise. Hybrid it may be, but the Royal will test every aspect of your game, even before you reach for your camera (and hopefully not for another ball) on the 16th tee.

# VILAMOURA (VICTORIA) ↗

**Palmer  2004  €€€**  **H:** M 24, L 28, J 28

✉ The Victoria Course, 8125-507 Vilamoura, Algarve

☎ +351 289 310 333

✎ reservas_golfe@lusotur.pt  www.vilamoura.net

🚗 ✈ Faro: N125-10 airport exit road for Faro; r after 3km for A22; after 4km r onto N125 for Almancil; 11km past 1st Almancil sliproad l at lights into Vilamoura estate; r at 3rd rbt (1.5km); l at 2nd rbt (1km); r into club after 500m.

| | m | p | | m | p |
|---|---|---|---|---|---|
| 1 | 408 | 4 | 10 | 371 | 4 |
| 2 | 327 | 4 | 11 | 352 | 4 |
| 3 | 517 | 5 | 12 | 500 | 5 |
| 4 | 372 | 4 | 13 | 183 | 3 |
| 5 | 529 | 5 | 14 | 388 | 4 |
| 6 | 199 | 3 | 15 | 288 | 4 |
| 7 | 417 | 4 | 16 | 190 | 3 |
| 8 | 154 | 3 | 17 | 538 | 5 |
| 9 | 404 | 4 | 18 | 423 | 4 |
| | 3327 | 36 | | 3233 | 36 |
| | | | | 6560 | 72 |

Long, large-scale, impressive, but currently a little soulless, American-style layout. Better front 9 over rolling, slightly parkland terrain; more demanding back 9, a bit flatter, with some severe, strategic, water hazards. Challenging bunkering and large undulating greens. Maturity will tell...

On our brief preview shortly before the course opened, we were, to a man, united that, with time, this American-style design should rank second to *Vilamoura (Old)* as the best at Vilamoura. With wide fairways and generally open ground, it seems an inviting course, but don't be fooled: Victoria is not such an innocent girl. She is long: too much off line on the front 9 and she'll spice up your life – stuck in this groove and "who do you

*5 is one big Mama of a p5: the back tee is a full 99m behind the next one – let your head go, and try it (if you dare). From there, however, ensure your driver doesn't have a mind of its own: play as left as you can or you'll significantly lengthen the hole. This view shows what you will have left: the bunkers begin well short of the green – lay up left or right?*

*Downhill long p4:1 immediately presents us with the movement of land through which Victoria's first 10 holes are woven. The ground drops away from the tee to a rolling fairway, protected on the right by bunkers, before evening out nearer the green, which wraps higher back left around the lengthy and optically illusionary '2 become 1' bunker.*

think you are?" she'll holler the rest of your way round. Into one too many water hazards on the back 9 and you'll wannabe fighting hard to save your score – or you'll be out of your mind. Indeed if you are prone to a shank, the becks and tarns all along the right-hand side of demanding left-to-right-sweeping p5:17 will drive you real mad; rid of this disease, you will still need good shots (three of increasing difficulty) to reach the raised green, which juts out into the water. Other aquatic penalties await you if you go left at either p4:11 or excellent p5:12, where the risk and reward over the amount of water you take on is perfectly balanced (the further right you go, the less water, but the longer the hole – and a wonderful little pimple nestles just in front of the putting surface on the 'safer' line, to throw off any slight mishit). With several other excellent-looking holes (e.g. slightly uphill to pulpit green p4:2 and weave-around-trees-and-bunkers p5:3) it was frustrating that the course was not yet open for us to play. The front 9 goes right from the clubhouse and the back 9 left, so this course is not posh, but 'soph' (the root of the Greek for 'wisdom') – with maturity possibly very appropriate!

*Longish p3:13 is indicative of the sensitive treatment of water at Victoria: although it seems a tee-water-green p3 (and is, if you go straight for a flag placed left), Palmer leaves enough room on the right (out of shot) for weaker players (or even those still learning to fly, as it were), whose strategy to play relatively safe is well accommodated.*

# ALTO

Cotton/Dobereiner 1991 €€    **H:** M 28, L 36, J 28/36

✉ Alto Golf, Quinta do Alto Poço – Apdo.1, A8501-906 Alvor, Algarve
☎ +351 282 460 870
✎ golf@altoclub.com    www.altoclub.com

🚗 ✈ Faro: N125-10 airport exit road for Faro; r after 3km for
A22; after 7km 2nd r sliproad onto A22 for Portimão; exit 4 (km18),
under N125 at end of long slip road, onto N531-1 for Alvor, whence
follow Portimão signs until you see sign for Alto Golf; follow signs.

| | m | p | | m | p |
|---|---|---|---|---|---|
| 1 | 162 | 3 | 10 | 410 | 4 |
| 2 | 364 | 4 | 11 | 152 | 3 |
| 3 | 419 | 5 | 12 | 136 | 3 |
| 4 | 400 | 4 | 13 | 416 | 5 |
| 5 | 437 | 5 | 14 | 262 | 4 |
| 6 | 401 | 4 | 15 | 370 | 4 |
| 7 | 201 | 3 | 16 | 604 | 5 |
| 8 | 323 | 4 | 17 | 160 | 3 |
| 9 | 376 | 4 | 18 | 532 | 5 |
| | 3083 | 36 | | 3042 | 36 |
| | | | | 6125 | 72 |

Lack of space forced
compromises in one of Sir
Henry Cotton's last designs
(implemented posthumously,
but before Benamor): unless
on top of your game, consider
irons off the tee at narrower
(but not necessarily shorter)
holes. Undulations add some
character, especially on back 9.

*At just over 600m, p5:16 is our longest Portuguese hole (but just shorter than
Andratx 6, Mallorca, Spain). This view (taken before the mid-2004 clean-up)
illustrates the narrow, tree-lined fairways of Alto, and also shows how the original
design had been allowed to overgrow: the water hazard, left, had become almost
invisible. But notice, in any event, how the bends in the fairway enhance the hole.*

# AROEIRA (2)

Steel  2000  €€

**H:** M 28, L 36, J 36

✉ Clube Golfe Aroeira, Herdade da Aroeira, 2815-207 Charneca de Caparica

☎ +351 21 297 110

✎ golf.reservas@aroeira.com   www.aroeira.com

🚗 ✈ Lisbon: exit airport following signs for IC19 Sintra onto 2ª Circular (but do not take IC19), then follow signs for A2 for Setúbal over 25 de Abril bridge; r at exit 1 IC20 (km6) for Caparica; l at lights at entrance to Caparica (after 6km) onto N377-1 (sign); straight over all junctions and up into forest; r fork after 6.4km (sign); r onto road coming in from l after 1.6km; l after 1.3km (sign); r after 600m (sign), through security; l for 1.2km; r at rbt; car park on l after 1 km.
N.B. Check in at *Aroeira 1* (page 176).

| | m | p | | m | p |
|---|---|---|---|---|---|
| 1 | 416 | 4 | 10 | 365 | 4 |
| 2 | 511 | 5 | 11 | 495 | 5 |
| 3 | 336 | 4 | 12 | 181 | 3 |
| 4 | 504 | 5 | 13 | 350 | 4 |
| 5 | 202 | 3 | 14 | 184 | 3 |
| 6 | 399 | 4 | 15 | 286 | 4 |
| 7 | 353 | 4 | 16 | 341 | 4 |
| 8 | 147 | 3 | 17 | 431 | 4 |
| 9 | 386 | 4 | 18 | 480 | 5 |
| | 3254 | 36 | | 3113 | 36 |
| | | | | 6367 | 72 |

This residential course, lined with majestic pines, tests distance judgment, putting and bunker play. Much water amidst flatter land away from the clubhouse, and at the closing hole of each loop of 9. Surprisingly, the housing stadium backdrop adds atmosphere.

*11 at Aroeira (2) is a medium length p5, from a high tee past some well-positioned fairway bunkers (out of shot) and left around pines. The fairway rises sufficiently en route for the deceptively bunkered green to conceal the putting surface (but not the flag) for the 2nd shot, so there are several features here which make distance judgment difficult – as on other holes.*

# BATALHA

Cameron & Powell   1996   €   **H:** M 28, L 36, J 36

✉ Batalha Golf, Rua do Bom Jesus, Aflitos, 9545-234 Fenais da Luz, São Miguel, Açores

☎ +351 296 498 559

✎ verdegolf@virtualazores.com   www.verdegolf.net

🚗 ✈ Ponta Delgada: from airport exit follow signs for Ribeira Grande; after 13km l for Pico de Pedra; after 1.5km l in PdP (sign); after 500m, r-l-l-r around church; follow road for 2km (course visible on l, 1km); l after church (sign); club entrance 700m on l.

| | A | | | B | | | C | |
|---|---|---|---|---|---|---|---|---|
| | m | p | | m | p | | m | p |
| 1 | 481 | 5 | 1 | 401 | 4 | 1 | 388 | 4 |
| 2 | 185 | 3 | 2 | 329 | 4 | 2 | 467 | 5 |
| 3 | 359 | 4 | 3 | 474 | 5 | 3 | 184 | 3 |
| 4 | 559 | 5 | 4 | 315 | 4 | 4 | 390 | 4 |
| 5 | 385 | 4 | 5 | 475 | 5 | 5 | 156 | 3 |
| 6 | 420 | 4 | 6 | 195 | 3 | 6 | 350 | 4 |
| 7 | 352 | 4 | 7 | 374 | 4 | 7 | 371 | 4 |
| 8 | 197 | 3 | 8 | 376 | 4 | 8 | 348 | 4 |
| 9 | 369 | 4 | 9 | 189 | 3 | 9 | 527 | 5 |
| | 3307 | 36 | | 3128 | 36 | | 3181 | 36 |
| AB | 6435 | 72 | AC | 6488 | 72 | BC | 6309 | 72 |

**C2 red:** drive up a slope more suited to Courchevel and then where's the green?

*Right to left dogleg p4:C8 looks relatively bland from the tee but, as the corner unfolds, one of Batalha's most attractive golfing vistas appears, enhanced by the view of C's 6th green, behind. The golf, however, could become most unattractive, if you find yourself in the wrong position on the sloping green, especially if you have already tasted sand.*

Hilly, partially tree-lined layout with wide-sweeping Atlantic views across stone walls, which occasionally come into play. Bunkered, generally raised greensites will test your short game. Several doglegs, and some challenging, generally long p3s. If time is short, play A and B.

# BELAS

Roquemore   2000   €€                    **H:** M 28, L 36, J 28/36

✉ Belas Golf, Club House, Alemeda do Aqueduto, Belas Clube de Campo, 2650-199 Belas, Lisbon

☎ +351 219 626 640

✎ golfe@planbelas.pt   www.belasgolf.com

🚗 ✈ Lisbon: exit airport following signs for IC19 Sintra onto 2ª Circular; follow signs for IC19 (via IC17 CRIL) onto IC19; exit onto CREL A9; A9 exit 3 (km10) for IC16 Belas; l fork after toll for N250 Belas; at bottom of hill r, immediately l over bridge and r up hill; l after 600m (sign); r after 100m (one way – sign); r after 200m; immediately l up to security; follow signs across Belas CdC estate to clubhouse.

|    | m    | p  |    | m    | p  |
|----|------|----|----|------|----|
| 1  | 383  | 4  | 10 | 496  | 5  |
| 2  | 501  | 5  | 11 | 358  | 4  |
| 3  | 410  | 4  | 12 | 372  | 4  |
| 4  | 350  | 4  | 13 | 347  | 4  |
| 5  | 205  | 3  | 14 | 179  | 3  |
| 6  | 506  | 5  | 15 | 455  | 5  |
| 7  | 195  | 3  | 16 | 322  | 4  |
| 8  | 320  | 4  | 17 | 150  | 3  |
| 9  | 422  | 4  | 18 | 409  | 4  |
|    | 3292 | 36 |    | 3088 | 36 |
|    |      |    |    | 6380 | 72 |

Pretty, rustic start, followed by residential holes – a few long, and some uphill. Sloping, bunkered greens, with water occasionally in play, especially at end of each loop of 9. Playable by all standards – from the appropriate tee (otherwise you may find some holes rather hard!).

*Some of the opening holes at Belas are set in a quiet rustic valley – a far cry from most of the rest of the course. The 2nd is a longish p5, whose sloping green is set beyond a stream, but, because the hole is significantly downhill, you may be tempted to reach it in two. No need to say more…*

# BENAMOR

Cotton   2000   €€                    **H:** M 28, L 36, J 28/36

✉ Benamor Golf, Quinta de Benamor, Conceição, 8800-067
   Tavira, Algarve

☎ +351 281 320 880

✎ secretaria@golfbenamor.com   www.golfbenamor.com

🚗 ✈ Faro: N125-10 airport exit road for Faro; r after 3km for A22;
after 7km r onto A22 for Spain; exit 16 (after km103) for Tavira; across
rbt onto N270 for Tavira; after 3km l at Vela ao Venta rbt; follow N125
for Vila Real de Santo António; club on l in Conceição (approx 6km).

| | m | p | | | m | p |
|---|---|---|---|---|---|---|
| 1 | 308 | 4 | | 10 | 156 | 3 |
| 2 | 153 | 3 | | 11 | 252 | 4 |
| 3 | 269 | 4 | | 12 | 162 | 3 |
| 4 | 237 | 4 | | 13 | 289 | 4 |
| 5 | 466 | 5 | | 14 | 345 | 4 |
| 6 | 379 | 4 | | 15 | 454 | 5 |
| 7 | 431 | 5 | | 16 | 398 | 4 |
| 8 | 195 | 3 | | 17 | 171 | 3 |
| 9 | 320 | 4 | | 18 | 512 | 5 |
| | 2758 | 36 | | | 2739 | 35 |
| | | | | | 5497 | 71 |

Suitable for all standards, a
rolling, moderately tree-lined
holiday layout with several short
p4s and rustic views from holes
away from main road. 2 watery
p3s and some sloping greens
add to the entertainment.

*18 at Benamor is an 'up and over' p5: from a lower tee, you drive up to an open
fairway on a ridge, followed (if you try for it in 2) by a blind shot over the end of the
ridge down to a green with an ecclesiastical backdrop. As our resort editor
demonstrates, play a little left of the bell tower – a rather long 2nd to a green defended
by bunkers: more than a quick prayer may well be needed to wing your ball home.*

# BOAVISTA

Swan   2002   €€                    **H:** M 28, L 36, J 36

✉ Boavista Golf, Apartado 62, 8601-901 Lagos, Algarve

☎ +351 282 000 111

✉ golf.reception@boavistagolf.com   www.boavistagolf.com

🚗 ✈ Faro: N125-10 airport exit road for Faro; r after 3km for A22; after 7km 2nd sliproad r onto A22 for Portimão; exit 1 for Vila do Bispo; straight over 1st rbt; 1st exit (r) at 2nd rbt onto N125; club entrance 100m on l.

| | m | p | | m | p |
|---|---|---|---|---|---|
| 1 | 340 | 4 | 10 | 404 | 4 |
| 2 | 148 | 3 | 11 | 179 | 3 |
| 3 | 475 | 5 | 12 | 377 | 4 |
| 4 | 201 | 3 | 13 | 512 | 5 |
| 5 | 305 | 4 | 14 | 227 | 3 |
| 6 | 194 | 3 | 15 | 390 | 4 |
| 7 | 323 | 4 | 16 | 510 | 5 |
| 8 | 454 | 5 | 17 | 284 | 4 |
| 9 | 312 | 4 | 18 | 418 | 4 |
| | 2752 | 35 | | 3301 | 36 |
| | | | | 6053 | |

A well-conceived, engaging, player's course with challenging greens and good bunkering, requiring several dramatic shots – tempered by some relatively hospitable forward tees. Hopefully the higher ground will remain free of residential development (under way nearer the clubhouse).

**14 red:** as a p3, a hole of such length should not be so deceptive – from the back tee the carry over the water is longer than it seems, plus the dead ground and the greenside bunker are hardly visible. Too unfair.

*You may think we should have awarded gold to Boavista's spectacular p3:6 over a chasm – a little overstated, perhaps. However, the subtleties of 11, another p3 whose bunkering, green slopes and banks really make you think on the tee (even before considering the effects of the wind), are closer to gold – an excellent example of understatement. A par here is just as good as at 6.*

# CASTRO MARIM (ATLANTIC)

Murray   2001   €                                    **H:** M 27, L 36, J 36

✉ Castro Marim Golf & Country Club, Apdo.70, 8950-909
Castro Marim, Algarve

☎ +351 281 510 330

✎ golfe@castromarimgolfe.com   www.castromarimgolfe.com

🚗 ✈ Faro: N125-10 airport exit road for Faro; r after 3km for
A22; after 7km r onto A22 for Spain; exit 18 (km129) for C.
Marim; l off slip road onto N122; ignore sign after 600m, r onto
slip road after bridge; r at T-junction for Monte Francisco; after
approx 300m, 2nd exit at rbt onto club entrance road; l to club at
rbt after 1.6km.

|   | m | p |    | m | p |
|---|-----|---|----|-----|---|
| 1 | 369 | 4 | 10 | 313 | 4 |
| 2 | 158 | 3 | 11 | 322 | 4 |
| 3 | 404 | 5 | 12 | 261 | 4 |
| 4 | 457 | 5 | 13 | 124 | 3 |
| 5 | 336 | 4 | 14 | 365 | 4 |
| 6 | 367 | 4 | 15 | 253 | 4 |
| 7 | 137 | 3 | 16 | 285 | 4 |
| 8 | 258 | 4 | 17 | 136 | 3 |
| 9 | 271 | 4 | 18 | 449 | 5 |
|   | 2757 | 36 |   | 2508 | 35 |
|   |   |   |   | 5265 | 71 |

Played mainly through
sometimes rather narrow
valleys (hit the fairway at 1 and
be prepared for more!), a hilly,
fairly tree-lined course with
some disarming (and
sometimes potentially
dangerous) short p4s; water
and doglegs abound. Vistas to
Spain over the 'wishbones'.

**3 red:** a good short p5 should invite a risk and reward 2nd shot to the green. Here we have a
very narrow uphill left to right banana fairway, after a long tee shot over water. There is no
chance of going for the green in two (the hillside is impossibly in the way); then an uphill
semi-blind green?!?

*11 at Castro Marim (Atlantic) is a downhill shortish p4, with the second over a
pond. You will probably not want to use a driver off the tee. Give yourself a firm
shot to the green: there isn't much margin for error, as there are also banks to the
right and behind. You'll be over the moon with a birdie!*

# ESTELA

Sottomayor  1988  €€          **H:** M 28, L 36, J 28/36

✉ Estela Golf Club, Rio Alto, Estela, 4490 Póvoa de Varzim

☎ +351 252 601 814

✎ Please book by phone    www.estelagolf.pt

🚗 ✈ Oporto: follow signs to IC1 North; IC1 North to exit 7;
whence, N13 to Estela; r off N13 and follow Golfe signs through
village to club (just before beach).

| | m | p | | | m | p |
|---|---|---|---|---|---|---|
| 1 | 459 | 5 | 10 | 373 | 4 |
| 2 | 146 | 3 | 11 | 336 | 4 |
| 3 | 411 | 4 | 12 | 171 | 3 |
| 4 | 164 | 3 | 13 | 457 | 5 |
| 5 | 392 | 4 | 14 | 352 | 4 |
| 6 | 382 | 4 | 15 | 493 | 5 |
| 7 | 473 | 5 | 16 | 345 | 4 |
| 8 | 311 | 4 | 17 | 158 | 3 |
| 9 | 362 | 4 | 18 | 359 | 4 |
| | 3100 | 36 | | 3044 | 36 |
| | | | | 6144 | 72 |

Enhanced by its wonderful
links site, with two out and
back loops along the shore,
this is a serious challenge in
the wind – especially with its
small, often raised, bunkered
greens, and some inland lakes.
Oh, that it had links turf: that
would make it special…

*164m for a p3 doesn't seem too daunting, but, in the windy conditions shown here,
Estela's 4th required our best 1-iron to find the green. At the time of our visit, tees
were being constructed nearer the angle of the photo (higher than our tee, but away
from drifting dunes). Thence, more directly into the same wind, you may well need a
wood. This setting (despite the fence, which plays the vital role of keeping the sand at
bay), plus the small, raised, bunkered green, made the award of gold easy.*

# ESTORIL

Gassiat/P M Ross  1945  €  **H:** M 28, L 36, J 28/36

✉ Golf do Estoril, Av. Da República, 2765-273 Estoril
☎ + 351 214 680 176
✎ reservas@golfestoril.com   www.hotel-estoril-palacio.com

✈ Lisbon: take A5 to exit 9 (km 19) N6-8 for Estoril; l fork on slip road exit (i.e. not back onto m-way); r at mini rbt (may be temporary); r after 400m (sign); club 500m on l at top of hill.

>27 7/8
<13

|  | m | p |  | m | p |
|---|---|---|---|---|---|
| 1 | 352 | 4 | 10 | 453 | 5 |
| 2 | 143 | 3 | 11 | 379 | 4 |
| 3 | 294 | 4 | 12 | 329 | 4 |
| 4 | 154 | 3 | 13 | 160 | 3 |
| 5 | 459 | 5 | 14 | 381 | 4 |
| 6 | 234 | 4 | 15 | 304 | 4 |
| 7 | 390 | 4 | 16 | 186 | 3 |
| 8 | 203 | 3 | 17 | 272 | 4 |
| 9 | 357 | 4 | 18 | 263 | 4 |
|  | 2586 | 34 |  | 2727 | 35 |
|  |  |  |  | 5313 | 69 |

Full of history and not to be underestimated, a relatively short, pretty, tree-lined course, whose narrow fairways and subtle, often hard-to-find greens require careful tee shots, and more. Recovery from adjoining highway construction is reaching maturity.

N.B. There is also a 9 hole course (2379m).

*This late afternoon view of left to right dogleg short p5:10 shows what you will need to do after a good drive. Most longer hitters will still require their 3-wood to reach the small, raised green, surrounded by bunkers and banks, but their shot will have to either run up onto, or pitch onto and hold, the putting surface. Both options difficult. So, better to lay up? Still difficult! Enjoy…*

# GRAMACHO

Fream   1991/2002   €€                          **H:** M 27, L 36, J 36

✉ Gramacho Course, Pestana Golf Resort Carvoeiro,
Apdo.1011, Carvoerio, Lagoa 8401-908, Algarve

☎ +351 282 340 900

✎ info@pestanagolf.com   www.pestanagolf.com

🚗 ✈ Faro: N125-10 airport exit road for Faro; r after 3km for
A22; after 7km 2nd sliproad on A22 for Portimão; exit 6 (km39); l
onto N124-1 over A22 for Carvoeiro; after 1.8km l fork for
Carvoeiro, leads to N125; after 800m almost U-turn r at lights (sign
Parque Aquatico); l at rbt after 1km; l 500m after Pinta rbt (1km);
clubhouse 700m up hill on r.

|   | m | p |   | m | p |
|---|---|---|---|---|---|
| 1 | 338 | 4 | 10 | 173 | 3 |
| 2 | 512 | 5 | 11 | 374 | 4 |
| 3 | 339 | 4 | 12 | 484 | 5 |
| 4 | 186 | 3 | 13 | 360 | 4 |
| 5 | 365 | 4 | 14 | 347 | 4 |
| 6 | 475 | 5 | 15 | 178 | 3 |
| 7 | 179 | 3 | 16 | 376 | 4 |
| 8 | 289 | 4 | 17 | 284 | 4 |
| 9 | 366 | 4 | 18 | 482 | 5 |
|   | 3049 | 36 |   | 3058 | 36 |
|   |   |   |   | 6107 | 72 |

Satisfying olive tree layout over
rolling land with plenty of
bunkers and widespread views.
The newer central 9 holes are
more open. Sloping greens and
some water. If you only have
time for one Carvoeiro course,
play Pinta.

*Whilst medium short p4:3 is not the most difficult hole at Gramacho, we liked the
use of land, hazards (the tree in the fairway to the right in this photo is well-
positioned for both play and aesthetics) and indeed the views from the hole. The
green is a little further than it seems and you only just see the bunker on the left.
Take enough club for your second shot.*

# LISBON SPORTS CLUB

F/M Hawtree   1964/92   €         **H:** M 28, L 36, J 36

✉ Lisbon Sports Club, Casal da Carregueira, 2605-213 Belas, Lisbon
☎ +351 214 310 077
✎ geral@lisbonclub.com   [no website]

🚗 ✈ Lisbon: exit airport following signs for IC19 Sintra onto 2ª Circular; follow signs for IC19 (via IC17 CRIL) onto IC19; exit onto CREL A9; A9 exit 3 (km10) for IC16 Belas; l fork after toll for N250 Belas; at bottom of hill l for 3.1km to Belas; straight across rbt (not r per sign) following sign to Club de Campo Belas; r for Pêro Pinheiro; club on l after 3.2km.

| | m | p | | m | p |
|---|---|---|---|---|---|
| 1 | 168 | 3 | 10 | 263 | 4 |
| 2 | 401 | 4 | 11 | 126 | 3 |
| 3 | 176 | 3 | 12 | 466 | 5 |
| 4 | 346 | 4 | 13 | 196 | 3 |
| 5 | 442 | 5 | 14 | 263 | 4 |
| 6 | 287 | 4 | 15 | 321 | 4 |
| 7 | 357 | 4 | 16 | 476 | 5 |
| 8 | 148 | 3 | 17 | 162 | 3 |
| 9 | 269 | 4 | 18 | 417 | 4 |
| | 2594 | 34 | | 2690 | 35 |
| | | | | 5284 | 69 |

Old-fashioned British-style course (belonging to historic club founded in 1922) running mainly through valleys with a variety of undulations, bunkering, streams and raised greens. Some challenging holes to finish. Better than its card suggests. Holes over road (14-16) added in M Hawtree remodelling.

*Although only 263m, measured around the left to right dogleg, p4:14 is a great test of the golfing mind. The drive is from a raised tee (out of shot) to the right. The question is which club to take and where to hit it: go for the green, play short of the stream, over it, pin high left? Over to you… Very nearly gold.*

# MONTADO

Sottomayor 1991 € **H:** M 28, L 36, J 36

✉ Urbanização do Golfe do Montado Lote N.º 1, Algeruz, 2951-051 Palmela

☎ +351 265 708 150

✒ reservas@golfdomontado.com.pt www.golfdomontado.com.pt

🚗 ✈ Lisbon: exit airport following signs for Sul and A12, over Vasco da Gama bridge, for Setúbal; at first lights after Setúbal toll, l for "porto, Alcácer"; after 700m l at lights (sign); follow road (through Brejos do Asso) for 5.7km, whence r at junction (sign); r after 2.8km (sign); club entrance 800m on r.

| | m | p | | | m | p |
|---|---|---|---|---|---|---|
| 1 | 311 | 4 | | 10 | 339 | 4 |
| 2 | 508 | 5 | | 11 | 124 | 3 |
| 3 | 148 | 3 | | 12 | 483 | 5 |
| 4 | 350 | 4 | | 13 | 328 | 4 |
| 5 | 337 | 4 | | 14 | 298 | 4 |
| 6 | 507 | 5 | | 15 | 317 | 4 |
| 7 | 324 | 4 | | 16 | 489 | 5 |
| 8 | 164 | 3 | | 17 | 150 | 3 |
| 9 | 394 | 4 | | 18 | 349 | 4 |
| | 3043 | 36 | | | 2877 | 36 |
| | | | | | 5920 | 72 |

Open fairways and relatively short p4s make this reasonably flat, partially tree-lined course attractive to all standards. Yet with raised, bunkered greens your short game must be electric to score well. Water and lilies. (Improvements by Santana da Silva began June 2004; revised, more watery course to measure 6445m.)

*After pylonic 3, medium p4:4 brings us to one of the course's more rustic corners, though houses are never far away. The bunkers may be to the left, but don't stray too far right – particularly near the green, where an otherwise delightful pond awaits a mishit…*

# MORGADO

Talley   2003   €€                    **H:** M 28, L 36, J 36

✉  Golfe do Morgado, Apdo. 293, Morgado do Reguengo,
   8501-912 Portimão, Algarve

☎  +351 282 402 152

✎  bookings@golfedomorgado.com   [no website]

🚗 ✈ Faro: N125-10 airport exit road for Faro; r after 3km for
A22; after 7km 2nd r slip road onto A22 towards Portimão; exit 5
(km22); r at rbt onto N266 for Monchique; after 5.5km l (sign);
follow signs for 6km (road becomes track after 3km). (New road
planned for 2005: l 700m along N266 after rbt.)

|    | m    | p  |    | m    | p  |
|----|------|----|----|------|----|
| 1  | 342  | 4  | 10 | 511  | 5  |
| 2  | 373  | 4  | 11 | 166  | 3  |
| 3  | 535  | 5  | 12 | 302  | 4  |
| 4  | 359  | 4  | 13 | 483  | 5  |
| 5  | 209  | 3  | 14 | 326  | 4  |
| 6  | 364  | 4  | 15 | 313  | 4  |
| 7  | 484  | 5  | 16 | 527  | 5  |
| 8  | 197  | 3  | 17 | 211  | 3  |
| 9  | 282  | 4  | 18 | 415  | 4  |
|    | 3145 | 36 |    | 3254 | 37 |
|    |      |    |    | 6399 | 73 |

Two fairly contrasting well-conceived 9 hole loops: front 9 flatter with lakes and good finish; back 9 more rolling. Bunkering perhaps too linksy for the inland rural context, open though it is. Large greens. Clubhouse has style. (Construction of Golfe dos Àlamos, 2nd course, began in 2004.)

*Morgado's short p4 9th is played around a slight dogleg: the very gently rising, open fairway gives a clear view of the green – across a sea of wild flowers in the spring. It's a pity the hole isn't a little shorter, to encourage mere mortals to consider going for the excellent slightly raised green in one shot.*

# PALHEIRO

Robinson   1994   €€                    **H:** M 28, L 36, J 36

✉ Palheiro Golfe, Sítio do Balancal, São Gonçalo, 9050-296
Funchal, Madeira

☎ +351 291 790 120

✎ reservations@palheirogolf.com   www.palheirogolf.com

🚗 ✈ Madeira: ER101 towards Funchal; exit for Boa Nova
(sign); r onto ER102; follow signs; 3km up hill; inside gate r fork to
clubhouse.

| | m | p | | | m | p |
|---|-----|---|---|----|-----|---|
| 1 | 342 | 4 | | 10 | 468 | 5 |
| 2 | 316 | 4 | | 11 | 159 | 3 |
| 3 | 179 | 3 | | 12 | 529 | 5 |
| 4 | 305 | 4 | | 13 | 129 | 3 |
| 5 | 141 | 3 | | 14 | 406 | 4 |
| 6 | 520 | 5 | | 15 | 478 | 5 |
| 7 | 190 | 3 | | 16 | 325 | 4 |
| 8 | 344 | 4 | | 17 | 403 | 4 |
| 9 | 365 | 4 | | 18 | 487 | 5 |
| | 2702 | 34 | | | 3384 | 38 |
| | | | | | 6086 | 72 |

Predominantly beautiful and challenging holes, with arboretum feel and sea views over Funchal – hilly, with undulating tightly bunkered greens. No significant water. Two new holes (15 & 16) by Santana da Silva (2003) have enhanced the course.

*Palheiro's left to right dogleg long p4 14th is in the middle of the arboretum area on the hillside, high above Funchal and the Atlantic beyond. But the hole scores marks for more than just aesthetics: from a high tee you play down to a rolling fairway and will need to place your drive carefully at the angle of the dogleg if you wish to attack the pin on an undulating, well-bunkered green. Anything short will be rejected – better to be pin high and right, where the bank allows a small margin for error.*

# PALMARES

Pennink 1975 €€          **H:** M 28, L 36, J 28/36

✉ Palmares Golf, Apdo.74, Meia Praia, 8600-901 Lagos, Algarve

☎ +351 282 790 500

✗ reservations@palmaresgolf.com    www.palmaresgolf.com

🚗 ✈ Faro: N125-10 airport exit road for Faro; r after 3km for A22; after 7km 2nd sliproad r onto A22 for Portimão; exit 3 for Odiáxere; l onto N125; r towards Palmares; follow signs for golfe; club entrance approx 4km from Odiáxere on l.

| | m | p | | | m | p |
|---|---|---|---|---|---|---|
| 1 | 418 | 4 | | 10 | 165 | 3 |
| 2 | 321 | 4 | | 11 | 271 | 4 |
| 3 | 287 | 4 | | 12 | 400 | 4 |
| 4 | 142 | 3 | | 13 | 386 | 4 |
| 5 | 550 | 5 | | 14 | 347 | 4 |
| 6 | 344 | 4 | | 15 | 212 | 3 |
| 7 | 462 | 5 | | 16 | 418 | 4 |
| 8 | 142 | 3 | | 17 | 458 | 5 |
| 9 | 317 | 4 | | 18 | 321 | 4 |
| | 2983 | 36 | | | 2978 | 35 |
| | | | | | 5961 | 71 |

Mature, tri-flavoured layout on top and side of, and below, coastal hill: 5 testing linksy holes, 7 parklandish and 6 tree-lined on slopes in between. Extensive sea views; sloping greens; some good bunkering. At least as long as its length.

*This photo of p4:6 would not win gold for its artistic qualities: it has some foreground, but, apart from the tee marker, no really obvious subject. But that is its point: it shows the hole from the player's view. 6 does not win its gold for aesthetic qualities, and there seems to be no really obvious target. The tee markers seem to be pointing in the wrong direction – but no: the fairway starts to the left (out of shot) before an almost right-angle turn, over undulations, to a green riskily driveable over water and sand. How would you play it?*

# PARQUE DA FLORESTA

Gancedo   1985   €€                    **H:** M 28, L 36, J 36

✉ Parque da Floresta Golf & Leisure Resort, Vale do Poço,
8650-060 Budens, Algarve

☎ +351 282 690 054

✐ golf@vigiasa.com    www.vigiasa.com

🚗 ✈ Faro: N125-10 airport exit road for Faro; r after 3km for
A22; after 7km 2nd sliproad r onto A22 for Portimão; exit 1 for Vila
do Bispo; straight over 1st rbt; 1st exit (r) at 2nd rbt onto N125;
1km beyond Budens, r into estate road leading to club.

|     | m    | p  |     | m    | p  |
|-----|------|----|-----|------|----|
| 1   | 305  | 4  | 10  | 438  | 5  |
| 2   | 359  | 4  | 11  | 150  | 3  |
| 3   | 166  | 3  | 12  | 420  | 5  |
| 4   | 443  | 5  | 13  | 396  | 4  |
| 5   | 113  | 3  | 14  | 385  | 4  |
| 6   | 363  | 4  | 15  | 150  | 3  |
| 7   | 183  | 3  | 16  | 299  | 4  |
| 8   | 296  | 4  | 17  | 376  | 4  |
| 9   | 488  | 5  | 18  | 331  | 4  |
|     | 2716 | 35 |     | 2945 | 36 |
|     |      |    |     | 5661 | 72 |

More difficult than its card
might suggest, with 2 loops of
9 in different valleys, a slightly
quirky, undulating course with
some spectacular shots to
often raised and/or elongated
sloping greens.

*The spectacular downhill short p3:5 is Parque da Floresta's most celebrated hole.
We have to confess that on our visit, with the photographer joining in as a last
resort 5th player, none of us (professional included) put the ball on the green! We
wish you better luck at this deceptively difficult little hole…*

# PINE CLIFFS

M Hawtree   1991   €€      **H:** M 36, L 36, J 36 – Minimum age: 6

✉ Pine Cliffs Resort, Praia de Falésia, 8200-909 Albufeira, Algarve
☎ +351 289 500 113
✎ sheraton.algarve@starwoodhotels.com   www.pinecliffs.com

🚗 ✈ Faro: N125-10 airport exit road for Faro; r after 3km for
A22; after 4km r onto N125 for Almancil; 12km past 1st Almancil
sliproad l onto N526 for Albufeira (sign); after 3.3km l for Quinta
do Paiva; l after 1km (sign for Sheraton Algarve); after 600m r for
Olhos d'Àgua; after 600m l into Sheraton Algarve Pine Cliffs Resort;
r through entrance; l and follow signs (car park 100m on r after
Academy; clubhouse through gap between apartment buildings).

|   | m | p |
|---|---|---|
| 1 | 267 | 4 |
| 2 | 144 | 3 |
| 3 | 319 | 4 |
| 4 | 129 | 3 |
| 5 | 395 | 4 |
| 6 | 198 | 3 |
| 7 | 355 | 4 |
| 8 | 270 | 4 |
| 9 | 150 | 3 |
|   | 2227 | 32 |

Pretty hotel golf course, where pines (and, at
its spectacular apex, cliffs) are as much a
hazard as bunkers. Undulating fairways lead to
good greensites. Clifftop sea views. A 9 holer
which easily stands on its own feet.

*Rarely in golf do you experience quite such a frighteningly delicious
cocktail of colours and emotions than at the eponymous p3 6th
(the championship tee is upper centre hard above the ocean, as
seen on title page spread), when your opponent, having hit, now
has no choice but to fly to Morocco to play his second shot – or
lose the hole, provided you carry the hazard yourself... Good luck!*

# PINHEIROS ALTOS

Fream   1992   €€€                          **H:** M 28, L 36, J 36

✉ Pinheiros Altos Campo de Golfe, Quinta do Lago, 8135-863 Almancil, Algarve

☎ +351 289 359 910

✎ golf@pinheirosaltos.pt   www.pinheirosaltos.pt

🚗 ✈ Faro: N125-10 airport exit road for Faro; r after 3km for A22; after 4km r onto N125 for Almancil; after 3km slip road r for Almancil; after 1.8km (in Almancil) l at lights (small blue signs on l); after 200m l fork for Quinta do Lago reaching "Q" rbt after 2.7km; 4th exit (fork back l – sign to club); l after 2.2km up hill; club on r after 400m.

| | m | p | | m | p |
|---|---|---|---|---|---|
| 1 | 365 | 4 | 10 | 325 | 4 |
| 2 | 194 | 3 | 11 | 374 | 4 |
| 3 | 308 | 4 | 12 | 450 | 5 |
| 4 | 329 | 4 | 13 | 587 | 5 |
| 5 | 156 | 3 | 14 | 201 | 3 |
| 6 | 542 | 5 | 15 | 303 | 4 |
| 7 | 429 | 4 | 16 | 304 | 4 |
| 8 | 525 | 5 | 17 | 124 | 3 |
| 9 | 369 | 4 | 18 | 301 | 4 |
| | 3217 | 36 | | 2969 | 36 |
| | | | | 6186 | 72 |

Several demanding shots are required on a course of two parts: the relatively hilly 'Pines' front 9, gives way to the comparatively open parkland 'Lakes' back 9 on flatter ground. Some tricky greens.

*The last hole at Pinheiros Altos, which brings us back up to the pines from the lower site of most of the second 9, is a relatively short p4, but a tiered green and heavy bunkering mean that any hesitance with your second will be severely penalised – whether by sand, a long potentially cross-tier putt, or both. The lone pines on the left can also cause problems.*

# QUINTA DA BELOURA

Roquemore 1994 €€  **H:** M 28, L 36, J 36

✉ Pestana Beloura Golf Resort, Rua das Sesmarias 3, Quinta da Beloura, Estrada de Albarraque, 2710-444 Sintra, Lisbon

☎ +351 219 106 350

✎ beloura.reservas@pestana.com  www.pestana.com

🚗 ✈ Lisbon: exit airport following signs for IC19 Sintra onto 2ª Circular; follow signs for IC19 (via IC17 CRIL) onto IC19; exit 13 for Cascais (not Cascais via IC16), l-hand lane; l onto N9 for Cascais at rbt after 1km (sign); l into QdB estate after 1.6km, through security after 300; l after 200m; follow road for 1.4km; r into one way street for club on r.

|    | m    | p  |    | m    | p  |
|----|------|----|----|------|----|
| 1  | 466  | 5  | 10 | 465  | 5  |
| 2  | 317  | 4  | 11 | 302  | 4  |
| 3  | 123  | 3  | 12 | 157  | 3  |
| 4  | 301  | 4  | 13 | 361  | 4  |
| 5  | 254  | 4  | 14 | 144  | 3  |
| 6  | 341  | 4  | 15 | 452  | 5  |
| 7  | 464  | 5  | 16 | 446  | 5  |
| 8  | 159  | 3  | 17 | 329  | 4  |
| 9  | 321  | 4  | 18 | 372  | 4  |
|    | 2746 | 36 |    | 3028 | 37 |
|    |      |    |    | 5774 | 73 |

Tree growth may add to the oasis feel (amidst industrial and residential developments) of a generally flat, mildly bunkered course with some water hazards – all of which puts better layouts into context.

*Quinta da Beloura's short p4 5th entertains us with the strategic challenge of whether to go for the green in one shot: downhill, and with a favourable wind, it is certainly on. The heroic placing of the bunkers inside the dogleg will provide satisfaction if carried, and, should you drive into the greenside bunkers, at least you will be in them in one shot, not two.*

# QUINTA DA MARINHA

Trent Jones Snr   1984   €€                    **H:** M 28, L 36, J 36

✉ Quinta da Marinha Golf, Rua do Clube, Casa 36, Quinta da
Marinha, 2750-715 Cascais, Lisbon

☎ +351 214 860 180

✎ golf@quintadamarinha.com   www.quintadamarinha.com

🚗 ✈ Lisbon: exit airport following signs for IC19 Sintra onto 2ª
Circular; follow signs for IC19 and then A5 Cascais (via IC17 CRIL);
onto A5 for Cascais till end – continue off slip road for 400m; r at
rbt (sign); after 400m l at rbt (sign); veer r after 1km (sign for
QdM, but not golf); l after 200m (sign); straight over all junctions
for 900m, then r (QdM sign); l after 400m (sign); l after 200m (sign
– ignore sign for golfe straight ahead); club on r after 600m.

|   | m | p |   |   | m | p |
|---|-----|---|---|---|------|---|
| 1 | 493 | 5 |   | 10 | 490 | 5 |
| 2 | 130 | 3 |   | 11 | 521 | 5 |
| 3 | 519 | 5 |   | 12 | 411 | 4 |
| 4 | 378 | 4 |   | 13 | 334 | 4 |
| 5 | 153 | 3 |   | 14 | 148 | 3 |
| 6 | 489 | 5 |   | 15 | 269 | 4 |
| 7 | 151 | 3 |   | 16 | 152 | 3 |
| 8 | 373 | 4 |   | 17 | 326 | 4 |
| 9 | 165 | 3 |   | 18 | 343 | 4 |
|   | 2851 | 35 |   |   | 2994 | 36 |
|   |     |   |   |   | 5045 | 71 |

**Don't underestimate the gentle
but subtle slopes of this mainly
pine-lined hotel/residential
course, especially around the
excellent, often heavily-
bunkered greensites. Sea views
on 2nd 9, closest to the shore
at 13.**

*An early morning view from the approach to p4:4 (left) to p3:5 (centre right),
through the trees over water (tee right, just out of shot). This shows the subtleties
built into Quinta da Marinha's greensites: you will see the little bank up to the
raised, sloping 4th green, and, if you look closely at the tree-trunk shadows cast
across the 5th green, the bank of the large tier rising to the left of the 5th flag.*

# QUINTA DA RIA

Roquemore   2003   €€                                    **H:** M 28, L 36, J 36

✉ **Quinta da Ria Golf, Quinta da Ria, 8900-057 Vila Nova de Cacela, Algarve**

☎ **+351 281 950 580**

✒ **qdria@mail.telepac.pt   www.quintadariagolf.com**

🚗 ✈ **Faro:** N125-10 airport exit road for Faro; r after 3km for A22; after 7km r onto A22 for Spain; exit 16 (after km103) for Tavira; across rbt onto N270 for Tavira; after 3km l at Vela ao Venta rbt; follow N125 for Vila Real de Santo António; r after 10.5km for Cacela Velha and sign for golfe; r after 800m into club drive.

|   | m | p |   |   | m | p |
|---|-----|---|---|----|-----|---|
| 1 | 465 | 5 |   | 10 | 422 | 4 |
| 2 | 139 | 3 |   | 11 | 482 | 5 |
| 3 | 342 | 4 |   | 12 | 278 | 4 |
| 4 | 340 | 4 |   | 13 | 188 | 3 |
| 5 | 113 | 3 |   | 14 | 321 | 4 |
| 6 | 442 | 5 |   | 15 | 356 | 4 |
| 7 | 360 | 4 |   | 16 | 453 | 5 |
| 8 | 358 | 4 |   | 17 | 161 | 3 |
| 9 | 344 | 4 |   | 18 | 390 | 4 |
|   | 2903 | 36 |   |   | 3051 | 36 |
|   |     |    |   |   | 5954 | 71 |

Sublime sea views from an olive, almond and carob tree course on subtly rolling land, with some desert-style bunkering. Several testing greens and some water, mainly lateral. Relatively gentle start belies tougher finish.

*10 is rated gold primarily for its strategic qualities. Drive on a line left of the olive tree left of the lake, and you risk a fairway bunker and/or leaving the olive tree in the way. Play right to the wide open fairway short of the lake, and your second will be straight down the line of the photo, with water all the way to a green that is long from the left, but thin from the right. (10 is only 422m – p4!)*

# QUINTA DO LAGO (NORTH)

Mitchell/Roquemore  1974/2003  €€€     **H:** M 28, L 36, J 36

✉ Quinta do Lago, 8135-024 Almancil, Algarve

☎ +351 289 390 700

✎ golf@quintadolago.com  www.quintadolago.com

🚗 ✈ Faro: N125-10 airport exit road for Faro; r after 3km for A22; after 4km r onto N125 for Almancil; after 3km slip road r for Almancil; after 1.8km (in Almancil) l at lights (small blue signs on l); after 200m l fork for Quinta do Lago reaching "Q" rbt after 2.7km; 3rd exit (l) onto QdL estate road; r at rbt '4' (2km); r into club.

>27 🌡 7/8
<13

| | m | p | | m | p |
|---|---|---|---|---|---|
| 1 | 367 | 4 | 10 | 358 | 4 |
| 2 | 180 | 3 | 11 | 465 | 5 |
| 3 | 482 | 5 | 12 | 329 | 4 |
| 4 | 380 | 4 | 13 | 374 | 4 |
| 5 | 345 | 4 | 14 | 154 | 3 |
| 6 | 319 | 4 | 15 | 370 | 4 |
| 7 | 504 | 5 | 16 | 160 | 3 |
| 8 | 153 | 3 | 17 | 326 | 4 |
| 9 | 380 | 4 | 18 | 480 | 5 |
| | 3110 | 36 | | 3016 | 36 |
| | | | | 6126 | 72 |

Play some of the Algarve's prettiest holes mostly in pine-lined valleys, tempered by some long green to tee walks on the newer mid-round loop, by Roquemore (extending the original 9 to 18). Good greensites.

*Quinta do Lago (North)'s p5 3rd is one of its most picturesque holes, in the middle of the beautiful run from the 1st to 5th greens. But these holes are no pushover, so make sure you enjoy the golf as well as the scenery. 3 is reachable in two by long hitters, who manage to pass the fairway bunker (foreground) and hold their ball in the left to right sloping fairway. If the ball kicks too far right or, worse still, stays up left, you will curse the trees instead of admiring their aesthetic input. (Actually, in your folly, you should also be appreciating their contribution to the design of the hole.)*

# SALGADOS

Vasconselos/Muir-Graves   1994   €€

✉  Salgados Golf Club, Vale Rabelho, Apdo.2362, 8200-917
Albufeira, Algarve

☎  +351 289 583 030

✎  salgados.golf@mail.telepac.pt   www.nexus-pt.com/salgados

🚗 ✈ Faro: N125-10 airport exit road for Faro; r after 3km for
A22; after 7km 2nd sliproad r onto A22 for Portimão; exit 8 (km42)
for Algoz; at end of slip road l on N524 for Pêra; after 2.5km
straight across N125 into Pêra, whence after 500m l onto rua
Almeida Garrett; after 1.4km l at rbt (sign); after 2km r (sign); after
500m r into club entrance road.

| | m | p | | m | p |
|---|---|---|---|---|---|
| 1 | 320 | 4 | 10 | 390 | 4 |
| 2 | 485 | 5 | 11 | 300 | 4 |
| 3 | 170 | 3 | 12 | 130 | 3 |
| 4 | 360 | 4 | 13 | 295 | 4 |
| 5 | 375 | 4 | 14 | 490 | 5 |
| 6 | 515 | 5 | 15 | 545 | 5 |
| 7 | 415 | 4 | 16 | 320 | 4 |
| 8 | 135 | 3 | 17 | 180 | 3 |
| 9 | 350 | 4 | 18 | 305 | 4 |
| | 3125 | 36 | | 2955 | 36 |
| | | | | 6080 | 72 |

Almost flatter than Florida:
lake-lined, strategically
bunkered, peaceful course
suited to straight hitters, which
will cost off-game players many
balls, as the water seems to be
everywhere. Some challenging
greensites. Wildlife, especially
birds, abound.

*This low level view from the tee of long p4:7, probably the toughest and best hole
at Salgados, emphasises the flat terrain. The fairway seems to turn around the
bunker, which, lying some 150m from the front of the green, is there to catch your
drive. This may encourage you to play out to the right, but the boundary fence and
water beyond it (both just visible, upper centre right) run the entire length of the
hole. So there is only one solution: hit it straight!*

# SANTO DA SERRA

Trent Jones Snr   1991   €€                **H:** M 28, L 36, J 36

✉ Clube de Golfe Santo da Serra, Santo da Serra, 9200-152 Machico, Madeira

☎ +351 291 550 100

✎ reservations@santodaserragolf.com
www.santodaserragolf.com

🚗 ✈ Madeira: exit from airport perimeter; leave dual carriageway at first exit; take ER211 from rbt and follow signs for Santo da Serra – club on r approx 6km up, up, up the hill.

N.B.
Take warm clothing

| Machico | | | Desertas | | | Serras | | |
|---|---|---|---|---|---|---|---|---|
| | m | p | | m | p | | m | p |
| 1 | 364 | 4 | 1 | 361 | 4 | 1 | 518 | 5 |
| 2 | 403 | 4 | 2 | 523 | 5 | 2 | 363 | 4 |
| 3 | 476 | 5 | 3 | 288 | 4 | 3 | 339 | 4 |
| 4 | 185 | 3 | 4 | 422 | 4 | 4 | 297 | 4 |
| 5 | 377 | 4 | 5 | 327 | 4 | 5 | 160 | 3 |
| 6 | 333 | 4 | 6 | 171 | 3 | 6 | 396 | 4 |
| 7 | 492 | 5 | 7 | 508 | 5 | 7 | 274 | 4 |
| 8 | 154 | 3 | 8 | 152 | 3 | 8 | 149 | 3 |
| 9 | 352 | 4 | 9 | 353 | 4 | 9 | 424 | 5 |
| | 3136 | 36 | | 3105 | 36 | | 2920 | 36 |
| MD | 6241 | 72 | MS | 6056 | 72 | DS | 6025 | 72 |

*A multipurpose spectacular clear day view from the heights of the 9th green down to golden p5:3 (whose green is seen behind and right of the foreground 9th flagstick), and the ensuing dramatic p3:4 (which seems on the brink of the distant ocean). Bottom right is the 3rd fairway: after a drive over a huge swale, the hole turns left past the bunker on the right: cut the corner…? 4, played over a ravine beyond the 3rd green, is visible below the uppermost bunker.*

Challenging layout with views as spectacular as some of M's downhill opening holes. But what goes down has to come up again: unless you are very fit, best not to play both M and D without a buggy, as both have huge climbs; S is less hilly. Tricky, small greens. Fickle, cloudy climate.

# VILAMOURA (LAGUNA)

Lee    1990/93    €€                          **H:** M 28, L 36, J 36

✉  Laguna Course, 8125-507 Vilamoura, Algarve

☎  +351 289 310 333

✎  reservas_golfe@lusotur.pt    www.vilamoura.net

🚗  ✈ Faro: N125-10 airport exit road for Faro; r after 3km for A22; after 4km r onto N125 for Almancil; 11km past 1st Almancil sliproad l at lights into Vilamoura estate; r at 3rd rbt (1.5km); l at 2nd rbt (1km); l into club after 400m.

| | m | p | | m | p |
|---|---|---|---|---|---|
| 1 | 470 | 5 | 10 | 484 | 5 |
| 2 | 133 | 3 | 11 | 372 | 4 |
| 3 | 357 | 4 | 12 | 181 | 3 |
| 4 | 196 | 3 | 13 | 405 | 4 |
| 5 | 315 | 4 | 14 | 334 | 4 |
| 6 | 300 | 4 | 15 | 507 | 5 |
| 7 | 321 | 4 | 16 | 354 | 4 |
| 8 | 474 | 5 | 17 | 153 | 3 |
| 9 | 378 | 4 | 18 | 377 | 4 |
| | 2944 | 36 | | 3167 | 36 |
| | | | | 6111 | 72 |

This open, well-bunkered flattish course with a strong links feel may well rank second – i.e. only after The Old – at Vilamoura, for the purist player (though there may soon be a rival in Victoria). Exposed, so tough in the wind, but there are forward tees... Lateral water aplenty.

*Laguna's shortish p4 7th is part of the front 9, opened in 1990 – not so far from gold, primarily because of the superb bunkering inside the corner of the dogleg. There is more fairway out to the right, but the closer you play to the bunkers on the left, the more straight will be your line into a green which slopes up to a higher level at the back. This kind of green slope means that a ball played from the side is less likely to run up the putting surface in a controlled manner than one played from straight on, so the advantage of keeping close to the bunker is subtle but very real. Big hitters cutting off the dogleg will get very close, and earn classic 'passing-the-test-of-heroic-golf design' satisfaction. Joe Lee continued the theme with the back 9, which opened in 1993.*

# VILAMOURA (MILLENNIUM)

Lee/M Hawtree   1990/2000   €€        **H:** M 28, L 36, J 36

✉ Millennium Course, 8125-507 Vilamoura, Algarve

☎ +351 289 310 333

✎ reservas_golfe@lusotur.pt   www.vilamoura.net

🚗 ✈ Faro: N125-10 airport exit road for Faro; r after 3km for A22; after 4km r onto N125 for Almancil; 11km past 1st Almancil sliproad l at lights into Vilamoura estate; r at 3rd rbt (1.5km); l at 2nd rbt (1km); l into club after 400m.

| | m | p | | m | p |
|---|---|---|---|---|---|
| 1 | 325 | 4 | 10 | 339 | 4 |
| 2 | 391 | 4 | 11 | 467 | 5 |
| 3 | 203 | 3 | 12 | 317 | 4 |
| 4 | 502 | 5 | 13 | 188 | 3 |
| 5 | 423 | 4 | 14 | 334 | 4 |
| 6 | 151 | 3 | 15 | 122 | 3 |
| 7 | 374 | 4 | 16 | 378 | 4 |
| 8 | 440 | 5 | 17 | 345 | 4 |
| 9 | 354 | 4 | 18 | 504 | 5 |
| | 3163 | 36 | | 2994 | 36 |
| | | | | 6157 | 72 |

Challenging course with outstanding early 5 hole foray into pine forest – remaining holes will become more demanding (and aesthetically satisfying) as trees mature. Excellent greensites. 1-9 are Hawtree – placed in front of Lee's original Vilamoura 3 third 9.

*Millennium's all too brief foray into a pine wood has produced some outstandingly beautiful holes, the best of which is long p4:5, a right to left dogleg slightly downhill around trees to a green that is a little further away than it looks (the rolling fairway foreshortens the view) – all in all a gilt-edged combination of golfing challenge (mental and physical) and hazard placement (trees, plus two bunkers around the green), with an excellent greensite (slopes).*

# VILAMOURA (PINHAL)

Pennink/Trent Jones Jnr   1975/1985   €€    **H:** M 28, L 36, J 36

⊠  Pinhal Course, 8125-507 Vilamoura, Algarve

☎  +351 289 310 333

✎  reservas_golfe@lusotur.pt   www.vilamoura.net

🚗 ✈ Faro: N125-10 airport exit road for Faro; r after 3km for A22; after 4km r onto N125 for Almancil; 11km past 1st Almancil sliproad l at lights into Vilamoura estate; straight over 3 rbts into avenue whence (3.6km from estate entrance) U-bend l onto other side of avenue and immediately fork r; straight over 2 rbts into club (600m).

| | m | p | | m | p |
|---|---|---|---|---|---|
| 1 | 498 | 5 | 10 | 348 | 4 |
| 2 | 400 | 4 | 11 | 333 | 4 |
| 3 | 560 | 5 | 12 | 168 | 3 |
| 4 | 362 | 4 | 13 | 522 | 5 |
| 5 | 177 | 3 | 14 | 130 | 3 |
| 6 | 394 | 4 | 15 | 319 | 4 |
| 7 | 389 | 4 | 16 | 339 | 4 |
| 8 | 147 | 3 | 17 | 496 | 5 |
| 9 | 359 | 4 | 18 | 412 | 4 |
| | 3286 | 36 | | 3067 | 36 |
| | | | | 6353 | 72 |

Enjoy the delightful older holes, mostly on the stronger front 9 of this gently rolling, pine-lined residential layout. Newer, slightly hillier, holes to accommodate housing development are relatively disappointing, but may improve a little with maturity.

**17 red:** a longish, uphill p5, which turns sharply right some 210m from the tee and before the main climb begins. On a hole of this length one should be allowed to hit a full drive. Of course one could try cutting the corner, but that would take one dangerously close to the 11th. 17 just doesn't work.

*Pinhal's downhill medium p4:4 is a right to left dogleg around trees, with water (out of shot) to the right of the sloping green. This is in the centre of the best part of the course, where the original Pennink holes (upgraded by Trent Jones Jnr in 1985) predominate. It is a great pity that a significant part of the original layout had to be sacrificed on the altar of property development.*

# VILA SOL

Steel   1990/2000   €€€          **H:** M 27, L 35, J 27/35

✉ Vila Sol Golf Course, 8125-307 Vilamoura, Algarve

☎ +351 289 300 522

✐ golfsecretary@vilasol.pt   www.vilasol.pt

🚗 ✈ **Faro:** N125-10 airport exit road for Faro; r after 3km for A22; after 4km r onto N125 for Almancil; 5.3km past first Almancil slip road l at 'Quatros Estradas' traffic lights for Quarteira (sign) onto N396; club 2.8km on r.

| | Prime | | | Challenge | | | Prestige | |
|---|---|---|---|---|---|---|---|---|
| | m | p | | m | p | | m | p |
| 1 | 381 | 4 | 1 | 355 | 4 | 1 | 488 | 5 |
| 2 | 407 | 4 | 2 | 456 | 5 | 2 | 166 | 3 |
| 3 | 385 | 4 | 3 | 360 | 4 | 3 | 368 | 4 |
| 4 | 190 | 3 | 4 | 159 | 3 | 4 | 301 | 4 |
| 5 | 392 | 4 | 5 | 506 | 5 | 5 | 524 | 5 |
| 6 | 515 | 5 | 6 | 177 | 3 | 6 | 320 | 4 |
| 7 | 180 | 3 | 7 | 346 | 4 | 7 | 147 | 3 |
| 8 | 499 | 5 | 8 | 369 | 4 | 8 | 398 | 4 |
| 9 | 292 | 4 | 9 | 366 | 4 | 9 | 369 | 4 |
| | 3241 | 36 | | 3094 | 36 | | 3081 | 36 |
| PC | 6335 | 72 | PP | 6322 | 72 | CP | 6175 | 72 |

Well-conceived, often quite tight, primarily pine-lined former Portuguese Open layout over gently rolling ground with several testing water hazards (including some compulsory carries). A few greens are more tricky than first appear. (Prestige 9 added in 2000. More housing is planned.)

*Vila Sol's p3 13th (i.e. 4th on the Challenge 9) looks benign enough in the late afternoon shadows. If you hit it straight, it is. But look at the bunker on the left, and the trees around it: the hole is tighter than it seems, as the trees act as aerial hazards for anything off line. This hole is one of the prettiest at Vila Sol (mostly in pines, the Challenge 9 is the aesthete's loop).*

# ALGARVE SHORT COURSES

## ADOLFO DA QUINTA   Swan   1993   Free

✉ Adolfo da Quinta, Sitio dos Caliços, 8700-069 Moncarapacho, Algarve

☎ +351 289 790 790

✎ info@adolfodaquinta.com

🚗 ✈ Faro: N125-10 airport exit road for Faro; r after 3km for A22; after 7km r onto A22 for Spain; exit 15 Olhão (km93); straight over rbt for Moncarapacho; club on l after 1km.

|   | m | p |
|---|---|---|
| 1 | 150 | 3 |
| 2 | 72 | 3 |
| 3 | 72 | 3 |

## BALAIA   Southern Golf   2001   €

✉ Balaia Golf Village, Apdo. 917, 8200-912 Albufeira, Algarve

☎ +351 289 570 422

✎ golf@balaiagolfvillage.pt   www.balaiagolfvillage.pt

🚗 ✈ Faro: N125-10 airport exit road for Faro; r after 3km for A22; after 4km r onto N125 for Almancil; 12km past 1st Almancil sliproad l onto N526 for Albufeira (sign); follow road for approx 7km; l into side road (sign) by sign "freguesia de Olhos d'Àgua"; r after 150m; l after 900m and follow signs to club.

|   | m | p |
|---|---|---|
| 1 | 73 | 3 |
| 2 | 139 | 3 |
| 3 | 67 | 3 |
| 4 | 160 | 3 |
| 5 | 106 | 3 |
| 6 | 83 | 3 |
| 7 | 148 | 3 |
| 8 | 126 | 3 |
| 9 | 82 | 3 |
|   | 984 | 27 |

## MARAGOTA   Cavaco   2003   €   H: M 28, L 36, J 36

✉ Maragota Golf, Colina Verde Aparthotel, Sítio da Maragota, 8700-078 Moncarapacho, Algarve

☎ +351 289 790 110

✎ reservations@golfcolinaverde.com
www.golfcolinaverde.com

🚗 ✈ Faro: N125-10 airport exit road for Faro; r after 3km for A22; after 7km r onto A22 for Spain; exit 15 Olhão (km93); straight over rbt for Moncarapacho; after 2.2km l at fork; after 700m l at lights; after follow road for 3km, r for 400m to club.

|   | m | p |
|---|---|---|
| 1 | 83 | 3 |
| 2 | 250 | 4 |
| 3 | 97 | 3 |
| 4 | 117 | 3 |
| 5 | 163 | 3 |
| 6 | 101 | 3 |
| 7 | 80 | 3 |
| 8 | 104 | 3 |
| 9 | 151 | 3 |
|   | 1146 | 28 |

## VALE DE MILHO   Thomas   1990   €

✉ Vale de Milho Golf, Apdo. 1273, 8400-911 Carvoeiro, Lagoa, Algarve

☎ +351 282 358 502   Rsrvd membs til 12 , Tue & Fri

✎ valedemilhogolf@mail.telepac.pt
www.valedomilhogolf.com

🚗 ✈ Faro: N125-10 airport exit road for Faro; r after 3km for A22; after 7km 2nd sliproad r onto A22 for Portimão: exit 6 (km 39); r onto N125 for Lagoa (8km); l onto N124-1 at 2nd traffic light junction for Carvoeiro; after 300m follow l fork in road; after 2.1km l (not signed) for Poço Partido; after 100m r (sign); after 1.1km l (sign); l after 500m (sign); l after 400m (sign); r after 200m (sign) club entrance 200m on l.

|   | m | p |
|---|---|---|
| 1 | 110 | 3 |
| 2 | 154 | 3 |
| 3 | 68 | 3 |
| 4 | 86 | 3 |
| 5 | 116 | 3 |
| 6 | 75 | 3 |
| 7 | 95 | 3 |
| 8 | 88 | 3 |
| 9 | 134 | 3 |
|   | 926 | 27 |

*Maragota's p3:4, from right of the green, with the sun about to set over a distant mountain. There are more slopes to this green than first meet the eye.*

Driving ranges aside, the Algarve is blessed with four fairly peaceful facilities for practice – for beginners or for those who just want to play 9 holes in relatively relaxed surroundings. **Balaia**, just outside Albufeira, is a pleasant p3 course within a village complex, but with a rustic feel (N.B. some of the holes here would be distinctly difficult for beginners). **Maragota**, towards Spain (near *Quinta de Cima* and *Quinta da Ria*) has one p4 and eight p3s, attached to a hotel; some water and elevated greens means that a few holes are not at all easy – at least not at this level. **Vale de Milho**, also a p3 course (near *Gramacho* and *Pinta*) is perhaps the best-designed of these layouts, and also the most popular. In addition, if you want a charming, well-appointed country hotel with occasional free golf, **Adolfo da Quinta** (3 p3 greens with 9 tees), near Maragota, might suit you. There are also two short courses at *Penina*, an academy in *Vilamoura* at Supergolf, another attached to *Quinta da Cima*, a 9 hole par 3 garden course at **Vila Vita Parc** (a hotel in Armação de Pêra), and sundry other practice facilities along the coast. (*Pine Cliffs* has its own separate entry and short courses at other clubs are referred to under their own entries.)

# USEFUL INFORMATION

## DESIGNERS OF RATED COURSES

**Javier Arana** (E 1904-1974) *Designer* Famous amateur player – first laid out courses in 1936, becoming respected contemporary designer – known for leaving lone trees in fairway. Arguably the greatest Spanish designer, but only ever designed in his home country: *El Saler, Club de Campo (Negro), Guadalmina (Sur), Neguri, Río Real,* and *Ulzama* the most notable. Died before finishing *Aloha* (with more of his input, it may have been ✈ – a very near miss).

**Severiano Ballesteros** (E 1957-) *Player* Nephew of golfing legend Ramon Sota, Seve grew up on the Colt-designed *Pedreña,* practising on the beach. Turned pro in 1974. Success soon followed in late 1970s and early 1980s: multiple Open and Masters Champion. Formed Trajectory Golf Course Design, 1986. First course is *Novo Sancti Petri*, 1990, latest (no. 14) *San Roque (New)* with Perry Dye, 2003. Also *Alhaurín, Los Arqueros, Izki,* 4th 9 at *Club de Campo* and 3rd 9 at *Pedreña.*

**Bob Cameron/Chris Powell** (GB 1952-/ GB 1949-) *Player/Designer* **Bob Cameron**, whose spiritual home is Lochiel Scotland, played the Tour in the mid 1970s. In the early 1980s (with Chris Cameron) managed Miller Buckley in Europe, USA and Australia. 1987 – formed Cameron Powell to construct and operate Abbey Park Golf and Country Club, UK. 1993 won SATA Azores Open at *Furnas*. **Chris Powell** from 1981 to 1986 managed Miller Buckley (with Chairman Sir Michael Bonallack) at the forefront of innovative golf development. Incorporated into Cotton Pennink Lawrie and Partners (which Chris was managing at the time). Also joint ventures with Arnold Palmer, Graham Marsh, and Bernhard Langer. Jointly responsible for *Batalha* and sensitive extension of *Furnas* (5-13), Azores.

**Harry Shapland Colt** (GB 1869-1951) *Designer* Cambridge-educated solicitor and distinguished amateur golfer, first assisted Douglas Rolland in design of Rye Golf Club, 1894. Secretary at Sunningdale, 1901-1913. Soon abandoned law practice and before WW1 became one of the world's leading course designers. Colt brought on many first-rate golf architects, including C H Alison and Alister MacKenzie. The first truly professional course architect – first to use a drawing board in preparing layout plans, and first to prepare tree planting plans. Many famous courses worldwide. In Iberia *Málaga, Pedreña, Puerta de Hierro (Arriba)* and *Sant Cugat.*

**Sir Henry Cotton** (GB 1907-1987) *Player* Public schoolboy turned pro golfer at 17. Won Open 3 times (only GB champion between 1914 and 1969). Like Gene Sarazen, helped professional golfers become respected in the game. Trained under Sir Guy Campbell as golf architect; worked with J. Hamilton Stutt, before setting up own practice in late 1950s. Pioneer of Algarve golf, knighted a few days before his death. Many courses in UK and Europe: *Vale do Lobo* (original 27 holes) and *Penina,* Portugal his most famous. *Alto* and *Benamor*, completed after his death, based on outline layouts, might have been better had he been involved in their implementation.

**Perry Dye**  (US 1952-) *Designer*  Son of golf architects Pete and Alice Dye, involved in business from early age, but after graduating formed own company concentrating on housing construction. When this failed returned to father's firm and set up own course design company, 1982, concentrating on real estate development courses in US. Collaborated with Seve Ballesteros to produce *San Roque (New)*.

**European Golf Design**  *Players/Designers*  Company responsible for design of courses using the talents of many European Tour players. Notably *PGA de Catalunya* by Neil Coles (GB 1934-) & Ángel Gallardo (E 1943-), Panorámica by Bernhard Langer (D 1957-) and Ribagolfe by Michael King (GB 1948-) and Peter Townsend (GB 1946-). EGD also do minor works on courses used regularly on Tour e.g. *Quinta do Lago* and *Santo da Serra*. In-house designers support players – Ross McMurray (GB 1964-) is believed to be mainly responsible for Panorámica and Ribagolfe. Also *Morgado* (both courses by Russell Talley, US 1959-).

**Ronald W Fream**  (US 1942-) *Designer*  Employed by RTJ from 1966-1969. Worked as construction manager to R F Lawrence in 1970 and then briefly associated with Robert Muir Graves. Formed golf design firm with Peter Thomson and John Harris. 1980 – left to operate own business. Work in Portugal: Estoril Sol (now Int Golf Academy), 1976, with Harris, Wolveridge & Thomson; *Gramacho, Pinta* and *Pinheiros Altos*.

**José (Pepe) Gancedo**  (E 1938-) *Designer*  Five-time amateur champion of Spain, branching into design, 1971. A successful businessman and an often colourful designer, not least of courses in Spain – notably *Golf del Sur, Monte Mayor* and *Torrequebrada*. Also *Lerma*, and *La Herrería* (remodelled 1-9).

**Robert von Hagge**  (US 1930-) *Player*  Son of course constructor Ben Hagge, agricultural engineering graduate, 1951. Spent a few years on Tour, then as club pro. 1957 – trained as designer under Dick Wilson, establishing own firm, 1963. Renowned as showman, added 'von' to his original name. 1968 – formed partnership with Bruce Devlin, Australia, opening a year later in US. In 1980s joined with Smelek and Baril, working on emerging markets – many notable courses around the world. Les Bordes (France), *Empordà* and *RHSE Club de Campo* (Spain) are fine examples.

**Frederick William Hawtree**  (GB 1916-2000) *Designer*  Educated Oxford. Joined father's firm Hawtree & Taylor, 1938. Captured by Japanese, WW2. Upon release started practice as Hawtree & Son, and continued after father's death (1955), designing courses worldwide. Notably *Platja de Pals*, Spain, 1966. Joined in firm by AHF Jiggens, 1969, and by son Martin, 1974. Also *Lisbon Sports*, Llavaneras, *Terramar* (superseded by current Fazio), *Son Vida*. (Son Martin, born in 1947, designed *Pine Cliffs*, the new holes and related remodelling at *Lisbon Sports*, and *Vilamoura (Millennium)* (1-9).)

**Arthur Wright Hills**  (US 1930-) *Designer*  Graduate of Michigan State. Successful with garden business until added 'Golf Architect' to yellow pages listing, 1966 – phone went red hot. Started design practice in 1967, mainly in Florida; recently famous for spectacular *Oitavos*, Portugal.

**Robert Trent Jones Snr** ('RTJ') (US 1906-2000; b. GB)  *Designer*  Moved to US aged 5. Scratch player, educated Cornell. 1930 – joined Stanley Thompson at Thompson, Jones & Co, a firm influential in promoting strategic design, with the principle "hard par easy bogey". By 1960s had become the most known and influential designer in history: by 1980 over 400 courses in play worldwide. Two sons, Robert Jnr and Rees, are both successful designers. Iberian courses (mainly overseen by Cabell Robinson): *El Bosque, Las Brisas, La Cañada* (1-9), *Mijas (Olivos & Lagos), Los Naranjos, Marbella Golf, Quinta da Marinha, Santo da Serra, Sotogrande, Troia, Valderrama* (remodelled from his original Sotogrande Los Aves).

**Robert Trent Jones Jnr** (US 1939-)  *Designer*  Educated Yale. Joined father's design firm, 1962. Set up own firm in California, 1973. Pioneer in Australasia, 1970s. Advocate of concept that course is a work of art within environment. More than 220 courses to date worldwide, including World Cup and other championship venues. Champion of environmental issues and bold bunkering, combining traditional shaping with modern concerns of visibility and maintenance. Asked which was his best course, replied: "The next course is always the best one". Courses include *Bonmont, Penha Longa, Puerta de Hierro (Abajo)*, most recently Al Cañada (Mallorca).

**Joe Lee** (US 1922-2003)  *Designer*  Whilst assistant pro at club in Florida lodged with Architect Dick Wilson. In 1952 quit job and assisted Wilson to complete construction of nearby course. Full partner in firm 1959 and completed 4 courses after Wilson's death in 1965. Continued with same team under own name creating many quality courses, notably *San Lorenzo* (assisted by Roquemore), Portugal. Also Vilamoura 3 *(now Laguna* and *Millennium 10-18)*.

**Bernhard von Limburger** (D 1901-1981)  *Designer*  Successful as amateur golfer for Germany between wars, then in design partnership with Karl Hoffman. End of WW2 fled advancing Russians and ended up building courses for Americans stationed in Germany. Notably designed *Atalaya (Old)* Spain.

**William Follet Mitchell** (US 1912-1974)  *Designer*  Respected greenkeeper. First helped Orin Smith with course construction in New England in late 1930s. Late 1940s-mid 1950s ran design construction company Mitchell Brothers with Samuel and Henry. Then worked alone, famous for coining the phrase "executive course". One of last designs was the original 27 holes at *Quinta do Lago,* Portugal, his only course outside US.

**Greg Norman** (AUS 1955-)  *Player*  First played golf aged 16, turned pro in 1976. Successful career through 1980s and 1990s – the first player ever to win order of merit either side of the Atlantic. >80 wins worldwide. Heads Great White Shark Enterprises, which includes a course design company. New *El Prat* courses are his first design in Iberia.

**José María Olazábal** (E 1966-)  *Player*  Won Spanish under 9 Championship aged 7. Glittering amateur and professional golf career (multiple US Masters Champion); still competitive. Established as a designer of quality courses, his *Sevilla* course hosting World Cup, 2004. Other courses include *Masía Bach,* Costa Ballena (Jerez) and Basozábal (San Sebastián).

**Arnold Palmer** (US 1929-) *Player* Charismatic attitude made him the people's champion through 1960s and 1970s. Bought Bay Hill in late 1960s, remodelling many holes. First worked as design consultant with Francis Duane, 1969-74; then joined Edwin Seay, forming Palmer Course Design. Usually delegates much of work to professionals in his firm. Many courses in the US and a few elsewhere, notably the first course in Communist China and *Vilamoura (Victoria),* Portugal (in house designer: Vicky Martz).

**John Jacob Frank Pennink** (GB 1913-1983; b. NL) *Designer* Oxford-educated, distinguished amateur golfer (Amateur Champion 1937 & 1938). 1954 – joined established design practice of CK Cotton; soon headed Cotton, Pennink, Lawrie and Partners. Designed around the world except in Americas. Woburn probably his most famous British course. In Portugal: *Vilamoura (Old),* Dom Pedro (partly remodelled into *Vilamoura Pinhal), Palmares,* and *Aroeira (1).*

**Gary Jim Player** (SA 1935-) *Player* Outstanding playing career; one of 'Big Three' in 1960s, with Nicklaus and Palmer. In 1970s associated with American architects Kirby, Griffiths, and Davies (whilst also first golf director at *La Manga*) and in 1980s became golf consultant for Florida-based Karl Litten. Many courses in America and Africa, Sun City being the most famous, plus *El Paraíso,* Escorpión, Almerimar, *Zaudín* in Spain.

**Chris Powell** (see under Bob Cameron)

**Robert Dean Putman** (US date of birth unknown) *Designer* Multiple course record holding amateur golfer and artist (educated at University of Fresno). First worked as artistic director for a TV station. Joined golf architect Bob Baldock as a draughtsman in the late 1940s. In 1954 formed his own modest firm based in California, designing in North America, Hawaii and the Far East. Considered golf design as an extension of his art and sculpture. In Spain designed *La Manga (North & South)* and *Villamartín,* as well as the contemporary Las Lomas-El Bosque course near Madrid.

**Cabell Robinson** (US 1941-) *Designer* Educated Princeton, Harvard (met Rees Jones, son of RTJ), and Berkeley. 1967 – worked for RTJ, establishing Spanish branch, 1970, in Iberia notably assisted with *Mijas,* Sotogrande Los Aves (now *Valderrama), Los Naranjos* and *Troia.* 1987 – established own Spanish-based firm; designs courses across Europe and Morocco, in Iberia most notably *Praia d'el Rey, Santana* and *La Reserva de Sotogrande.* Also *Palheiro, Castillo de Gorraiz* and *La Cala.*

**William A 'Rocky' Roquemore Jnr** (US 1948-) *Designer* Floridian designer Joe Lee employed Rocky as construction foreman in 1969. By 1971 primary associate handling all work outside Florida. Received little public acknowledgment, although actively involved in e.g. *San Lorenzo (*long attributed solely to Lee). Lengthy association with late 20th/21st century Portuguese golf boom, most notably *Quinta de Cima.* Also *Quinta da Ria, Quinta do Peru, Vale do Lobo* (9 new holes at *Royal* and general remodelling), *Quinta do Lago* (9 new holes at *North), Belas* and *Quinta da Beloura.*

**Philip Mackenzie Ross** (GB 1890-1974) *Designer* In Army, WW1. 1920 – met Tom Simpson, who employed him as a construction manager. Mid 1920s – late 1930s partner in Simpson & Ross. From end of 1930s worked alone across Britain and Continent. Notable courses include:

Portugal – *Estoril* (remodelling), *Furnas* (original 9) and *Oporto* (remodelling); Spain – *Málaga* with Tom Simpson, *Maspalomas* (remodelling); most famous for remodelling Turnberry, Scotland after WW2.

**Francisco López Segalés** (E 1951-) *Designer* Followed father's footsteps as Golf Superintendant at *La Moraleja*, 1973. 1982 – started course design, full-time as Segalesgolf from 1990, remaining consultant to La Moraleja until 2001. Designed and built many courses including *Son Antem (East & West)*, *Ulzama* (10-18). Worked with Piñero on *Monte Paraíso*.

**Tom Simpson** (GB 1877-1964) *Designer* Wealthy Cambridge-educated lawyer and scratch golfer. First became interested in design when home club, Woking, was remodelled by its members. By 1910 closed legal practice and joined Herbert Fowler. After WW1 joined by Abecromby & Croome. Hired PM Ross as assistant in 1920s. By late 20s split from Fowler, forming partnership with creative Ross. In 30s called in famous lady golfer Molly Gourlay, thus becoming first designer to solicit a woman's opinion on the art. Always oversaw construction, so was not as prolific as some. Colourful character: made site visits in Silver Rolls Royce, wearing embroidered cape and beret. Retired at outbreak of WW2, but continued to write into 1950s. In Spain worked on *Terramar* (layout superseded by current Fazio), *Málaga, San Sebastián, Puerta de Hierro*.

**Donald Steel** (GB 1937-) *Designer* Scratch amateur golfer. Educated Cambridge, became golf writer in 1961. Then joined firm of CK Cotton, Pennink, Lawrie and Partners, 1965. 1971 – full partner, responsible for many courses in UK plus in Iberia Miramar, *Aroeira (2)* and *Vila Sol*.

**Blake Stirling** (US 1952-) *Designer* Son of golf pro, educated University of Colorado, successful amateur and 3 year pro playing career, regaining amateur status in 1980. Masters in Landscape Architecture at Colorado 1985. Worked for Killian Design, 1986-1987, before joining Dye Designs working on many courses until 1993. Moved to Ken Kavanagh's practice until 1997. 1998 – commissioned to build *El Cortijo* and moved to Canaries, since which time designed several courses in Spain, including Golf Layos (near Toledo), Logroño Municipal, Sherry Golf (Jerez), all of which he considers at least as good as *El Cortijo*. Also remodelled *Guadalmina (Sur)*.

**Dave Thomas** (GB 1934-) *Player* After successful playing career joined Peter Alliss in late 1960s to design and build courses in UK. For a while in 1980s concentrated on construction, but now established as a popular course designer in Europe including *Almenara, La Cañada (10-18), La Manga (West), Marbella Club* and *San Roque (Old)*, Spain.

*If any reader has corrections or relevant information relating to these biographies, we would be pleased to receive them (preferably by email).*

## TOP 5 DESIGNERS
### (by number of rated courses)

| | |
|---|---|
| Trent Jones Snr | 7 rated (of 11 in book) |
| Arana | 6 rated (of 7) |
| PM Ross | 4 rated (of 5) |
| von Hagge | 4 rated (of 4) |
| Colt | 4 rated (of 4) |

## DESIGNERS VS PLAYERS
### (by number of rated courses)

| | |
|---|---|
| Designers | 22 |
| Players | 11 |

# Recommended Reading

There is a whole library of books on golf design. We include only a brief listing, to get you further into the subject.

*The Anatomy of a Golf Course*, Tom Doak, 1992
*The Architects of Golf*, Geoffrey Cornish & Ronald Whitten,
    (formerly published as *The Golf Course*, 1988)
    We are indebted to the authors of this book, which we have used as a
    principal source for many of the designer biographies
*Golf Architecture*, Dr Alister MacKenzie, 1920
*The Links*, Robert Hunter, (reprinted) 1999
*Some Essays on Golf Course Architecture*, Colt & Alison, 1920
*The World Atlas of Golf*, Hamlyn (ed Ward-Thomas and Rowlinson), 2001

Many of these books are out of print, but a good source for second hand books on golf design is Rhod McEwan Golf Books – www.rhodmcewan.com

# Glossary of Golf Design Terms

**Aesthetics** The quality of the visual, sensual (and occasionally aural) impression provided during the experience of playing individual holes and the golf course as a whole.
**Blind (or blind shot)** Situation in which the player cannot see the target from any point on a hole where the player should be if playing the hole reasonably as intended by the designer.
**Dogleg** Golf hole which turns a distinct corner from the original line of play from the tee.
**Double dogleg** Golf hole which turns two distinct corners from the initial line of play – the second turn normally being in the opposite direction to the first.
**Enhancement** Embellishment of an existing design, generally without re-routing, nor to the extent that the course is so changed as for the work to constitute remodelling (e.g. addition of bunkers and tees, or tree amendment).
**Fair** A course or a hole is fair when its features are openly presented to the player, so that playing errors are due to the player himself making such errors, rather than due to an aspect of the course of which the player is not given reasonable notice.
**Greensite** The whole complex of a green and its immediate surroundings, including humps, swales, bunkers and other immediately adjoining features.
**Hazard** Design feature (whose definition has widened with developments in design), which makes the playing of the hole more challenging, e.g. bunkers, water, trees, swales (especially when combined with short grass), humps, and long grass (i.e. longer than normal rough – undesirable because of ball searches).
**Heroic design** A type of design which gives the player an opportunity to take on risks (e.g. cutting corner of dogleg by driving over bunkers, water or even rough) resulting in higher chances of lower score; success should render heroic satisfaction. There should always be room for an alternative stratgey. (A classic example of such a hole is do-I-have-a-go-for-the-green-in-1-but-then-I-must-carry-the-water? p4:10 at The Brabazon Course, The Belfry, England.)
**Holiday Course** Related to, and in some ways the forerunner of, the Resort Course, often shorter and less demanding than a traditional design, also intended to be fun and more relaxing; generally to be found in holiday locations.

**Links**  The original terrain of golf: ground which 'links' the land to the sea, also often used for common grazing. Its sandy soil, giving a base for springy turf, was generally formed by the sea, wind, and animals that lived there. The often uneven surfaces mean that links golf can seem a little unfair to the uninitiated, but such courses really test the player's resolve to keep going, despite bad luck – on such courses, the best player inevitably wins. There is little such ground outside Great Britain, Ireland and land adjoining the North Sea and English Channel. The term is often misused (generally for marketing purposes) to denote land adjoining the sea, on which golf is played (e.g *Alcaidesa* Links). The most links-like ground we have seen in Iberia is at *Oporto*, but links features (i.e. sand but not the springy turf of true links) are to be seen most notably at *Estela, Málaga, Maspalomas, Praia d'el Rey* and *El Saler*.

**Penal design**  A type of design where the perfect shot is rewarded but almost anything else is severely punished; in such design, the designer gives the player no option but to take on risks (the do-or-die island green p3:17 at TPC Sawgrass, Florida is a classic example).

**Remodel**  A golf course is remodelled when the work carried out significantly changes the design of holes, although not necessarily involving re-routing (e.g. changing the bunkering, moving tees and/or significantly changing greens)

**Renovation**  Making good defects to the design and condition of a golf course – a process more of repair than change.

**Re-routing**  Adjustment to a course layout involving significant changes in the sites of tees and greens, so that the course (or parts of it) takes a different route around the land on which it is sited.

**Resort Course**  A golf course designed to be more user friendly than a traditional course, often without significant rough, generally found in lavish holiday locations and designed to be appealing, fun and bold in appearance.

**Restore**  A golf course is restored if the work carried out generally returns it to how its designer originally designed it (though increasingly with sensitive and sympathetic adjustments to allow for the extra distance achievable with modern equipment).

**Reverse camber**  On a dogleg hole, land which slopes in the opposite direction to the turn in the hole and therefore does not help the ball go round the corner – generally an undesirable feature.

**Routing**  The way the holes are laid out over the land used for the golf course, and how the holes relate to the terrain and its opportunities or restrictions. The quality of the routing is crucial and generally closely related to the overall quality of the course because of the strong influence it can have on both the golfing test and aesthetic merits (or demerits).

**Run offs**  Short grass slopes on, and immediately adjoining, greens which cause misplaced shots to run off the green into nearby fairway, rough or hazards. The concept of short grass as a hazard should not be undervalued in golf design.

**Semi-blind (or semi-blind shot)**  As for blind shot, except the player can see part but not all of the target (or relevant ground between himself and the target).

**Strategic design**  The type of design which offers the player a choice of different ways to play a golf hole, ideally where risk and reward are balanced (i.e. riskier option may result in fewer strokes if successfully executed). St Andrews (Old) is the classic example of a strategic golf course.

**Swales**  Gentle depressions (often near greens) designed to catch or deflect the slightly errant shot and sometimes also test a player's distance judgment.

# TOP TENS (LISTED IN ALPHABETICAL ORDER)

## Playing Challenge
Empordà (Links)
Furnas
Oitavos
Platja de Pals
PGA de Catalunya
El Prat (Yellow)
Quinta do Lago (South)
RHSE Club de Campo (Norte)
Troia
Valderrama

## Mental Challenge
Empordà (Forest)
Furnas
Málaga
Marbella Golf
Oitavos
Quinta de Cima
La Reserva de Sotogrande
RHSE Club de Campo (Norte)
Valderrama
Vilamoura (Old)

## Use of Land
Empordà (Forest)
Empordà (Links)
Marbella Golf
PGA de Catalunya
Praia d'el Rey
El Prat (Red)
Puerta de Hierro (Arriba)
La Reserva de Sotogrande
Troia
Vilamoura (Old)

## Quality of Hazards
Empordà (Forest)
Empordà (Links)
Pedreña
PGA de Catalunya
El Prat (Red)
El Prat (Yellow)
Puerta de Hierro (Arriba)
RHSE Club de Campo (Norte)
San Lorenzo
Troia

## Aesthetics
Empordà (Forest)
Furnas
Monte Mayor
Pedreña
PGA de Catalunya
Platja de Pals
El Prat (Red)
Quinta de Cima
Ulzama
Vilamoura (Old)

## Greensites
Las Brisas
Empordà (both courses – sorry, cheating!)
Furnas
PGA de Catalunya
Praia d'el Rey
Quinta de Cima
El Prat (Red)
El Prat (Yellow)
La Reserva de Sotogrande
RHSE Club de Campo (Norte)

## Variety
Furnas
Oitavos
El Prat (Red)
Puerta de Hierro (Arriba)
La Reserva de Sotogrande
RHSE Club de Campo (Norte)
San Lorenzo
Sevilla
Sotogrande
Vilamoura (Old)

## Stylistic Integrity & Consistency
Furnas
Penina (Championship)
PGA de Catalunya
Puerta de Hierro (Arriba)
RHSE Club de Campo (Norte)
San Lorenzo
Sevilla
Troia
Ulzama
Vilamoura (Old)

## Fairness
Empordà (Forest)
Furnas
Málaga
Oitavos
Puerta de Hierro (Arriba)
El Saler
San Lorenzo
Sevilla
Sotogrande
Vilamoura (Old)

## Routing
Furnas
Bonmont
Oitavos
Pedreña
Puerta de Hierro (Arriba)
RHSE Club de Campo (Norte)
El Saler
San Lorenzo
Sotogrande
Vilamoura (Old)

## History
Club de Campo (Negro)
Málaga
Pedreña
Penina (Championship)
Puerta de Hierro (Arriba)
El Saler
Sant Cugat
Sotogrande
Valderrama
Vilamoura (Old)

## Negatives* (Bottom 10)
Alto
Benalup
Cabopino
Castro Marim
La Dama de Noche
Isla Canela
Islantilla
La Noria
Santa María
Valle del Este

* A negative is not necessarily a sign of a bad hole, so much as an avoidable feature.

# COURSES BY AIRPORT
## LISTED IN ★/ALPHA ORDER

*Particularly enjoyable courses are set in italics*

**PORTUGAL**

**Oporto**
↗
**Oporto**
*Estela*

**Faro**
★★
*Vilamoura (Old)*

★
*Penina (Chmpshp)*
*Quinta de Cima*
*San Lorenzo*

↗
*Pinta*
*Quinta do Lago (S)*
Vale do Lobo
  (Ocean & Royal)
*Vilamoura*
  *(Victoria)*

*Adolfo da Quinta*
Alto
*Balaia*
Benamor
Boavista
Castro Marim
Gramacho
Isla Canela
Islantilla
Maragota
Morgado
Parque da Floresta
*Palmares*
*Pine Cliffs*
Pinheiros Altos
Quinta da Ria
Quinta do Lago (N)
Salgados
Vale de Milho
Vilamoura (Laguna
  Millennium &
  Pinhal)
Vila Sol

**Santander**
★ *Pedreña*

**Lisbon**
★★
*Oitavos*
*Troia*

★
*Praia d'el Rey*
*Quinta do Peru*

↗
*Aroeira 1*
Penha Longa

Aroeira 2
Belas
*Estoril*
Lisbon Sports Club
Montado
Quinta da Marinha
Quinta de Beloura

**S**

**Sevilla**
↗
*Sevilla*
Zaudín

**Jerez**
Montecastillo
Novo Sancti Petri (A & B)

**Ponta Delgada**
★★
*Furnas* Batalha

**Tenerife (Sur)**
★
*Golf del Sur*
Las Américas

**Funchal**
Santo da Serra
*Palheiro*

**Gran Canaria**
↗
El Cortijo
Maspalomas

Salobre

**Gibraltar**
★★
*Sotogrande*

★
*La Reserva de*
  *Sotogrande*
*Valderrama*

↗
**San Roque (New)**

Alcaidesa
Almenara
Benalup
La Cañada
Montenmedio
San Roque (Old)

# FRANCE

**Bilbao**
↗ *Neguri*

**San Sebastián**
San Sebastián

**Vitoria**
zki

**Iruña/Pamplona**
★
*Ulzama*

Castillo de Gorraiz

**Girona**
★★
*Empordà (Forest)*
*PGA de Catalunya*

★
*Empordà (Links)*
*Platja de Pals*

**Madrid**
★★
*RSHE Club de*
*Campo*
*(Norte)*
*Puerta de*
*Hierro*
*(Arriba)*

★
Club de Campo
(Negro)
*Puerta de*
*Hierro (Abajo)*
RHSE Club de
Campo (Sur)

La Herrería
Lerma
La Moraleja (1)
La Moraleja (2)

**Barcelona**
★
*El Prat (Red)*

↗
**Bonmont**
*El Prat (Yellow)*
**Sant Cugat**

Masía Bach
Terramar

**SPAIN**

**Valencia**
★
*El Saler*
↗
**El Bosque**
Mediterráneo

**Palma de Mallorca**
↗
**Son Antem (West)**

Andratx
Son Antem (East)
Son Muntaner
*Son Vida*

**Alicante**
↗
*La Manga (North*
*South & West)*
Villamartín

 **Almería**
Desert Springs
Valle del Este

| **Málaga** | *Mijas (Lagos)* | Atalaya (New) | Los Flamingos | Monte Paraíso |
|---|---|---|---|---|
| ★ | *Los Naranjos* | Cabopino | Greenlife | La Noria |
| *Las Brisas* | *Río Real* | La Cala (North, | Guadalhorce | *El Paraíso* |
| *Málaga* | *Torrequebrada* | South & | Guadalmina | Santa Clara |
| | *Santana* | Academy) | (Norte) | Santa María |
| ↗ | | *Coto la Serena* | Lauro | La Siesta |
| *Atalaya (Old)* | Alhaurín | La Dama de | Marbella Club | El Soto |
| **Guadalmina** | *Aloha* | Noche | Mijas (Olivos) | La Quinta |
| **(Sur)** | Los Arqueros | La Duquesa | Miraflores | La Zagaleta |
| *Marbella Golf* | Artola | Estepona | *Monte Mayor* | |

# EXCELLENCE

**The Best Spanish 18** *(with correct hole numbers)*

| | hole | p | | hole | p |
|---|---|---|---|---|---|
| **Platja de Pals** | 1 | 4 | **RSHE Club de Campo (North)** | 10 | 5 |
| **Sotogrande** | 2 | 5 | **Empordà (Forest)** | 11 | 4 |
| *La Cala (Academy)* | 3 | 3 | **Málaga** | 12 | 5 |
| *Monte Mayor* | 4 | 5 | **Valderrama** | 13 | 4 |
| Bonmont | 5 | 3 | Ulzama | 14 | 4 |
| Mijas (Lagos) | 6 | 4 | **La Manga (West)** | 15 | 5 |
| **Sotogrande** | 7 | 4 | PGA de Catalunya | 16 | 3 |
| **Golf del Sur (Links)** | 8 | 4 | **Villamartín** | 17 | 3 |
| **Puerta de Hierro (Arriba)** | 9 | 4 | **Puerta de Hierro (Abajo)** | 18 | 4 |

**The Best Portuguese 18** *(with correct hole numbers)*

| | hole | p | | hole | p |
|---|---|---|---|---|---|
| **Vilamoura Old** | 1 | 4 | *Quinta da Ria* | 10 | 4 |
| **Troia** | 2 | 3 | **Oitavos** | 11 | 4 |
| *Santo da Serra* | 3 | 5 | Furnas | 12 | 4 |
| **Furnas** | 4 | 4 | **Quinta do Peru** | 13 | 5 |
| *Vilamoura (Millennium)* | 5 | 4 | *Palheiro* | 14 | 4 |
| *Palmares* | 6 | 4 | Vale do Lobo (Ocean) | 15 | 3 |
| San Lorenzo | 7 | 4 | **Vale do Lobo (Royal)** | 16 | 3 |
| Oporto | 8 | 3 | Quinta do Lago (South) | 17 | 5 |
| *Morgado* | 9 | 4 | Vilamoura (Old) | 18 | 4 |

**Spanish Gold**

| | | | | | |
|---|---|---|---|---|---|
| | | | **El Prat (Yellow)** | 12 | 3 |
| *La Cala (South)* | 17 | 3 | **Puerta de Hierro (Abajo)** | 18 | 4 |
| *La Cala (Academy)* | 3 | 3 | **Puerta de Hierro (Arriba)** | 8 | 4 |
| **Empordà (Forest)** | 11 | 4 | **Puerta de Hierro (Arriba)** | 9 | 4 |
| **Golf del Sur (Links)** | 8 | 4 | **RHSE Club de Campo (Norte)** | 10 | 5 |
| **Golf del Sur (South)** | 2 | 3 | **El Saler** | 8 | 4 |
| **Las Brisas** | 12 | 5 | **El Saler** | 17 | 3 |
| **Málaga** | 12 | 5 | **Santana** | 4 | 5 |
| **La Manga (West)** | 15 | 5 | **Sant Cugat** | 1 | 4 |
| **Marbella Golf** | 2 | 5 | **Sotogrande** | 2 | 5 |
| *Monte Mayor* | 4 | 5 | **Sotogrande** | 7 | 4 |
| **Pedreña** | 8 | 4 | **Valderrama** | 1 | 4 |
| **PGA de Catalunya** | 11 | 3 | **Valderrama** | 13 | 4 |
| **Platja de Pals** | 1 | 4 | **Villamartín** | 17 | 3 |

**Portuguese Gold**

| | | | | | |
|---|---|---|---|---|---|
| *Estela* | 4 | 3 | **Praia d'el Rey** | 4 | 4 |
| **Furnas** | 2 | 3 | *Quinta da Ria* | 10 | 4 |
| **Furnas** | 4 | 4 | **Quinta do Peru** | 13 | 5 |
| **Oitavos** | 11 | 4 | *Santo da Serra* | M3 | 5 |
| *Palmares* | 6 | 4 | **Troia** | 2 | 3 |
| **Penina (Championship)** | 13 | 3 | **Vale do Lobo (Royal)** | 16 | 3 |
| *Pine Cliffs* | 6 | 3 | *Vilamoura (Millennium)* | 5 | 4 |
| **Pinta** | 3 | 4 | **Vilamoura (Old)** | 1 | 4 |

**Back to Back Gold**

| | | | |
|---|---|---|---|
| **Puerta de Hierro (Arriba)** | 8–9 | 4s | |

Gold holes are set in bold

*Unrated courses are set in italics*

## Spectacular holes *(glitter but not gold)*

| | | |
|---|---|---|
| Alcaidesa | 13 | downhill shortish p5: view to Gibraltar |
| Andratx | 8 | downhill long p4: view and vertigo |
| Boavista | 6 | long p3 over chasm |
| Bonmont | 5 | downhill p3 over chasm |
| Cabopino | 3 | downhill short p4: view and more vertigo |
| La Cañada | 18 | downhill p4: long carry over chasm and distant sea view |
| Castillo de Gorraiz | 8 | downhill long p3: bunker in front, water behind; views |
| El Cortijo | 13 | downhill long p3 to raised, be-palmed bunkered green |
| La Duquesa | 8 | shortish downhill p3: distant sea view and less vertigo |
| Lisbon Sports | 14 | just reachable p4 over stream: what to do on the tee? |
| Marbella Golf | 12 | downhill p4 from high gun-platform tee with sea view |
| Monte Mayor | 3 | seemingly impossible downhill long p3 in beautiful setting |
| Oporto | 8 | linksy medium p3 with bunkered two-tier green – wind! |
| Palheiro | 3 | downhill medium bunkered p3; Funchal through trees |
| Parque da Floresta | 5 | downhill short p3 with small raised bunkered green |
| Platja de Pals | 11 | downhill short p3 over trees (or under ?!?) |
| P de Hierro (Ab) | 17 | long downhill p3 over bunker |
| Santo da Serra | M4 | long downhill p3 over chasm with Atlantic vista |
| San Lorenzo | 7 | medium p4: green surrounded by water and bunkers |
| San Roque (New) | 4 | downhill p3 over chasm; very long from Seve's tee |
| Torrequebrada | 16 | downhill left to right p4 over chasm and lake |
| Vilamoura (Old) | 6 | long downhill p3 with raised bunkered green |

---

### Best 9 holes extended into 18
| | |
|---|---|
| Furnas | 1-4; 14-18 |
| Ulzama | 1-9 |

### Best clubhouse bar
Puerta de Hierro

### Best clubhouse restaurant
Greenlife (El Lago – dinner)

### Best *Sangría*
Artola

### Best opening hole
Vilamoura (Old)

### Best finishing hole
Puerta de Hierro (Abajo)

### Best site for a golf course
Pedreña

### Best use of a bad site for a golf course
Empordà (Links) – former paddy field

### Best sites with most potential for improvement
Izki

### Best 1st tees
Puerta de Hierro (setting: two p3s and distant mountains, especially when snow-capped)
Valderrama (history, and gets you thinking…)

### Best 18th tees
La Manga (West) – retrospective
La Cañada (back tee – not for the faint-hearted!)

### Best for views
Alcaidesa (Straits of Gibraltar)
Batalha (mid-Atlantic over walled green fields)
La Herrería (El Escorial monastery)
Izki (wild scenery)
Neguri (sea and mountains)
Oitavos (sea and mountain)
Palheiro (Funchal from 19th)
Pedreña (sea, bay and mountains)
Santo da Serra (Madeira/Porto Santo)

### Best conditioned course (2004 – and always has been)
Valderrama

# SHORTCOMINGS

## Spanish Red

| | hole | p |
|---|---|---|
| Almenara (Alcornoques) | 9 | 5 |
| Almenara (Lagos) | 5 | 4 |
| Atalaya (New) | 3 | 4 |
| Benalup | 5 | 5 |
| Cabopino | 5 | 4 |
| Cabopino | 6 | 4 |
| Cabopino | 12 | 5 |
| Cabopino | 14 | 5 |
| Castillo de Gorraiz | 6 | 4 |
| Castillo de Gorraiz | 18 | 4 |
| La Dama de Noche | 6 | 4 |
| Estepona | 9 | 4 |
| **Guadalmina (Sur)** | 13 | 4 |
| Islantilla (Yellow) | 1 | 5 |
| Islantilla (Yellow) | 3 | 5 |
| **La Manga (West)** | 17 | 5 |
| La Noria | 2 | 4 |
| La Noria | 4 | 4 |
| La Noria | 5 | 4 |
| Miraflores | 15 | 3 |
| **El Prat (Red)** | 6 | 3 |
| Santa Clara | 7 | 4 |
| Santa María | 11 | 4 |
| **Son Antem (West)** | 12 | 4 |
| **Valderrama** | 17 | 5 |
| Valle del Este | 9 | 5 |

## Sporting Red

| | | |
|---|---|---|
| Benalup | 5 | 5 |

(becomes p4 if you get it right!)

## Portuguese Red

| | hole | p |
|---|---|---|
| Batalha | 2 | 5 |
| Boavista | 14 | 3 |
| Castro Marim | 3 | 5 |
| **San Lorenzo** | 18 | 4 |
| **Vale do Lobo (Ocean)** | 8 | 5 |
| Vilamoura (Pinhal) | 17 | 5 |

## Back to Back Red

| | |
|---|---|
| Cabopino | 5-6 |

## Iberia's Reddest Spot

| | |
|---|---|
| Cabopino | 5,6,12,14 |

## Weakest opening hole

Isla Canela

## Weakest Finishing Hole

Castillo de Gorraiz

## Weakest design

9 holes: La Noria
18 holes: Castro Marim

## Weakest for views

Miraflores: cranes (but there isn't room for much more building, so this is temporary – or is it?!)
Quinta de Beloura: industrial-cum-residential development
*Weakest setting with some surprisingly good views:* El Cortijo

## Unfortunate deletions

Sant Cugat: near gold p3 twixt 2 & 3
Vale do Lobo (Ocean): p3 twixt 8 & 9
Rated courses are set in bold

# OTHER LISTINGS

### Golf courses with more than one style/recurring feature

Los Arqueros: residential front 9; rustic-for-how-much-longer? back 9
Empordà (Links): different 'pseudo-links' style for each 9
Gramacho: original 9 with 2 greens/hole; newer 9 with 1 green/hole, in middle
Guadalhorce: undulating front 9; flat back 9
La Herrería: remodelled front 9; original back 9
La Manga (West): 2 original 9s made into 18; back 9 in forest
Los Naranjos: different vegetation for each 9: front non-orange, back oranges
Palheiro: open 6-9, 12; arboretum: the rest
Palmares: 3 distinct sections: links, parkland & tree-lined
Pinheiros Altos: pine-lined and hilly 1-11, 18; flat and watery 12-17
Quinta do Lago (N) & Vale do Lobo (Royal): Roquemore 9 inserted in middle
Son Vida: narrow-valleyed 1-12; open 13-18
Vale do Lobo (Ocean): hotchpotch.

## Unusual hazards
**Bakehouse** Alto 2
**Archaeology** El Prat (Yellow) 9
**Black bunkers, rocks and unusual mounds** Golf del Sur
**Building in front of tee (how long will it last?)** Empordà (Links) 16
**Darkness (if off line on Thursday nights!)** La Dama de Noche
**Desert theme features/hardpan** Desert Springs, Valle del Este
**Ha-ha** Son Muntaner 10
**Island bunker in shape of Gran Canaria** El Cortijo 4
**Modern Art sculptures** Montenmedio

**Obelisk** Isla Canela 13
**Palm trees as aerial bunkers** El Cortijo generally, especially 5 & 18
**Pylons in line of play** La Noria, (Montado – less so)
**'Roman' columns & statue** Los Flamingos
**Ruin** Lisbon Sports 15
**Shrine** Son Vida 11
**Walls** Andratx 7, Gramacho 16
**Well(s)** Vale do Lobo (Ocean) 3 & 6 (and several other courses)
**Windfalls – avocados** Santana
**Windfalls – oranges** Los Naranjos
**Windfalls – olives** Ubiquitous

---

## Longest Drive
**Airport to clubhouse**
Lerma (200km, approx)
**Road to clubhouse**
Morgado 6km (but being rectified)
**18th green to clubhouse**
Atalaya (New) (600m, approx)

## Nearest the Pin
Airport to clubhouse
Málaga (wheels barely up)

## Mandatory to play with member
Puerta de Hierro (Arriba & Abajo)
La Reserva de Sotogrande
La Zagaleta

## Apparent Highest Security
La Moraleja (2)
Valderrama

## Most eccentric greens
Empordà (Links)
9, 11 and 13, in particular
*Unrated course mentioned in the despatches:* Los Flamingos

## Back to Nature: least pollution (aural, visual and atmospheric)
| | |
|---|---|
| Batalha | Santo da Serra |
| Furnas | Ulzama |
| Izki | |

## Lonely Heart
La Coruña: (P M Ross, 1962) best course (possible ✈) – excluded only because not in a golf 'destination'

*Singing in the rain – well not quite! La Dama de Noche was very wet for (l to r) photographer Nic fforde (the shadow), Sam & Peter Millhouse and William fforde.*

## Easy to walk
La Dama de Noche
Isla Canela
Málaga
Maspalomas
Oporto
Penina (all courses)
El Saler
Salgados
Son Antem (East & West)

## Hardest run of holes
Troia (12-18, all from back tee)

## Hardest back-to-back combination
Oitavos 17-18
Valderrama 17-18

## Three of a kind
Marbella Club  6, 7 & 8: all p5s

## Hard Hat Areas
Castro Marim (Atlantic) (14-16)
Santa Clara (4-6)

## Hard to walk
Andratx (N.B. several stiff climbs to back tees off buggy path)
La Cala (North)
Marbella Club (6-7: crampons?!)
Monte Mayor (green fee includes buggy: sense!)
Santo da Serra (on a site with such a drop, why two 9 hole loops with clubhouse at the highest point on the course – out and back routing would surely have been better?)

## Hardest to find
Izki (in the middle of nowhere)

La Moraleja (both courses)
Neguri
Zaudín

## 62 steps
La Cala (South) 17 – up to back tee; then straight back down again… but still gold!

## Longest Walks from Green to Tee
Andratx (especially 2-3)
Marbella Club (especially 6-7; 10-11)
Quinta do Lago (North)
Vale do Lobo (Royal esp. 16-17 & Ocean 8-9)

## Understated Clubhouse Beauty
Morgado
San Lorenzo
Vilamoura (Old)

## Clubhouse Elegance
Puerta de Hierro
Marbella Golf

## Unmentionable clubhouses
Too many to mention, particularly in Spain – mainly for overstatement

## Unusual Number of Holes
Adolfo da Quinta        3 (excellent hotel location for a practice break)
La Cala (Academy)     6 (a very near miss for the only course to have neither yellow nor red holes)

## Back-to-back p3s on full-length course
| Oitavos | 13 & 14 |
| Atalaya (New) | 12 & 13 |

---

## Honourable Omissions
*Courses to be (re-)considered for a second edition*

### Spain
**Basozábal** (Olazábal, 1992, extended to 18 holes, near San Sebastián – looks good, from the road)
More in **Balearics** (including Al Cañada, Trent Jones Jnr, 2003, on the sea, which he considers his best in Iberia) and **Canaries** (we have generally respected airport-

convenience in all these islands)
**La Coruña** (see Lonely Heart p 235)
**Costa Ballena** (Olazábal, 1996, west of Jerez – we like all the 'Chema' courses we've seen)
**Costa Brava** (Hamilton Stutt, 1968 – by repute)
**Escorpión** (Kirby, 1975, our preference for other Valencia courses

led to omission)

**Fontanals & Cerdaña** (Arana, 1929 & Espinosa, 1994 – by repute; in Pyrenees, rather too far from Barcelona airport)

**Girona** (F Hawtree, 1990 – by repute)

**Jarama RACE** (Arana, 1967 – 5, 13 17 & 18 provisionally rated green)

**Layos** (Stirling & Martín, 2001 – by repute, and near Toledo, which is worth seeing)

**Montanyà** (Thomas, 1989 – by recommendation: Pyrenean views)

**Panorámica** (Langer, 1995 – our preference for *Bonmont* and *Mediterráneo* led to omission)

**Platja D'Aro** (Espinosa, 1990, south of Platja de Pals – initial impression: some green holes & good views)

**Sherry Golf, Jerez** (Stirling & Martín, 2003 – Stirling considers it his best to date)

## Portugal

**Estoril Sol** (Fream, Harris, Thomson & Wolveridge, 1976 – 9 holes alongside *Penha Longa*; a useful practice course; aka Academia International de Golfe)

**Montebelo** (Stilwell & Kenyon, 2000 – remote, with mountain views)

**Quinta do Brinçal** (formerly Golden Eagle, Roquemore, 1994 – by itself NE of Lisbon; worth a visit)

**Ribagolfe** (1 & 2) (King & Townsend, 2004 – near Lisbon: inspected and have rating potential, especially (2))

**Terceira** (Azores, designer unknown, 1954)

**Vidago** (PM Ross, 1936, 9 holes)

And perhaps a few of about 30+ in Iberia generally "planned" to open every year…?

# A FEW PLACES TO STAY

In general, we refer you to tour operator or travel guides, but would draw your attention to the following, which for various reasons have caught our attention:

**Barcelona – golf, wine and food: El Trapiche** – a 'must' for the golf-wine-&-food *cognoscenti*: restored 18th century Catalan *masía* (farmhouse), with stunning view of the dramatic Montserrat mountain. 5 en-suite double+ bedrooms on B&B basis (€€ for room), with dinner optional. Guests dine together, as if part of the family. The *simpatico* atmosphere, memorable cooking, and host's liberal generosity with the wine (included in the price) mean that guests tend to return. Close to Barcelona courses, wine tours, etc.

*El Trapiche at sunset with Montserrat behind and distant snow-clad Pyrenees.*

*See the Nasrid Palace at the Alhambra, Granada, before you die...*

No smoking. ☎ +34 937 31 469 ✉ michael.johnston@bmlisp.com ✈
Barcelona: AP7 (as for *Masía Bach*) but proceed to exit 27 (Sant Sadurní):
take BP2427 up the hill, following signs for (old) N340/A7; 600m above Els
Casots l onto unmarked track just after km3 to masía.

**Basque French-Spanish border**  Overlooking the Spanish border just south
of Hendaye, the French frontier town, hotel/restaurant Bakéa's perfectly
adequate and inexpensive French hotel rooms (€ for double) belie the
magnificent Franco-Basque cuisine (N.B. foie gras), savourable on a peaceful
shaded terrace (summer)/simple dining room (winter), which earns ∗s from
restaurant guides. Economic base for *San Sebastián, Ulzama, Castillo de
Gorraiz, Neguri,* Basozábal and Biarritz (Colt). First/last motorway exit in
France, follow signs to Biriatou. ✉ contact@bakeafr ☎ +33 5 59 20 76 36

**Costa del Sol**  Artola Hotel: friendly and surprisingly quiet (ensure you have
garden facing rooms), adjoining A7 (directions as for its golf course). We
recommend it not because it has a pitch & putt course, which is irrelevant
for most players, but as a pleasant, simple comfort alternative to tourist
hotels (€€ for double). ✉ hotelartola@inves.es ☎ +34 952 831 390

**Estela**  Estalagem São Félix Parque at Monte de São Félix – on the top of a
hill a few km inland from *Estela* at Laundos. A very quiet and secluded hotel.
We enjoyed its value for money, views, food and comfortable rooms (€€ for
double). ✉ sfelixparque@iol.pt ☎ +351 252 607 176

**Madeira**  Estalagem Casa Velha do Palheiro: wonderfully off-piste elegant
and discreet, slightly 'olde worlde' hotel adjoining *Palheiro*, with peaceful
garden in arboretum surroundings (€€€ for double).
✉ info@casa-velha.com ☎ +351 291 794 901

**Madrid**  Hotel Monte Real (good breakfast) has been our regular in Madrid for
its proximity to *Puerta de Hierro, Club de Campo* and the Madrid ring roads,
whence other clubs (Arroyofresno, 17 – €€€ for double).
✉ montereal@hotelmontereal.com ☎ +34 913 162 140. For an up-market
stay in Central Madrid, we liked Orfila (Orfila, 6 – €€€€ for double).
✉ inforeservas@hotelorfila.com ☎ +34 917 027 770

**Mallorca**  Arabella Sheraton Golf Hotel Son Vida: adjoins *Son Vida* and
close to *Son Muntaner*– excellent food (€€€€ for double).
✉ arabella@arabella.es ☎ +34 971 787 100 Marriott Son Antem hotel:
adjoins *Son Antem (East & West)* – well-equipped spa (€€€€ for double).

✏ mhrs.pmigs.reservations@marriott.com ☎ +34 971 129 100

**Portugal/Lisbon** *Hotel chain* Tivoli – quality hotels, including: Vilamoura – Tivoli Marinotel, between marina and beach (€€€€ for double) (good breakfast) ✏ marinotel@mail.telepac.pt +351 289 303 303; Lisbon – Tivoli Tejo, convenient for airport (€€€ for double) ✏ reservas.htt@tivolihotels.com ☎ +351 218 915 100; Tivoli Lisboa, central (€€€€ for double) ✏ reservas.htl@tivolihotels.com ☎ +351 213 198 900; new hotel planned for *Vilamoura (Victoria)*. Owned by Banco Espirito Santo, which is also understood to own/have interests in several courses, including *Salgados* and Ribagolfe, and therefore to be well placed to make golf reservations.

**Sevilla** Alfonso XIII: expensive hotel, but one of those experiences. Lavishly decorated in Moorish-influenced Andalusian style (bedrooms as well as public rooms). Dine out in central courtyard in summer months (San Fernando, 2 – €€€€ for double) ✏ www.westin.com ☎ +34 954 917 000

# NON-GOLFING DIVERSIONS

Please refer to travel guides, but we particularly enjoyed the following:

**Barcelona**: old central area, countless museums and galleries plus (as yet unfinished) La Sagrada Familia church.

**Basque country**: the best food in Iberia – tapas bars and restaurants (from basic good to world-class gourmet) in and near San Sebastián (refer to well-known restaurant guides).

**Bilbao**: Guggenheim museum.

**Burgos**: cathedral.

**Catalunya**: wine – Cava (sparkling) (Codorníu: AP7 exit 27 downhill for Sant Sadurní – follow road; after approx 2km r down hill, following signs to Cordoníu on r – vast cellars and fabulous architecture, washrooms included (!); very comprehensive tour; shop); Penedés (Torres: AP7 exit 28; take BP2121 northwest from Vilafranca del Penedés, l 200m after km2, signed Torres Visites; state-of-the-artish, not too long, tour; shop).

**Costa del Sol – Málaga**: cathedral and tapas bars in streets southwest of it; new Picasso Museum; **Gibraltar**: take the tour as a group in a taxi (from just inside the border – or Casemates) – views to Africa, crystal caves, apes and siege tunnels – memorable.

**Girona**: cathedral & old Jewish quarter.

**Granada**: not for golf (though there is an Espinosa course there), but the Alhambra is one of those places you must see before you die… Important: book tickets well in advance by phone from +34 902 224 460 and pay by credit card. Do not miss the Nasrid Palace (nor your specified ticket time to see it), and also the Generalife gardens.

**Jerez**: tour a sherry bodega – Gonzalez Byass (near centre) do good English-language tours; shop.

**Lisbon**: old city centre.

**Madrid**: Prado, Reina Sofía and Thyssen art galleries; Basque and fish restaurants; nightlife and much more. El Escorial monastery (very close to *La Herrería*).

**Oporto**: port lodges and tours (e.g. Sandeman, central on south bank of Douro).

**São Miguel, Azores**: beautiful verdant island with extinct volcanic scenery (especially Caldeira das Sete Citades) – away from it all.

**Toledo:** old town, El Greco, Alcázar, circunvalación view (Layos course nearby)

# INDEX

---

**Golf design advice from**
greg@gregturnergolf.com

**Golf photos from**
look@pocket-golf.com

**Golf tuition from**
peter@gogolf4life.com

**English-speaking Spanish lawyer:** Juan de Zavala: jzv@aza.as

---

**Faro**
*Vilamoura (Old)* ✱✱
*Penina (Chmpshp)* ★
*Quinta de Cima*
*San Lorenzo*
*Pinta* ✱
*Quinta do Lago (S)*
Vale do Lobo
(Ocean & Royal)
*Vilamoura
(Victoria)*
*Adolfo da Quinta
Alto*
*Balaia*
Benamor
Boavista
Castro Marim
Gramacho
Isla Canela
Islantilla
Maragota
Morgado
Parque da Floresta
*Palmares*
*Pine Cliffs* ★
Pinheiros Altos
Quinta da Ria
Quinta do Lago (N)
Salgados
Vale de Milho
Vilamoura (Laguna
*Millennium* &
Pinhal)
Vila Sol

**PORTUGAL**

**Lisbon**
*Oitavos* ✱✱
*Troia* ★
*Praia d'el Rey* ★
*Quinta do Peru*
*Aroeira 1* ✱
*Penha Longa* ★
*Aroeira 2*
Belas
*Estoril*
Lisbon Sports Club
Montado
Quinta da Marinha
Quinta de Beloura

**Oporto**
Oporto
*Estela* ✱

**Jerez**
Montecastillo
Novo Sancti Petri (A & B)

**Sevilla**
Sevilla
Zaudin ✱

**Gibraltar**
*Sotogrande* ✱✱
*La Reserva de
Sotogrande* ★
*Valderrama* ★
Alcaidesa
Almenara
Benalup
La Cañada
Montenmedio
San Roque (Old)

**San Roque (New)** ✱

**Santander**
★ Pedreña

**Funchal**
*Santo da Serra* ★
Palheiro

**Ponta Delgada**
*Furnas* ✱✱
Batalha

**Gran Canaria**
*El Cortijo* ✱
Maspalomas ★
Salobre

**Tenerife (Sur)**
*Golf del Sur* ★
Las Américas